low fat vegetarian

low fat vegetarian

180 delicious recipes for healthy soups, salads, main courses
and desserts, shown in over 750 photographs

Editor: Anne Sheasby

southwater

This edition is published by Southwater,
an imprint of Anness Publishing Ltd, 108 Great Russell Street,
London WC1B 3NA; info@anness.com

www.southwaterbooks.com; www.annesspublishing.com;
twitter: @Anness_Books

If you like the images in this book and would like to investigate
using them for publishing, promotions or advertising, please visit
our website www.practicalpictures.com for more information.

A CIP catalogue record for this book is available from
the British Library.

Publisher: Joanna Lorenz
Editor: James Harrison
Designer: Graham Webb, Design Principals
Production Controller: Rosanna Anness

PUBLISHER'S NOTE
Although the advice and information in this book are believed to be
accurate and true at the time of going to press, neither the authors
nor the publisher can accept any legal responsibility or liability for
any errors or omissions that may have been made nor for any
inaccuracies nor for any loss, harm or injury that comes about from
following instructions or advice in this book.

NOTES

Bracketed terms are intended for American readers.

For all recipes, quantities are given in both metric and imperial
measures and, where appropriate, in standard cups and spoons.
Follow one set of measures, but not a mixture, because they are
not interchangeable.

Standard spoon and cup measures are level. 1 tsp = 5ml,
1 tbsp = 15ml, 1 cup = 250ml/8fl oz.

Australian standard tablespoons are 20ml. Australian readers
should use 3 tsp in place of 1 tbsp for measuring small quantities.

American pints are 16fl oz/2 cups. American readers should
use 20fl oz/2.5 cups in place of 1 pint when measuring liquids.

Electric oven temperatures in this book are for conventional
ovens. When using a fan oven, the temperature will probably
need to be reduced by about 10–20°C/20–40°F. Since ovens
vary, you should check with your manufacturer's instruction
book for guidance.

The nutritional analysis given for each recipe is calculated per
portion (i.e. serving or item), unless otherwise stated. If the recipe
gives a range, such as Serves 4–6, then the nutritional analysis
will be for the smaller portion size, i.e. 6 servings. The analysis
does not include optional ingredients, such as salt added to taste.

Each recipe title in this book is followed by a symbol that
indicates the following:

★ = 5g of fat or less per serving
★★ = 10g of fat or less per serving

Some of the recipes in this book may contain raw or lightly
cooked eggs – these recipes are not recommended for babies
and young children, pregnant women, the elderly and those
convalescing. Medium (US large) eggs are used unless
otherwise stated.

Ideally, home-made low-fat stock should be used for all
relevant recipes in this book (see recipe on page 12).
Alternatively, good quality stock cubes or bouillon powder
can be used.

Main front cover image shows Italian Stuffed Peppers –
for recipe, see page 143.

CONTENTS

BEING VEGETARIAN

Many people think that vegetarianism is a relatively new trend, but in many countries around the globe, vegetarianism, in one form or another, has been the natural way to eat for many hundreds, if not thousands, of years. Today, there are millions of people who are vegetarians.

Although some vegetarian dishes are high in calories and fat, many can be enjoyed as part of a healthy low-fat eating regime, and with a few basic guidelines, a low-fat vegetarian diet is simple to achieve.

Defining vegetarianism

There are various forms of vegetarianism: you might be a vegan, a lacto-vegetarian, a fruitarian or on a macrobiotic diet. According to the Vegetarian Society, the definition of a vegetarian is "someone living on a diet of grains, pulses, nuts, seeds, vegetables and fruits with or without the use of dairy products and eggs (preferably free-range)".

A vegetarian does not eat any meat, poultry, game, fish, shellfish or crustacea, or meat by-products such as gelatine or animal fats.

A typical vegetarian diet includes a wide range of different food groups such as cereals/grains, pulses, nuts, seeds, fruit and vegetables, as well as dairy or soya products, eggs and vegetable oils and fats. These form the basis of a healthy and nutritious eating regime.

There are several different kinds of vegetarian diets. The most common vegetarians are Lacto-ovo-vegetarians who avoid meat, poultry and fish, etc, but include dairy products and eggs in their diet. Lacto-vegetarians are the same as Lacto-ovo-vegetarians, but they do not eat eggs.

Vegans, on the other hand, follow a much stricter eating regime and do not eat meat, poultry and fish, dairy products, eggs, or any other animal product. Fruitarians eat a diet which consists mainly of raw

fruit, grains and nuts. Very few processed or cooked foods are eaten. Finally, some people choose a macrobiotic diet, which is a diet followed for spiritual and philosophical reasons. This specific diet progresses through ten levels, becoming increasingly restrictive. Although not all levels are vegetarian, each level gradually eliminates animal products until the highest level eventually reaches a brown rice diet.

As long as you eat a wide variety of foods, life never need be dull if you choose to follow a vegetarian diet. By its very nature, a balanced vegetarian diet tends to be naturally low in saturated and total fat, high in dietary fibre and complex carbohydrates, and high in many protective vitamins and minerals. A well-balanced vegetarian diet should provide all the nutrients, vitamins and minerals your body needs.

Through vegetarian cooking, you can mix and match the vibrant colours, textures and flavours of vegetables, fruits, pulses and grains with many other exciting ingredients, and experiment with a wide variety of interesting and unusual foods to create all kinds of delicious and tempting dishes from many parts of the world.

Choosing vegetarian food

Many vegetarian foods available in shops and supermarkets are clearly marked on their packaging as being 'suitable for vegetarians'. Some food products also carry the 'V' (vegetarian) symbol and others carry vegetarian symbols familiar to particular countries such as the 'two green leaves' symbol. Some vegetarian foods carry a Vegetarian Society symbol, which indicates that they are approved and meet specific criteria that ensures the foods are absolutely suitable for vegetarians. Other food products,

Left: Rice is perfect for experimenting with many different vegetarian options.

such as cheese, may also include additional useful information, for example advice that the cheese is made using 'non-animal rennet'.

Nutrition and the vegetarian diet

In a vegetarian diet, protein, which is made up of amino acids, is needed for the growth and repair of all body cells. Protein is provided by foods such as eggs, milk, yogurt, cheese and soya bean products, such as tofu and tempeh, all of which contain many of the essential amino acids we need.

Other foods such as beans, peas, lentils, grains, nuts and seeds also provide a valuable source of protein.

Carbohydrates, which divide into simple and complex carbohydrates, supply the body with energy. Simple carbohydrates tend to be found in sugars and sweet foods, which should only be eaten in moderation. Complex carbohydrates on the other hand are a vital part of a healthy diet and these are provided by foods such as rice, pasta, bread, potatoes and other vegetables, as well as many fruits. Many of these complex carbohydrate foods also provide fibre, vitamins and minerals.

Above: Sweat mushrooms in a little stock rather than butter or use raw in salads. Reconstituted dried mushrooms are excellent for adding intense flavour to sauces, rice and pasta dishes.

Vitamins and minerals have many vital functions and important roles, such as keeping the nervous system and other tissues healthy, helping to maintain healthy eyes, skin and hair, and to protect against disease. A balanced vegetarian diet should supply many of these, although some vegetarians choose to increase their intake of vitamins and minerals with supplements such as vitamin B12, calcium, iron and zinc.

How to use this book

There are over 180 delicious and easy-to-follow low-fat vegetarian recipes for all the family to enjoy. Our tempting selection of recipes ranges from soups, appetizers and snacks, salads and side dishes, to light meals, main course dishes and suppers. It also includes a tasty collection of delicious desserts and home-baked breads, cakes and bakes.

The following pages give lots of useful and informative advice, including helpful hints and tips on low-fat and fat-free vegetarian ingredients and low-fat or fat-free cooking techniques. You will find practical tips on how to reduce fat and saturated fat in your diet and an interesting and useful insight into many of the different ingredients typically found in the vegetarian kitchen and used widely in vegetarian cooking.

Each recipe gives a nutritional breakdown, providing at-a-glance calorie and fat contents (including saturated fat content), as well as other key nutrients such as protein, carbohydrate, cholesterol, calcium, fibre and sodium.

As its title suggest, all the recipes in this cookbook are low in fat – the majority containing five grams or less of fat per serving, and some containing less than one gram. The only exceptions are in the chapter entitled 'Main Courses', where the more substantial of the recipes contain ten grams of fat or less per serving.

Below: Tomatoes on the vine contain vitamin C, folic acid, potassium and lycopene – an antioxidant that can help prevent cancer.

For ease of reference, throughout the recipe section, all recipes with a single ★ following the recipe name contain five grams of fat or fewer, and those with ★★ contain ten grams of fat or fewer. All the recipes contain even less fat than typical vegetarian recipes yet they are still full of delicious flavour and appeal.

Above: Onions have excellent culinary and medicinal values for the vegetarian.

A HEALTHY VEGETARIAN DIET

A healthy vegetarian diet is one that provides you with all the nutrients you need. By eating the right types, balance and proportions of foods, you are more likely to feel healthy, have plenty of energy and have a higher resistance to disease. You will be less likely to develop illnesses such as heart disease, cancers, bowel disorders and obesity.

By choosing a variety of foods every day, you will ensure that you are supplying your body with all the essential nutrients, including vitamins and minerals, it needs. To get the balance right, it is important to know just how much of each type of food you should be eating.

It is recommended that you eat plenty of fruits and vegetables (at least five portions a day, not including potatoes) and foods such as cereals, pasta, rice and potatoes; moderate amounts of dairy products (and meat, fish and poultry if you follow a non-vegetarian diet), and only small amounts of foods containing fat or sugar.

By choosing a good balance of foods from these groups every day, and by choosing lower-fat, lower-sugar and lower-salt alternatives, we will be supplying our bodies with all the nutrients they need for optimum health.

THE ROLE OF FAT IN THE DIET

Most people eat fats in some form or other every day. We all need a small amount of fat in our diet to maintain a healthy, balanced eating plan. However, many of us eat far too much fat and you should be looking to reduce your overall fat intake, especially of saturated fats (as in butter, cream, milk, etc), as this contributes to a rise in blood cholesterol levels and may lead to coronary heart disease. Instead you should choose unsaturated fats such as olive and sunflower oils, which are high in

Above: Broad (fava) beans provide potassium and iron for the vegetarian diet.

monounsaturated and polyunsaturated fat and low in saturated fat, as these are healthier types of fat and are thought actually to help lower cholesterol levels. If you use these types of fat in moderation, they can be enjoyed as part of a low-fat diet – especially if combined with regular exercise.

Some other ingredients typically used in vegetarian cooking, such as cheese and yogurt, can be high in fat, but they can be substituted with lower-fat versions such as reduced-fat cheeses or low-fat yogurts. In many recipes, the quantity of the high-fat food can often simply be reduced to lower the fat content of the dish. When preparing recipes, you will be surprised at how small an amount of oil you need, for example when sautéing vegetables. Foods such as pasta and rice are also ideal for a low-fat diet as they are naturally high in carbohydrates and low in fat. By cutting down on the amount of fat you eat and making simple changes to your diet, you will soon be reducing your overall fat intake and enjoying a much healthier lifestyle, and you'll hardly notice the difference.

Left: Vegetables such as cauliflower and broccoli should be staples of a vegetarian diet and are best steamed or stir-fried or added washed and raw in salads.

The daily intake of fat should be limited to no more than 30–35 per cent of the total number of calories. Since each gram of fat provides nine calories, for anyone eating 2,000 calories a day, the total daily intake should be no more than around 70g fat.

As a general rule, the total intake of saturated fats should be no more than approximately ten per cent of the total number of calories.

TYPES OF FAT

All fats in our foods are made up of building blocks of fatty acids and glycerol, and their properties vary according to the way they are combined.

There are two main types of fat, which are referred to as saturated and unsaturated. The unsaturated group of fats is divided into two further types – polyunsaturated and monounsaturated fats. There is usually a combination of these types of unsaturated fat in foods that contain fat, but the amount of each type varies from one kind of food to another.

Saturated fats

These fats are usually hard at room temperature. They are not essential in the diet, and should be limited, as they are linked to increasing the level of blood cholesterol, which can increase the likelihood of heart disease.

The main sources of saturated fats are animal products, such as fatty cuts of meat and meat products, spreading

Above: With a deep green skin and firm, pale flesh, courgettes (zucchini) provide perfect bulk for vegetable stews. They are low in calories with a high water content.

fats, such as butter, lard and margarine, that are solid at room temperature, and full-fat dairy products such as cream and cheese. However, there are also saturated fats of vegetable origin, notably coconut and palm oils, and some margarines and oils, which, when processed, change the nature of the fat from unsaturated fatty acids to saturated ones. These fats are labelled "hydrogenated" (for example hydrogenated vegetable oil), and should be limited. Saturated fats are also found in many processed foods, such as chips (French fries), savoury snacks and crisps (US potato chips), as well as cookies, and cakes.

Polyunsaturated fats

There are two types of polyunsaturated fats: that of vegetable or plant origin (known as omega 6), which is found in sunflower oil, soft margarine and seeds, and that from oily fish (known as omega 3), such as salmon, herring, mackerel and sardines. Both fats are usually liquid at room temperature. Small amounts of polyunsaturated fats are essential for good health and are thought to help reduce the blood cholesterol level. It is generally agreed that polyunsaturated fats are healthier than saturated fats, but like all fats they

are high in calories and should be eaten sparingly. They also provide essential fatty acids for healthy skin and the development of body cells.

Monounsaturated fats

Foods such as rapeseed oil, olive oil, some nuts, including almonds and pecans, olives and avocados all contain monounsaturated fats. These fats are generally thought to have the beneficial effect of reducing the blood cholesterol level, so it's fine to include them in moderation in the diet.

PLANNING A LOW-FAT DIET

You can still cut down on sources of fat even in a vegetarian diet, by reducing your intake of butter, oils, margarine, cream, full cream (whole) milk and full-fat cheese. Low-fat calcium-fortified soya-based beverages, for example, can provide calcium in amounts similar to milk. Also try to build meals around protein sources that are naturally low in fat, such as beans, rice and lentils, and don't overload meals with high-fat cheeses to replace the meat. Basically, aim to limit the intake of saturated fats, cholesterol, added sugars and salt. For example it's natural to add dressings, sauces, marinades and relishes for moistness and flavour, but there are low-fat versions you can make yourself (see page 14) or purchase off the shelf.

By educating yourself and being aware of which foods are high in fats, particularly saturated fats, and by making simple changes to your diet, you can reduce the total fat content of your diet quite considerably.

Fill up on very low-fat foods, such as fruits and vegetables, as well as foods that are high in carbohydrates, such as pasta, rice, bread and potatoes.

Cutting down on fat doesn't mean sacrificing taste. It's easy and enjoyable to follow a sensible healthy eating plan without forgoing all your favourite foods.

Above: Fresh, organic vegetables are well worth the extra cost for taste and health.

THE CHOLESTEROL QUESTION

Cholesterol is a fat-like substance that plays a vital role in the body. It's the material from which many essential hormones and vitamin D are made. Too much saturated fat encourages the body to make more cholesterol than it uses or can rid itself of. Cholesterol is carried around the body, attached to proteins called high-density lipoproteins (HDL), low-density lipoproteins (LDL), and very low-density lipoproteins (VLDL or triglycerides).

After a meal the LDLs carry the fat in the blood to the cells where it's required. Any surplus should be excreted from the body, however, if there is too much LDL in the blood, some of the fat will be deposited on the walls of the arteries. This furring up gradually narrows the arteries and is one of the most common

causes of heart attacks and strokes. In contrast, HDLs appear to protect against heart disease. Whether high triglyceride levels are risk factors remains unknown.

For some people, an excess of cholesterol is a hereditary trait; in others, it's mainly the result of consumption of too much saturated fat. In both cases it can be reduced by a low-fat diet.

CUTTING DOWN ON FAT IN THE VEGETARIAN DIET

Most of us eat about 115g/4oz of fat every day. Yet just 10g/¼oz, about the amount in a single packet of crisps (US potato chips) or a thin slice of Cheddar cheese, is all we actually need.

Follow the simple "eat less, try instead" suggestions below to discover how to reduce the fat in your diet.

• Eat less butter or hard margarine.
• Try reduced-fat, low-fat or fat-free spreads. Try low-fat cream cheese or low-fat soft cheese for sandwiches and toast.
• Eat fewer full-fat dairy products such as full cream (whole) milk, cream, butter, hard margarine, crème fraîche, whole-milk yogurts and hard cheese.
• Try instead semi-skimmed (low-fat) or skimmed milk, low-fat or reduced-fat milk products, low-fat yogurts, low-fat fromage frais and low-fat soft and low-fat cream cheeses, reduced-fat hard

cheeses such as Cheddar, and reduced-fat crème fraîche.
• Use lots of low-fat protein products such as peas, beans, lentils or tofu.
• Do not cook with hard cooking fats, such as hard margarine.
• Try instead polyunsaturated or mono-unsaturated oils, such as sunflower, corn or olive oil for cooking (but don't use too much).
• Eat fewer rich salad dressings, and less full-fat mayonnaise.
• Try instead reduced-fat or fat-free mayonnaise or dressings. Make your own salad dressings at home with low-fat yogurt or fromage frais.
• Eat less fried food.
• Try instead fat-free cooking methods such as grilling (broiling), baking, microwaving or steaming whenever possible. Try cooking in non-stick pans with only a very small amount of oil.
• Eat fewer deep-fried and sautéed potatoes.
• Try instead low-fat starchy foods such as pasta, couscous and rice. Choose baked or boiled potatoes.
• Eat less added fat in cooking.
• Try instead to cook with little or no fat. Use heavy, good-quality non-stick pans so that the food doesn't stick. Try using a small amount of spray oil in cooking to control how much fat you are using.

HOW TO COOK A LOW-FAT MEAL

Once you get into the habit, it's easy to cook without fat. For example, whenever possible, grill (broil), bake, microwave and steam foods without the addition of fat, or try stir-frying with little or no fat. Alternatively, try using a low-fat or fat-free stock, wine or fruit juice for cooking, instead of fat.

• By choosing good-quality, non-stick cookware, you'll find that the amount of fat needed for cooking foods can be kept to an absolute minimum. If you do need a little fat for cooking, choose an oil that is high in unsaturates, such as olive or sunflower oil, and use as little as possible, or try an unsaturated spray oil.

• When baking low-fat cookies and cakes, use good-quality non-stick bakeware that doesn't need greasing before use, or use baking parchment and only lightly grease before lining.
• Look for non-stick coated fabric sheets. This re-usable non-stick material is amazingly versatile, as it can be cut to size and used to line cake tins (pans), baking sheets or frying pans. Heat-resistant up to 290°C/550°F and microwave-safe, it will last for up to five years.
• Sauté vegetables in low-fat or fat-free stock, wine or fruit juice instead of oil.
• Try a low-fat type of oil or just vinegar or lemon juice for salad dressings.
• Parcel-cooking vegetables and fruit allows the food to cook in its own juices

The steam created holds in all the flavour and nutrient value and eliminates the need for oil or fats. Enclose food in individual foil or greaseproof parcels, add extra flavourings such as wine, herbs and spices, if liked, twist or fold parcel ends to secure and ensure juices can't run out, then bake, steam or cook on a barbecue.

• When grilling (broiling) foods, the addition of fat is often unnecessary. If the food shows signs of drying, lightly brush with a small amount of unsaturated oil, such as olive, sunflower or corn oil.
• Microwaved foods rarely need the addition of fat, so add herbs or spices for extra flavour and colour.

• Steaming and boiling are easy, fat-free ways of cooking many foods. Cook vegetables in a covered pan over a low heat with a little water so they cook in their own juices.
• Try poaching foods such as fruit in a fat-free stock or syrup.

• Try braising vegetables in the oven in low-fat or fat-free stock, wine or simply water with the addition of some chopped fresh or dried herbs.
• When serving vegetables resist the temptation to add a knob (pat) of butter or margarine. Instead, sprinkle with chopped fresh herbs or ground spices.

• Don't pan-fry vegetables, such as onions, mushrooms, carrots and celery, in oil or butter. Instead, put the sliced vegetables into a non-stick saucepan or frying pan with about 150ml/¼ pint/⅔ cup low-fat stock. Cover and cook for 5 minutes or until the vegetables are tender and the stock has reduced. If you like, add 15ml/1 tbsp dry wine or wine vinegar for a little piquancy and continue cooking for a further few minutes until the vegetables are dry and appear lightly browned.

LOW-FAT SPREADS IN COOKING

There is a huge variety of low-fat and reduced-fat spreads available in stores. Generally speaking, any very low-fat spreads with a fat content of around 20 per cent or less have a high water content. These are unsuitable for cooking and can only be used for spreading.

STOCKS, SAUCES AND FLAVOURINGS

Using ingredients like vinegar, lemon juice, herbs, tomato and garlic means you needn't worry about giving up on taste and flavour to achieve satisfying low-fat sauces.

LOW-FAT VEGETABLE STOCK

A good home-made vegetable stock is invaluable in the kitchen, forming the basis for many vegetarian soups, appetizers and main course dishes. Below is a low-fat vegetable stock recipe which is economical and easy to make. You could vary the ingredients in the vegetable stock according to taste and availability.

MAKES ABOUT 2.4 LITRES/4 PINTS/10 CUPS

INGREDIENTS
  2 large onions, coarsely chopped
  2 leeks, sliced
  3 garlic cloves, crushed
  3 carrots, coarsely chopped
  4 celery sticks, sliced
  a large strip of pared lemon rind
  12 fresh parsley stalks
  a few fresh thyme sprigs
  2 bay leaves
  2.4 litres/4 pints/10 cups water

1 Put the prepared vegetables in a large pan. Add the lemon rind, with the parsley, thyme and bay leaves. Pour in the water and bring to the boil. Skim off the foam that rises to the surface.

2 Lower the heat and simmer, uncovered, for 30 minutes. Strain, season to taste and leave to cool.

BOUQUET GARNI

A little bundle of herbs is perfect for adding flavour to vegetable stocks, soups and stews. Tying the herbs in a bundle means that the bouquet garni is easy to remove after cooking. A traditional bouquet garni comprises sprigs of parsley, thyme and a bay leaf, but you can vary the herbs according to the dish and/or main ingredients. Rosemary and oregano are a good combination, while mint, chervil, basil, chives and tarragon go well together.

1 Using a short length of string about 15 cm (6 in) in length, tie together a bay leaf with sprigs of thyme and parsley. Work from the thickest part.

2 Alternatively, you can place the herbs in the centre of a square of muslin (cheesecloth) and then tie them into a neat bundle using a short length of string to close the opening.

3 Use the bouquet garni immediately or freeze. (Herbs tied in muslin are better suited for freezing than string-tied herbs.)

LOW-FAT TOMATO SAUCE

MAKES ABOUT 350ML/12FL OZ/1½ CUPS

INGREDIENTS
  10ml/2 tsp olive oil
  1 onion, finely chopped
  1 garlic clove, crushed
  400g/14oz can chopped tomatoes
  15ml/1 tbsp tomato purée (paste)
  15ml/1 tbsp chopped fresh mixed
    herbs (parsley, thyme, oregano, basil)
  pinch of granulated sugar
  salt and ground black pepper

1 Heat the oil in a non-stick pan and cook the onion and garlic gently until softened. Stir in the tomatoes, tomato purée, herbs, sugar, salt and pepper.

2 Simmer, uncovered, for 15–20 minutes, stirring occasionally, until the mixture has reduced and is thick. Use immediately or store in the refrigerator.

COOK'S TIP

Use this sauce on pizzas or pasta. It also tastes excellent with vegetables. Spoon it over cooked cauliflower, top with a little grated reduced-fat cheese and grill.

Stock Energy 5Kcal/21kJ; Protein 0.3g; Carbohydrate 0.2g, of which sugars 0g; Fat 0.3g, of which saturates 0g; Cholesterol 0mg; Calcium 1mg; Fibre 0g; Sodium 336mg.
Sauce Energy 160Kcal/673kJ; Protein 4.7g; Carbohydrate 19.7g, of which sugars 18.2g; Fat 7.6g, of which saturates 1.3g; Cholesterol 0mg; Calcium 78mg; Fibre 6g; Sodium 79mg.

LOW-FAT SAUCES AND STOCKS

Adding sauces can mean introducing an unwelcome amount of fat into a recipe, so that dishes which start out low in fat may end up being served in a rich, high-fat coating. Unfortunately, it is not possible simply to introduce a low-fat spread into most sauce recipes. The traditional roux method for making a sauce won't work successfully using low-fat spreads because of their high water content, which evaporates on heating, leaving insufficient fat to blend with the flour. Below are three quick and easy low-fat cooking methods to try out, plus some low-fat vegetarian alternatives to classic richer sauces.

• The All-in-One Method: Place 25g/ 1oz/2 tbsp each of low-fat spread and plain flour in a saucepan with 300ml/ ½ pint/1¼ cups skimmed milk. Bring to the boil, stirring continuously until the sauce is thickened and smooth.

• Using Cornflour to Thicken: Blend 15ml/1 tbsp cornflour with 15–30ml/ 1–2 tbsp cold water, then whisk into 300ml/½ pint/1¼ cups simmering stock or milk, bring to the boil and cook for 1 minute, stirring continuously.

• Using Stock to Replace Fat: Sweat your vegetables, such as onions, mushrooms and leeks, in a pan using a small amount of vegetable stock rather than frying in fat. This will help reduce fat intake.

LOW-FAT VARIATIONS OF CLASSIC SAUCES

• **Mayonnaise** You can buy commercially made reduced-calorie mayonnaise or, to make further fat and calorie savings, substitute half the stated quantity with low-fat natural yogurt or low-fat fromage frais. This works well for mayonnaise-based dips or sauces like Thousand Island, which have tomato purée or ketchup added.

• **Hollandaise** This sauce is classically made with egg yolks, butter and vinegar and can't be made with low-fat spreads. However, some fat saving can be made by using less butter and including buttermilk.

1 Place 3 egg yolks in a bowl with the grated rind and 15ml/ 1 tbsp juice from 1 lemon.

2 Heat gently over a pan of water, stirring until thickened.

3 Gradually whisk in 75g/3oz/6 tbsp softened butter, in small pieces, until smooth.

4 Whisk in 45ml/3 tbsp buttermilk and season. Reserve for special occasions.

• **Vinaigrette Dressings** Buy reduced-calorie and oil-free dressings and check the labels carefully. Or, if you like the real thing, simply use less.

• **Vegetable Purées** Many recipes are traditionally thickened by adding cream, beurre manié (a butter and flour paste) or egg yolks, all of which add unwanted fat to the sauce. If cooked vegetables are included in the recipe, blend some down in a food processor to make a purée, then stir back into the juices to produce this low-fat version of a thickened vegetable sauce.

Above: if you use olive oil, portion it out using tablespoons to keep tabs on the calories. Low-fat butter contains about half the fat of butter. Consume in moderation.

DRESSINGS, MARINADES AND RELISHES

Fortunately today there is a very good choice of ready-made low-fat sauces to give your meals a bit of zing, but it's also easy to experiment with your own selection of ingredients. Try these.

LOW-FAT FRENCH DRESSING

Serve this tasty low-fat French-style dressing drizzled over mixed salad leaves, tomato salads, or chargrilled vegetables.

MAKES ABOUT 200ML/7FL OZ/SCANT 1 CUP

INGREDIENTS
    105ml/7 tbsp white grape juice
    60ml/4 tbsp extra-virgin olive oil
    30ml/2 tbsp red wine vinegar or
      tarragon vinegar
    5–7.5ml/1–1½ tsp Dijon or
      wholegrain mustard
    5–10ml/1–2 tsp chopped mixed fresh
      herbs (such as parsley, thyme,
      oregano and basil or chives)
    a pinch of caster (superfine) sugar
    salt and ground black pepper

1 Put the grape juice, olive oil, vinegar, mustard, chopped herbs, sugar, salt and pepper into a small bowl. Whisk the ingredients together thoroughly.

2 Alternatively, put all the ingredients into a clean screw-top jar, seal.

3 Shake well until thoroughly mixed and adjust the seasoning to taste. Serve immediately, or keep in a screw-top jar in the refrigerator for up to 3 days.

LOW-FAT TOMATO SALAD DRESSING

Drizzle this flavourful low-fat salad dressing over roast vegetables such as peppers and courgettes, or simply serve it with a mixed green or baby leaf salad.

MAKES ABOUT 200ML/7FL OZ/SCANT 1 CUP

INGREDIENTS
    105ml/7 tbsp tomato juice
    60ml/4 tbsp extra-virgin olive oil
    30ml/2 tbsp cider vinegar
    15ml/1 tbsp tomato ketchup
    5ml/1 tsp Dijon mustard
    2.5ml/½ tsp caster (superfine) sugar
    1 clove garlic, crushed (optional)
    a few drops of Tabasco
      sauce (optional)
    salt and ground black pepper

1 Put the tomato juice, olive oil, vinegar, tomato ketchup, mustard, sugar, garlic and Tabasco sauce, if using, and salt and pepper into a small bowl. Whisk the ingredients together until thoroughly mixed.

2 As an alternative, you can put the ingredients into a pre-cleaned screw-top jar, seal and shake well.

3 The dressing is immediately ready to serve or to save in the jar in the refrigerator for a few days.

QUICK-FIX OIL-FREE DRESSING

1 Whisk together 90ml/6 tbsp low-fat natural (plain) yogurt and 30ml/2 tbsp freshly squeezed lemon juice.
2 Season to taste with freshly ground black pepper.
3 If you prefer, wine, cider or even orange juice could be used in place of the lemon juice.
4 Add chopped fresh herbs, crushed garlic, mustard, honey, grated horseradish or other flavourings.
5 Mix well, or shake thoroughly in a pre-washed screw-top jar. Adjust to taste. It's ready to serve immediately, or to store.

Above: Try adding honey, mustard, garlic, herbs, shallots, or chillies to add flavour and body to low-fat dressings.

GRAPEFRUIT AND YOGURT DRESSING

This oil-free dressing makes a healthy change from vinaigrette.

MAKES ABOUT 250ML/8FL OZ/1 CUP

INGREDIENTS
    30ml/2 tbsp pink grapefruit juice
    15ml/1 tbsp sherry vinegar
    1 garlic clove, crushed
    5ml/1 tsp wholegrain mustard
    150ml/¼ pint/⅔ cup low-fat natural
      (plain) yogurt
    15ml/1 tbsp chopped fresh herbs

Mix the juice and vinegar in a bowl. Add garlic and mustard, whisk in the yogurt and herbs. Serve with mixed salad leaves or drizzle over cold cooked vegetables.

COOK'S TIP

For vinaigrette dressings, the usual ratio of oil to vinegar is 3 to 1. Try to reverse it so you have 3 parts vinegar to 1 part oil. Or simply replace some of the oil with water, juice or fat-free broth.

French Energy 480Kcal/1981kJ; Protein 2.4g; Carbohydrate 15.1g, of which sugars 12.3g; Fat 46.7g, of which saturates 6.4g; Cholesterol 0mg; Calcium 119mg; Fibre 0g; Sodium 12mg.
Tomato Energy 451Kcal/1863kJ; Protein 2g; Carbohydrate 10.7g, of which sugars 9.9g; Fat 45.3g, of which saturates 6.3g; Cholesterol 0mg; Calcium 24mg; Fibre 0.8g; Sodium 486mg.
Grapefruit Energy 113Kcal/474kJ; Protein 9.1g; Carbohydrate 14.8g, of which sugars 14.1g; Fat 3.1g, of which saturates 0.8g; Cholesterol 2mg; Calcium 329mg; Fibre 0.8g; Sodium 132mg.

FRESH TARRAGON DRESSING

Serve this light and tasty dressing with cooked cold or warm asparagus, or with mixed salad leaves.

MAKES ABOUT 325ML/11FL OZ/
GENEROUS 1¼ CUPS

INGREDIENTS
175g/6oz low-fat soft cheese
150ml/¼ pint/⅔ cup reduced-fat single (light) cream or low-fat natural (plain) yogurt
15–30ml/1–2 tbsp chopped fresh tarragon
10–15ml/2–3 tsp tarragon vinegar
salt and ground black pepper

1 Put the soft cheese into a small bowl and stir or mash until smooth, then stir in the cream or yogurt until well blended.

2 Stir in the tarragon and vinegar to taste, mixing well, then season to taste with salt and pepper.

3 Cover and leave to stand in a cool place for 30 minutes before serving, to allow the flavours to develop. Taste and adjust the seasoning before serving.

QUICK IDEAS FOR MARINADES

• Mix olive oil with chopped fresh herbs such as parsley, chives, garlic, chervil and basil. Add a splash or two of lemon juice and season with salt and pepper.
• Combine groundnut oil, toasted sesame oil, dark soy sauce, sweet sherry, rice vinegar and crushed garlic. Use as a marinade for tofu or tempeh.
• Mix together olive oil, lemon juice, sherry, honey and crushed garlic and use as a marinade for vegetable kebabs.

CUCUMBER RELISH

A cool, refreshing relish, this can be used as a dip, or as a sauce with vegetable kebabs. Serve when still fresh, so that the pieces are still crunchy. As cucumber is very refreshing add some ice cubes for extra chill.

INGREDIENTS
½ cucumber
2 celery sticks, chopped
1 green (bell) pepper, seeded and chopped
1 garlic clove, crushed
300ml/½ pint/1¼ cups low-fat natural (plain) yogurt
15ml/1 tbsp chopped fresh coriander (cilantro)
ground black pepper

1 Dice the cucumber and place in a large bowl.

2 Add the celery, green pepper and crushed garlic.

3 Stir in the yogurt and fresh coriander. Season with the pepper. Cover and chill.

CHILLI RELISH

This warm and spicy relish is ideal served with vegetarian snacks. If you prefer a slightly milder flavour, remove the seeds from the chilli before serving.

INGREDIENTS
2 large tomatoes
1 red onion
10ml/2 tsp chilli sauce
15ml/1 tbsp chopped fresh basil
1 fresh green chilli, finely chopped
pinch of salt
pinch of granulated sugar

1 Finely chop the tomatoes and place in a mixing bowl.

2 Finely chop the onion and add to the tomatoes with the chilli sauce.

3 Stir in the fresh basil, chilli, salt and sugar.

TOMATO RELISH

This cooked relish may be served hot or cold. It has a concentrated flavour, making it ideal with pasta or vegetable kebabs.

INGREDIENTS
10ml/2 tsp olive oil
1 onion, chopped
1 garlic clove, crushed
25g/1oz/2 tbsp plain (all-purpose) flour
30ml/2 tbsp tomato ketchup
300ml/½ pint/1¼ cups passata (bottled strained tomatoes)
5ml/1 tsp granulated sugar
15ml/1 tbsp chopped fresh parsley

1 Heat the oil in a non-stick pan. Add the onion and garlic clove and sauté for 5 minutes, stirring from time to time.

2 Stir in the flour and cook for a further minute.

3 Stir in the tomato ketchup, passata, sugar and fresh parsley. Bring to the boil. Chill and use as required.

COOK'S TIP
•Passata is a smooth liquid made from sieved tomatoes. It is used as a base for recipes such as soups and sauces.
• All these relishes should be used as quickly as possible for optimum flavour. They will keep in the fridge for 3–4 days.

Tarragon Energy 330Kcal/1378kJ; Protein 35.1g; Carbohydrate 18.6g, of which sugars 18.4g; Fat 16.1g, of which saturates 9.8g; Cholesterol 44mg; Calcium 578mg; Fibre 2.3g; Sodium 906mg.

VEGETABLES

Naturally low in fat and bursting with vitamins and minerals, vegetables are one food group that should ideally make up the bulk of our daily diet. The most common vegetables contain less than 1g fat, although the humble pea ranks 1.5g per 100g/3½oz portion. Vegetables have always played an essential role in vegetarian cooking. They are sometimes served as dishes in their own right, and sometimes as accompaniments. Either way, there is a vast range of imaginative low-fat recipes from all over the world, incorporating vegetables, from salads to hearty vegetable stews. A whole variety of flavourings, such as herbs, can bring out the best flavour in vegetables.

ROOTS AND TUBERS

Vegetables such as carrots, swedes, parsnips and potatoes are a comforting and nourishing food, and it is not surprising that they should be popular in the winter. Their sweet, dense flesh provides sustained energy, valuable fibre, vitamins and minerals.

Carrots

The best carrots are not restricted to cold winter months. Summer welcomes the slender sweet new crop, often sold with their green, feathery tops, which are best removed after buying as they rob the root of moisture and nutrients. Buy organic carrots if you can because high pesticide residues have been found in non-organic ones. As an added bonus, organic carrots do not need peeling. Look for firm, smooth carrots – the smaller they are, the sweeter they are. Carrots should be prepared just before use to preserve their valuable nutrients. They are delicious raw, and can be steamed, stir-fried, roasted or puréed.

Beetroot (Beet)

Deep, ruby-red in colour, beetroot adds a vibrant hue and flavour to all sorts of dishes. It is often pickled in vinegar, but is much better roasted, as this emphasizes its sweet earthy flavour. Raw beetroot can be grated into salads or used to make relishes. It can also be added to vegetarian risottos or delicious soups. If cooking beetroot whole, wash carefully, taking care not to damage the skin or the nutrients and colour will leach out. Trim the stalks to about 2.5cm/1in above the root. Small beetroots tend to be sweeter and more tender than the larger ones.

Parsnips

This vegetable has a sweet, creamy flavour and is delicious roasted, puréed or steamed. Parsnips are best purchased after the first frost of the year as the cold converts their starches into sugar, enhancing their sweetness. Scrub before use and only peel if tough. Avoid large roots, which can be woody.

Celeriac

This knobbly root is closely related to celery, which explains its flavour – a cross between aniseed, celery and parsley. Similar in size to a small swede (rutabaga), it has ivory flesh and is one of the few root vegetables that must be peeled before use. When grated and eaten raw in salads, celeriac has a crunchy texture. It can also be steamed, baked in gratins or combined with potatoes and mashed with butter or margarine and grainy mustard. Celeriac can also be used in vegetarian soups and broths.

Swedes

The globe-shaped swede (rutabaga) has pale orange flesh with a delicate sweet but earthy flavour. Trim off the thick peel, then treat it in the same way as other root vegetables: grate raw into salads; dice and cook in vegetable casseroles and soups; steam, then mash, season to taste, and serve as an accompaniment.

Turnips

The humble root vegetable has many health-giving qualities, and small turnips with their green tops intact are especially nutritious. Their crisp, ivory flesh, which is enclosed in white, green and pink-tinged skin, has a pleasant, slightly peppery flavour, the intensity of which depends on their size and the time of harvesting. Small turnips can be eaten raw. Alternatively, steam, bake or use in vegetable casseroles and soups.

Potatoes

There are thousands of potato varieties, and many lend themselves to particular cooking methods. Small potatoes, such as Pink Fir Apple and Charlotte, and new potatoes, such as Jersey Royals, are best steamed. They have a waxy texture, which retains its shape after cooking, making them ideal for salads. Main crop potatoes, such as Estima and Maris Piper, are more suited to roasting, baking or mashing, and can be used to make chips (French fries). Discard any potatoes with green patches as these indicate the presence of toxic alkaloids called solanines.

Vitamins and minerals are stored in, or just below, the skin, so it is best to use potatoes unpeeled. New potatoes and special salad potatoes need only be scrubbed.

Potatoes are not in themselves fattening – it is added ingredients such

Above: Parsnips are very low in saturated fat, cholesterol and sodium. The vegetables also contain plenty of dietary fibre and Vitamin C. Above all they are a tasty and versatile addition to many quite different dishes.

as cheese and butter and the cooking method that can bump up the calories. Steam rather than boil and bake instead of frying to retain valuable nutrients and to keep fat levels down.

Jerusalem artichokes

The Jerusalem artichoke is an entirely different vegetable to the globe artichoke. It is, in fact, a tuber belonging to the sunflower family. Jerusalem artichokes look rather like knobbly potatoes, and can be treated as such. They have a lovely distinctive flavour and are good in vegetarian soups. They are also delicious baked, braised, lightly sautéed or puréed.

Radishes

There are several types of this peppery-flavoured vegetable, which is a member of the cruciferous family. The round ruby red variety is most familiar; the longer, white-tipped type has a milder taste. Mooli or daikon radishes are white and very long; they can weigh up to several kilos or pounds. Radishes can be used to add flavour and a crunchy texture to salads and stir-fries.

BRASSICAS AND GREEN LEAFY VEGETABLES

This large group of vegetables boasts an extraordinary number of health-giving properties especially for some cancers and cardiovascular diseases. Brassicas range from the crinkly-leafed Savoy cabbage to the small, walnut-sized Brussels sprout. Green, leafy vegetables include spinach, spring greens and Swiss chard.

Broccoli

This nutritious vegetable should be a regular part of everyone's diet. Two types are commonly available: purple-sprouting, which has fine, leafy stems and a delicate head, and

Below: Potatoes for baking or boiling.

calabrese, the more substantial variety with a tightly budded top and thick stalk. Choose broccoli that has bright, compact florets. Yellowing florets, a limp woody stalk and a pungent smell are an indication of overmaturity. Trim stalks before cooking, though young stems can be eaten, too. Serve raw in salads or with a dip. If you cook broccoli, steam or stir-fry it to preserve the nutrients and keep the cooking time brief to retain the vivid green colour and crisp texture.

Cauliflowers

The cream-coloured compact florets should be encased in large, bright green leaves. To get the most nutrients from a cauliflower, eat it raw, or bake or steam lightly. Cauliflower has a mild flavour and is delicious tossed in a light vinaigrette dressing or combined with tomatoes and spices.

Cabbages

Frequently overcooked, cabbage is best eaten raw, or cooked until only just tender. There are several different varieties: Savoy cabbage has substantial, crinkly leaves with a strong flavour and is perfect for stuffing; firm white and red cabbages can be shredded and used raw in salads (as can Chinese leaves (Chinese cabbage)); while pak choi (bok choy) is best cooked in stir-fries or with noodles.

Brussels sprouts

These are basically miniature cabbages that grow on a long tough stalk. They have a strong nutty flavour. The best are small with tightly packed leaves – avoid any that are very large or turning yellow or brown. Sprouts are sweeter when picked after the first frost. They are best cooked very lightly, so either steam or, better still, stir-fry to keep their green colour and crisp texture, as well as to retain the vitamins and minerals.

Spinach

For years we have been told to eat up our greens. Research into their health benefits now indicates that eating dark green leafy vegetables, such as spinach, spring greens, chard and kale on a regular basis may protect us against certain forms of cancer as well as supplying vitamins and iron to the vegetarian diet. Spinach is rich in fibre which can help to lower harmful levels of LDL cholesterol. Young, tender spinach leaves can be eaten raw and need little preparation, but older leaves should be washed well, then picked over and the tough stalks removed. Spinach is delicious combined with eggs.

Above: Broccoli is versatile, offers a superb source of vitamin C and calcium, and a great taste.

Above: Spinach wilts dramatically when cooked so allow at least 250g/9oz raw weight per person.

Swiss chard

A member of the beet family, Swiss chard has large, dark leaves and thick, white, orange or red edible ribs. It can be used in the same way as spinach, or the stems may be cooked on their own. Swiss chard is rich in vitamins and minerals although, like spinach, it contains oxalic acid.

Spring greens (collard)

These leafy, dark green young cabbages are full of flavour and are rich in vitamin C and beta carotene.

PUMPKINS AND SQUASHES

Widely popular in the USA, Africa, Australia and the Caribbean, pumpkins and squashes come in a tremendous range of shapes, colours and sizes. Squashes are broadly divided into summer and winter types: cucumbers, courgettes and marrows fall into the summer category, while pumpkins, butternut and acorn squashes are winter varieties.

Acorn squash

This small to medium-size squash has an attractive, fluted shape and looks rather like a large acorn – hence its name. The orange flesh has a sweet flavour and slightly dry texture, and the skin colour ranges from golden to dark green. Its large seed cavity is perfect for stuffing.

Butternut squash

A large, pear-shaped squash with a golden brown skin and vibrant orange flesh. The skin is inedible and should be removed along with the seeds. Roast, bake, mash or use in soups or vegetable casseroles. The flesh has a rich, sweet,

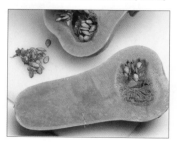

creamy flavour when cooked and makes a good substitute for pumpkin.

Pumpkins

Small pumpkins have sweeter, less fibrous flesh than the larger ones, which are perhaps best kept for making into lanterns. Deep orange in colour, pumpkin can be used in both sweet and savoury dishes, such as pies, soups, vegetable casseroles, soufflés and even ice cream. Avoid boiling pumpkin as it can become waterlogged and soggy. The seeds are edible and highly nutritious.

Winter squashes

These have tough inedible skins, dense, fibrous flesh and large seeds. Most winter squashes can be used in both sweet and savoury dishes.

Summer squashes

Picked when still young, summer squash have thin edible skins and tender, edible seeds. Their delicate flesh cooks quickly.

Pattypan squash

These pretty, baby squash resemble mini flying saucers. They are similar in taste to a courgette and are best steamed or roasted. They may be yellow or bright green, and although they can be expensive to buy, there is no waste. Pattypan squash will only keep for a few days in the fridge.

Courgettes (zucchini)

These summer squash typically have shiny green skin, a sweet delicate flavour and a crisp texture. They are at their best when they are small. The green variety is most common, but yellow ones are sometimes available.

Left: Butternut squash is delicious baked in an oven for 30 minutes or until the flesh is soft. Cut in half, scoop out the seeds and bake cut-side down. Serve in the skin, or remove the flesh and mash with a low-fat spread or yogurt.

Above: Marrows

Courgettes can be sliced or grated and eaten raw, or they can be cooked, combining well with other vegetables such as peppers, tomatoes and aubergines (eggplant). The larger courgettes become, the less flavour they have. When buying, choose firm, shiny specimens. Do not buy flabby courgettes or those with blemished skins. In countries such as Italy and France, the golden courgette flowers are also highly prized for eating. Courgettes are available almost all year round, but are best in spring and summer. They are perhaps best known as a key ingredient with tomatoes and onions in the popular vegetarian dish ratatouille.

Marrows

The 'grown-up' courgettes (zucchini), marrows have a pleasant, mild flavour and are best baked either plain or with a stuffing. Spices, chillies and tomatoes are particularly good flavourings.

Cucumbers

Probably cultivated as long ago as 10,000 BC, cucumbers were popular vegetables with the Greeks and the Romans. The long, thin, smooth-skinned variety is most familiar. Their refreshing, mild flavour makes cucumbers perfect to use raw in salads or thinly sliced as a sandwich filling. However, they can also be pickled and cooked in other ways, such as steaming, baking or stir-frying.

SHOOT VEGETABLES

This highly prized collection of vegetables, each honoured with a distinctive flavour and appearance, ranges from the aristocratic asparagus to the flowerbud-like globe artichoke.

Above: Fennel bulb, when cooked, has a subtle aniseed flavour.

Fennel bulb/Florence fennel

So called to distinguish it from the feathery green herb, fennel bulb or Florence fennel resembles a fat white root with overlapping leaves and green, wispy fronds. It has a delicate but distinctive flavour of aniseed and a crisp, refreshing texture. It can be eaten raw, dressed with a low-fat vinaigrette or served in a mixed salad. It can also be lightly sautéed, baked or braised. When cooked, the aniseed flavour becomes

more subtle and the texture resembles cooked celery. Choose firm, rounded bulbs, in which the outer layers are crisp and white, and if possible, buy those with the feathery green fronds intact.

Asparagus

Highly prized as a luxury vegetable all over Europe, asparagus has a very short growing season, from spring to early summer, and is really only worth eating during this period. Both green and white asparagus are cultivated. The green variety is grown above ground, so that the entire spear is bright green, and is harvested when it is about 15cm/6in high. The fat white spears with their pale yellow tips are grown under mounds of soil to protect them from the light.

Asparagus spears can be boiled, steamed, grilled (broiled) or roasted in a little olive oil, and served as a first course with a light sprinkling of freshly grated Parmesan cheese, or served with a light vinaigrette. Asparagus spears make an ideal accompaniment to low-fat vegetarian meals and asparagus tips also make a luxury addition to risottos.

Celery

Like asparagus, celery was once grown primarily for medicinal reasons. Serve raw, steam or braise. Celery leaves have a tangy taste and are also useful for adding flavour to stocks. Low in calories, but rich in vitamin C and potassium, celery is a recognized diuretic and sedative.

Left: Although they are both artichokes, the tightly packed heads of the green leafy globe artichoke (left) are not to be confused with the root vegetable Jerusalem artichoke (right).

Right: Jerusalem artichokes have a very distinctive flavour and are delicious baked, braised, lightly sautéed or puréed.

Above: If you're trying to eat five portions of fruit and vegetables a day then about five or six asparagus spears counts as one portion. Asparagus is a great source for B vitamin folate.

Globe artichokes

Tall vegetables that grow a round head (hence the name globe) on a long stem and are visibly striking when cultivated, globe artichokes produce edible, slightly nutty-flavoured heads (flower buds). Look for artichoke heads with tightly packed leaves, as open leaves indicate that the vegetable is too mature. When an artichoke is old, the tops of the leaves will turn brown. If possible, buy artichokes that are attached to their stems, as they will stay fresh for longer. Artichokes will keep fresh for several days if you place the stalks in water.

Otherwise wrap them in clear film (plastic wrap) and keep in the vegetable drawer of the refrigerator for a day or two.

Above: Tomatoes form the basis of many healthy vegetarian dishes, especially soups and sauces.

VEGETABLE FRUITS

By cultivation and use, tomatoes, aubergines and peppers are all vegetables, but botanically they are classified as fruit. Part of the nightshade family, they have only relatively recently become appreciated for their health-giving qualities.

Tomatoes

Sun-ripened and full of flavour, tomatoes form an essential ingredient for many healthy vegetarian recipes. The smallest tomatoes are cherry tomatoes, which are sweet and tasty. Medium tomatoes are also delicious and good for slicing. Plum tomatoes have thick walls and fewer seeds and so are ideal for tomato-based sauces. Beefsteaks are the largest type of tomato and are the best for stuffing or for slicing for salads. Bright red fruits literally bursting with aroma and flavour, tomatoes are essential ingredients in low-fat, no-fat dishes.

They can be eaten raw, sliced and served with a trickle of extra virgin olive oil and some torn fresh basil leaves. Raw ripe tomatoes can be chopped with herbs and garlic to make a fresh-tasting pasta sauce. Tomatoes can be grilled (broiled), lightly fried, baked, stuffed or stewed and made into tasty low-fat sauces and soups. Tomatoes are at their best when they have ripened naturally in the sun.

Choose your tomatoes according to the way you wish to use them. As well as fresh tomatoes, canned and sun-dried tomatoes are invaluable store cupboard (pantry) items, together with passata (bottled strained tomatoes) and tomato purée (paste). Remember, dry-packed sun-dried tomatoes are lower in fat than the oil-packed ones.

Aubergines (eggplant)

Originating in Asia, aubergines today feature in vegetarian dishes from many other countries. The plump purple variety is the most common. Look for firm, shiny-skinned specimens with green stalks, that are heavy for their size. A light aubergine may have a dry, spongy inside and could contain a lot of seeds. Do not buy those with wrinkled or damaged skins. Aubergines will keep in the refrigerator for up to a week and are a very versatile vegetable. They can be grilled (broiled), baked, stuffed, stewed or lightly sautéed, either on their own or with other vegetables, and since they absorb flavours well, they can be used with most seasonings.

Peppers

Capsicums, or bell peppers as they are also known, come in a range of colours including green, red, yellow, orange and even a purplish-black, though they all have the same sweetish flavour and crunchy texture. Peppers are commonly used in vegetarian dishes. They can be eaten raw or lightly roasted in salads or as an antipasto, and can be cooked in a variety of ways – roasted and dressed with a light olive oil or vinaigrette dressing, grilled (broiled) or stuffed and baked. To make the most of their flavour, grill (broil) peppers until charred, then rub off and discard the skins. Peppers have a great affinity with other ingredients such as olives, capers, aubergines (eggplants), courgettes (zucchini) and tomatoes.

BEANS AND PEAS

Most of these vegetables are delicious eaten fresh, but can also be bought frozen. High in nutritional value, these popular vegetables are available all year.

Above: (Bell) peppers are a very healthy food, being naturally low in fat and rich in vitamin C.

Other types of pea include mangetouts (snow peas) and sugar snap peas, which can be eaten whole, including the pod.

Broad (fava) beans

These beans are at their best in late spring or early summer when they are small and tender, or cooked and skinned later in the season. When young they can be cooked and eaten, pods and all. Cooked broad beans have a milder flavour than raw. Dried broad beans are popular in the Middle East where they are cooked with spices or added to vegetable stews.

Green beans

French, runner and dwarf beans are eaten whole. They should be bright green and crisp textured. Simply top and tail and lightly cook or steam them. Serve green beans hot, or leave to cool slightly and serve as a warm salad with a squeeze of fresh lemon juice or a vinaigrette dressing.

Corn

Corn cobs are best eaten soon after picking, before their natural sugars start to convert into starch when the flavour fades and the kernels toughen. Remove the green outer leaves and cook whole or slice off the kernels with a sharp knife. Baby corn cobs can be eaten raw, and are good in stir-fries.

Above: Garlic is available fresh, dried powdered and in liquid form.

THE ONION FAMILY

Both onions and garlic contain allicin, which stimulates the body's antioxidant mechanisms, raising levels of beneficial HDL cholesterol and combating the formation of clogged arteries. They are an absolute must in cooking and add flavour to a huge range of savoury dishes. Delicate leeks, sweet shallots and tangy spring onions (scallions) are members of the onion family.

Onions

These strongly flavoured vegetables are an essential component of virtually all savoury low-fat vegetarian dishes. Red- or white-skinned onion varieties have a sweet, mild flavour and are good used raw in salads. Large, Spanish (Bermuda) onions are also mild and a good choice when a large quantity of onions is called for in a recipe.

Leeks

With a sweeter, less overpowering flavour than onions, leeks should be a mainstay of the vegetarian diet. They have a very small bulb and a long whitish cylindrical stalk of superimposed layers that flows into green, tightly wrapped, flat leaves. Cultivated leeks are usually about 30cm (1ft) long. Leeks make a perfect base for soups and stews. They are excellent braised and served with a tasty sauce.

Garlic

Used crushed, sliced or even whole, garlic develops a smooth, gentle flavour with long, slow cooking. Used raw in salads, light sauces, dressings and marindades, garlic adds a delicious, strong flavour. Garlic also has a medicinal value, being a decongestant and helping to lower blood pressure and blood cholesterol.

MUSHROOMS

Button (white), open cup and flat mushrooms are used in vegetarian dishes all year round. Regional wild species such as ceps, chanterelles and oyster mushrooms are to be found in the markets during autumn. Mushrooms can be sliced and eaten raw, dressed with a dash of extra virgin olive oil, or they can be lightly brushed with olive oil and grilled (broiled).

LETTUCES

Nutritionally, lettuce is best eaten raw, but it can be braised, steamed or made into a soup. Large-leafed varieties can be used to wrap around a filling.

Cos lettuce

The cos or romaine lettuce has long, sturdy leaves and a strong flavour. Little Gem (Bibb) is a baby version of cos and has firm, densely packed leaves.

Iceberg lettuce

Crisp lettuce with a round, firm head of pale green leaves. It has a mild, slightly bitter flavour and is perfect in salads.

Oak leaf

Red tinged and soft textured with a slightly bitter flavour.

Lollo rosso

The pretty, frilly leaves of lollo rosso are green at the base and a deep, autumn-red around the edge. Its imposing shape means it is best mixed with other leaves if used in a salad or as a base for roasted vegetables.

Frisée lettuce

Also known as curly endive, frisée has spiky, ragged leaves that are dark green on the outside and fade to an attractive pale yellow-green towards its centre. It has a distinctive bitter flavour that is enhanced by a robust low-fat dressing.

Radicchio

The crisp leaves of radicchio taste slightly bitter and can be eaten raw or cooked. Radicchio is delicious grilled (broiled) and drizzled with a little olive oil and sprinkled with black pepper, or shredded and stirred into risotto or spaghetti. The raw leaves look pretty in salads.

Rocket (arugula)

Classified as a herb, rocket is popular in salads, or as a starter with thin shavings of Parmesan cheese. It has a strong, peppery flavour, which is more robust in wild rocket. Lightly steamed rocket has a milder flavour than the raw leaves but it is equally delicious.

Sorrel

The long pointed leaves of sorrel have a refreshing, sharp flavour that is best when mixed with milder tasting leaves.

Watercress

The hot, peppery flavour of watercress complements milder tasting leaves and is classically combined with fresh orange. It does not keep well and is best used within two days of purchase. Watercress is a member of the cruciferous family and shares its cancer-fighting properties.

Above, clockwise from left: frisée lettuce, oak leaf, cos, butterhead and iceberg lettuces

FRUIT

Fruit is used extensively in vegetarian cuisine. It is used in both sweet and savoury dishes and complements both flavours well. Raw fruit may also be eaten on its own as a simple dessert. Many fruits are naturally low in calories and fat and provide plenty of vitamin C.

ORCHARD FRUITS

Soft fruit from cultivated fruit trees grown mostly in temperate climates, these include apples, plums and pears.

Apples

There are thousands of varieties of apple, though the choice in supermakets is somewhat limited. Some of the most well-liked eating varieties are harvested in the UK, North America, Canada, Australia, New Zealand and South Africa. Popular varieties include Golden and Red Delicious, Braeburn, Jonagold, Fuji, Cox's Orange Pippin, Granny Smith, Gala, and Pink Lady. The Bramley Seedling, with its thick, shiny, green skin and tart flesh, is the most familiar cooking apple and is perfect for baking, or as the basis of apple sauce. Some less well-known varieties, many of which have a short season, are often available from farm shops.

Apples are delicious when they are eaten raw with their skin on. However, this versatile fruit is often used in vegetarian breakfast dishes, main meals, salads, desserts, pies and even soups. Large cooking apples are ideal puréed, stewed or baked, but their tartness means that sugar has to be added. Some varieties of eating apple are just as good

Below: A selection of larger cooking apples on the left and eating apples to the right.

cooked and don't need any added sugar. When buying apples, choose bright, firm fruits without any bruises. Store apples in a cool place, away from direct sunlight.

Apricots

The best apricots are sunshine gold in colour and full of juice. They are delicious baked or used raw in salads. An apricot is at its best when truly ripe. Immature fruits are hard and tasteless and never seem to attain the right level of sweetness.

Cherries

There are two types of cherry: sweet and sour. Some are best eaten raw like the popular Bing, while others, such as Morello, are best cooked.

Choose firm, bright, glossy fruits that have fresh, green stems. Discard any that are soft, or have split or damaged skin.

Peaches and nectarines

Among the most delicious summer fruits, peaches and nectarines need plenty of sun to ripen them and are grown in China, Japan, and neighbouring Asian countries, as well as the Mediterranean and North America. Peaches may be yellow-, pink- or white-fleshed, with a velvety, fuzzy skin. Nectarines are smooth-skinned, with all the luscious flavour of peaches. They also come in yellow and white varieties and, like peaches, the white nectarines have a finer flavour. Look for bruise-free specimens that just give when squeezed gently and choose fruits with an intense, sweet scent. Peaches and nectarines are interchangeable in recipes, whether cooked or raw. They can both be macerated in fortified wine or spirits, or poached in white wine and syrup. Peaches and nectarines are also delicious served with raspberries or made into fruit drinks and smoothies, low-fat ice creams and sorbets.

Pears

Succulent pears have been popular for thousands of years and were extensively cultivated by the Greeks and the Romans. Pears come into their own in the late summer and

Above: Look for peaches that have a background of yellow or cream colour plus a rosy blush on their cheeks.

autumn with the arrival of the new season's crops. Particular favourites are green and brown-skinned Conference; Williams, with its thin, yellow skin and sweet, soft flesh; plump Comice, which has a pale yellow skin with a green tinge; and Packham, an excellent cooking pear.

Pears can be used in both sweet and savoury vegetarian dishes; they are excellent in salads, and can be baked, poached in syrup, and used in low-fat crumbles and bakes.

Choose firm, plump fruits that are just slightly underripe. Pears can ripen in a day or so and then they pass their peak very quickly and become woolly or squashy. To tell if a pear is ripe, feel around the base of the stalk, where it should give slightly when gently pressed, but the pear itself should remain firm.

Plums

Ranging in colour from pale yellow to dark, rich purple, plums come in many different varieties, although only a few are available in shops. They can be sweet and juicy or slightly tart; the latter are best cooked in low-fat desserts, or made into a delicious jam. Sweet plums can be eaten as they are, and are good in fruit salads, or they can be puréed and combined with low-fat custard or low-fat yogurt to make a fruit fool.

Plums should be just firm, and not too soft, with shiny, smooth skin that has a slight "bloom". Store ripe plums in the fridge. Unripe fruits can be kept at room temperature for a few days to ripen.

Quince

Fragrant, knobbly fruits, with a thin, yellow or green skin, quinces can be either apple- or pear-shaped. They are too hard and sour to eat raw and the seeds are poisonous and should not be consumed. Their high pectin content makes for good jellies and, in Spain and France, quinces are used to make a fruit paste that is served with soft cheeses.

CITRUS FRUITS

Juicy, acidic and brightly coloured, citrus fruits such as oranges, grapefruit, lemons and limes are best known for their slightly bitter taste and high vitamin C content.

Oranges

Varieties of this popular fruit include seedless navel oranges, red-fleshed blood oranges and Seville oranges.

NUTRITIONAL CITRUS

Eating an orange a day will generally supply an adult's requirement for vitamin C, but citrus fruits also contain phosphorus, potassium, calcium, beta carotene and fibre. Pectin, a soluble fibre that is found in the flesh and particularly in the membranes of citrus fruit, has been shown to reduce cholesterol levels. The membranes also contain bioflavonoids, which have powerful antioxidant properties. Drink fresh fruit juice when you can, as bottled, canned and concentrated citrus juices have reduced levels of vitamin C.

Seville (Temple) oranges, the bitter marmalade variety, have a very short season, just after Christmas. Oranges should have unblemished shiny skins and feel heavy for their size, which indicates that they contain plenty of juice and that the flesh is not dry. Orange varieties vary in levels of sweetness. Choose unwaxed oranges if you intend to use the rind in recipes.

Grapefruit

The flesh of the grapefruit ranges in colour from vivid pink and ruby red to white; the pink and red varieties are sweeter. Heavier fruits are likely to be juicier. Served juiced, halved or cut into slices, grapefruit can provide a refreshing start to the day. The fruit also adds a refreshing tang to vegetarian salads. Cooking or grilling (broiling) mellows the tartness, but keep cooking times brief to preserve the nutrients. A glass of grapefruit juice before bed is said to promote sleep.

Lemons

These bright yellow citrus fruits are low in calories and fat and rich in vitamin C. They have an aromatic flavour which enhances many dishes and they are very versatile. Depending on the variety, lemons may have a thick indented skin or be perfectly smooth. Their appearance does not affect the flavour, but they should feel heavy for their size. Buy unwaxed lemons if you intend to use the rind in recipes. The rind also imparts a wonderful flavour to savoury vegetarian dishes, light salad dressings and low-fat desserts.

The juice can be squeezed to make a drink, or it can be added to tea, low-fat dressings and sauces. Lemons are also antioxidants, and prevent discoloration when brushed over fruits and vegetables that tend to turn brown when cut.

Limes

Once considered to be rather exotic, limes are now widely available. Avoid fruits with a yellowing skin as this is a sign of deterioration. The juice has a sharper flavour than that of lemons and if you substitute limes for lemons in a

Above: Lemons have an aromatic flavour, which enhances many vegetarian dishes. Try to choose organic, unwaxed ones but keep in the fridge as they go mouldy.

recipe, you will need to use less juice. Limes are used a great deal in Asian cooking and the rind can be used to flavour low-fat vegetarian curries, marinades and dips. Coriander, chillies, garlic and ginger are all natural partners.

BERRIES AND CURRANTS

These baubles of vivid red, purple and black are the epitome of summer and autumn, although they are now likely to be available all year round.

Strawberries

These are the favourite summer fruits and do not need any embellishment. Serve ripe (avoid those with white or green tips) and raw, on their own, or with a little low-fat natural yogurt. Wash only if absolutely necessary and just before serving.

Raspberries

Soft and fragrant, raspberries are best served simply and unadulterated – maybe with a spoonful of low-fat natural (plain) yogurt. Those grown in Scotland are regarded as the best in the world. Raspberries are very fragile and require the minimum of handling, so wash only if really necessary.

They are best eaten raw as cooking spoils their flavour and vitamin C content.

Blueberries

Dark purple in colour, blueberries come from the family which includes cranberries and bilberries. When ripe, the berries are plump and slightly firm, with a natural "bloom". Avoid any that are soft and dull-skinned, and wash and dry carefully to avoid bruising. Cultivated blueberries are larger than the wild variety. Both types are sweet enough to be eaten raw (though they can be tart) but are also good cooked in low-fat muffins, used for jellies and jams, or made into a sauce to serve with nut or vegetable roasts. Unwashed blueberries will keep for up to a week in the refrigerator.

Blackberries

These are a familiar sight in early autumn, growing wild in hedgerows. Cultivated blackberries are generally much larger than the wild fruits. Juicy and plump, blackberries can vary in sweetness, which is why they are so often cooked. Wash them carefully to prevent bruising the fruits, then pat dry with kitchen paper. Use in low-fat fruit desserts, or make into jams and jellies. The berries can also be lightly cooked, then puréed and sieved to make a sauce to serve with other fruits or low-fat ice cream.

Look for firm, glossy berries and currants. Make sure that they are not squashed or mouldy. Ripe fruits generally do not keep well and are best eaten on the day of purchase – store in the refrigerator. Unripe fruits can be kept for longer.

Gooseberries

A favourite fruit of Northern Europe, gooseberries are relatively rare in other parts of the world. They range from the hard and sour green type to the sweeter, softer purple variety. The skin can vary from smooth and silky to fuzzy and spiky. Slightly unripe, tart gooseberries make wonderful low-fat crumbles or jams and jellies. Ripe, softer fruits can be puréed and mixed with low-fat yogurt or custard, to make a delicious fruit fool. Gooseberries are a good source of vitamin A.

Right: Blackcurrants go well with apples and pears.

Blackcurrants and redcurrants

These small, pretty fruits are usually sold in bunches on the stem. To remove the currants from the stalk, run the prongs of a fork down through the clusters, taking care not to damage the fruit. Wash the fruits carefully. Raw blackcurrants are quite tart, but this makes them ideal for cooking in fruit desserts such as low-fat crumbles or pies. They make delicious jams and jellies, and are especially good in summer pudding when they are partnered by other berries. Sweeter whitecurrants make a delightful addition to fruit salads.

GRAPES, MELONS, DATES, OLIVES AND FIGS

These fruits were some of the first ever to be cultivated and are therefore steeped in history. They are available in an immense variety of shapes, colours and sizes, and with the exception of melons, they can also be bought dried.

Grapes

Fresh grapes are naturally low in fat while being rich in potassium and vitamins. Grapes tends to be heavily sprayed so you should always wash them thoroughly after purchase. Beneath the skin the flesh is always pale green and juicy. Buy bunches of grapes with fruit of equal size and not too densely packed on the stalk.

Right: Melons come in many different varieties, sizes, shapes and colours. The riper the melon, the sweeter the flavour. Melons can be served for breakfast, as an appetizer, dessert or snack.

Melons

This fruit comes in many different varieties, sizes, shapes and colours, including cantaloupe, Charentais, Galia, honeydew and Ogen, which are orange- and green-fleshed varieties, and also the wonderful pink-fleshed watermelon. Melons are often served in slices and decorated with other fresh fruits, simply as dessert fruit on their own. Ripe melons should yield to gentle pressure from your thumbs at the stalk end and have a fragrant, slightly sweet scent. If they smell highly perfumed and musky, they will probably be overripe. Melons contain mostly water, are naturally low in calories and fat, and provide some vitamin C.

Figs

Fresh figs are delicious served simply on their own either raw or lightly cooked. They vary in colour, from dark purple to green to a golden yellow, but all are made up of hundreds of tiny seeds, surrounded by soft pink flesh, which is perfectly edible. Choose firm, unblemished fruit that just yields to the touch. Figs are highly perishable so use quickly. Fresh figs can also be served with low-fat Greek (US strained plain) yogurt and honey, or stuffed with raspberry coulis and served as a dessert. Poached in a little water or wine flavoured with cinnamon or nutmeg, they make an excellent appetizer or accompaniment.

Above: Dates go particularly well with oranges and make a good addition to fruit salads.

Dates

When plump and slightly wrinkled, fresh dates have a rich honey-like flavour and dense, slightly chewy texture. They are delicious stoned (pitted) and served with low-fat Greek (US strained plain) yogurt. Dried dates can be used in the same way, but fewer are needed as the flavour is concentrated.

Olives

The fruit of one of the earliest known trees native to the Mediterranean, olives are popular in vegetarian cooking. There are many varieties, differing in size and taste. Colour depends purely on ripeness – the fruit changes from yellow to green, purple, brown and finally black when fully ripened. Fresh olives are picked at the desired stage, then soaked in water, bruised and immersed in brine to produce the familiar-tasting result. Olives are available loose, bottled or canned and may be whole or pitted. They are sometimes stuffed with pimientos or nuts, or bottled with flavourings such as garlic and chilli. Olives are quite high in monounsaturated fat and low in saturated fat, and should be used in moderation.

TROPICAL FRUIT

This exotic collection of fruits ranges from the familiar bananas and pineapples to the more unusual papayas and passion fruit.

Pineapples

These distinctive looking fruits have a sweet, exceedingly juicy and golden flesh. Unlike most other fruits, pineapples do not ripen after picking, although leaving a slightly unripe fruit for a few days at room temperature may reduce its acidity. Choose pineapples that have fresh green spiky leaves, are heavy for their size, and are slightly soft to the touch.

Papaya

Also known as pawpaw, these pear-shaped fruits come from tropical regions. When ripe, the green skin turns a speckled yellow and the pulp is a glorious orange-pink colour. The numerous edible, small black seeds taste peppery when dried. Peel off the skin using a sharp knife or a vegetable peeler before enjoying the creamy flesh which has a lovely perfumed aroma and sweet flavour. Ripe papaya is best eaten raw, while unripe green fruit can be used in cooking.

Mangoes

The skin of these luscious, fragrant fruits can range in colour from green to yellow, orange or red. Their shape varies tremendously, too. An entirely green skin is a sign of an unripe fruit, although in Asia, these are often used in salads. Ripe fruit should yield to gentle pressure and, when cut, it should reveal a juicy, orange flesh. Preparing a mango can be fiddly. Serve sliced, or purée and use as a base for low-fat ice creams and sorbets.

Bananas

A concentrated bundle of energy, bananas are also full of valuable nutrients. The soft and creamy flesh can be blended into smooth, sweet drinks, mashed and mixed with yogurt, or the fruits can be baked and barbecued whole. Bananas also make an ideal weaning food for babies as they rarely cause an allergic reaction.

If you wish to buy ripe bananas, choose yellow (or red) fruits that are patched with brown. Bananas with patches of green can be ripened at room temperature. Completely green bananas rarely ripen properly. Store bananas at cool room temperature.

Pomegranates

Golden, apple-shaped fruits with a tough skin, pomegranates contain hundreds of seeds covered with a deep pink flesh that has a delicate, slightly tart flavour. Try sprinkling over sweet dishes such as fruit salads. A good source of vitamin C.

OTHER TROPICAL FRUIT

Kiwi fruit, which is also known as the Chinese gooseberry, has a brown, downy skin and vivid green flesh that is peppered with tiny black seeds. It is extremely rich in vitamin C.

Passion fruit is a dark purple, wrinkly, egg-shaped fruit, which hides a pulpy, golden flesh with edible black seeds. Cut in half and scoop out the inside with a spoon. Passion fruit is rich in vitamins A and C.

Left: Sweet, red-skinned bananas and the more familiar large and small yellow-skinned varieties.

LOW-FAT DAIRY PRODUCE

Skimmed and semi-skimmed (low-fat) milk, half-fat and reduced-fat hard cheeses, cottage cheese, mozzarella light, feta and ricotta are all medium- to low-fat options when it comes to cooking with dairy produce.

MILK

Skimmed milk contains half the calories of full-fat milk and only a fraction of the fat, but nutritionally it is on a par, retaining the same vitamins, calcium and other minerals. Semi-skimmed (low-fat) milk has a fat content of only 1.5-1.8 per cent. In baking try using buttermilk which contains only 0.1 per cent fat. Avoid cream, but if you want to use it, choose half-fat single (light) cream with 12 per cent fat – still a quarter that of double (heavy) cream.

Soya milk

The most widely used alternative to milk is soya milk made from pulverized soya beans. It is suitable for both cooking and drinking and is used to make yogurt, cream and cheese. Soya milk is interchangeable with cow's milk, although it has a slightly thicker consistency and a nutty flavour. It is a valuable source of protein, calcium, iron, magnesium, phosphorus and vitamin E. It's also low in calories and contains no cholesterol.

Rice milk (with fewer nutrients) and goat's milk (with 20 per cent less cholesterol) are other milk alternatives.

Below: Choose reduced-fat or low-fat varieties of cheese.

MARGARINE

Vegetable margarine contains the same amount of fat as butter, which contains 80 per cent saturated fat, but the fat in margarine is polyunsaturated. This was once considered to give margarine greater health benefits. But margarine manufacturing processes change the fats into trans fats, or hydrogenated fats. Studies have shown that trans fats may be more likely than the saturated fat in butter to damage the heart and blood vessels.

SPREADS

Lower fat margarines are called spreads. They contain less than 80 per cent fat and those that are under 65 per cent fat can be classified as reduced fat. When the fat content falls below 41 per cent, a spread can be called low fat or half fat. Very low-fat spreads may contain gelatine (from animal tissues) and therefore are unsuitable for vegetarians. Olive oil based spreads are rich in monounsaturated fats and are said to reduce cholesterol levels. They can be used for cooking. When buying margarine and spreads always choose good-quality brands that contain no hydrogenated fats. Margarines and spreads absorb other flavours, so keep well-wrapped. Always store these products in the fridge; unsalted butters will keep for up to two weeks, other butters for up to a month, and margarines and spreads will keep for about two months.

CHEESE

Many low-fat varieties of cheese including Gruyère, Cheddar, Red Leicester, Danish blue, Dolcelatte, Parmesan, mozzarella, feta and many goat's cheeses are readily available and are suitable for vegetarians. Full-fat cheeses such as Parmesan can also be used sparingly to add extra flavour, but because of their high-fat content, they should only be used in small amounts. Look out for vegetarian Parmesan cheese, which goes a long way to adding delicious flavour to many vegetarian dishes, from pasta and polenta to risotto and pizzas.

Cottage cheese

Lower in fat than most other cheeses (between 2 and 5 per cent), cottage cheese is not usually used for cooking but is good in salads and dips. It makes a fine accompaniment to soft fruits and is best eaten as fresh as possible.

Quark

A soft, white cheese made from fermented skimmed milk, quark is virtually fat free, but check the label as some varieties are enriched with cream.

YOGURT

The fat content of this valuable health food ranges from 0.5g per 100g for very low-fat to virtually fat-free yogurts to 4g per 100g and above. Yogurt is used as a marinade, a dip and to enrich vegetarian soups and stews. Choose low-fat, reduced-fat or fat-free varieties, to keep the fat content of your vegetarian dishes down. Lower-fat yogurts can also be used instead of cream, but are best used in uncooked dishes.

Crème fraîche and fromage frais

These are excellent alternatives to cream. Crème fraîche is a thick, sour cream with a milky, lemony taste. The half-fat version has a fat content of 15 per cent. Fromage frais is a fresh, soft cheese available as virtually fat-free (0.4 per cent fat) and in a more creamy variety, which contains 7.9 per cent fat.

Below: Reduced-fat or low-fat Greek (US strained plain) yogurt is ideal for use in low-fat desserts, dips and marinades.

SOYA PRODUCE

Soya beans are incredibly versatile and are used to produce an extensive array of by-products that can be used in cooking – tofu, tempeh, textured vegetable protein, flour, miso, and a variety of sauces. The soya bean is the most nutritious of all beans. Rich in high-quality protein, it is one of the few vegetarian foods that contains all eight essential amino acids that cannot be synthesized in the body and are vital for the renewal of cells and tissues.

Tofu

Also known as beancurd, tofu is made in a similar way to soft cheese. The beans are boiled, mashed and sieved to make soya "milk", and the "milk" is then curdled using a coagulant. The resulting curds are drained and pressed to make tofu, and there are several different types to choose from.

Firm tofu

This type of tofu is sold in blocks and can be cubed or sliced and used in vegetable stir-fries, kebabs, salads, soups and casseroles. Alternatively, firm tofu can be mashed and used in bakes and burgers. The bland flavour of firm tofu is improved by marinating, because its porous texture readily absorbs flavours and seasonings.

Silken tofu

Soft with a silky, smooth texture, this type of tofu is ideal for use in sauces, dressings, dips and soups. It is a useful dairy-free alternative to cream, soft cheese or yogurt, and can be used to make creamy desserts.

Other forms of tofu

Smoked, marinated and deep-fried tofu are also available in health food stores as well as Oriental and other supermarkets.

Deep-fried tofu is fairly tasteless, but it has an interesting texture. It puffs up during cooking and, underneath the golden, crisp coating, the tofu is white and soft, easily absorbing the flavour of other ingredients. It can be used in much the same way as firm tofu and, as it has been fried in vegetable oil, it is suitable for vegetarian cooking.

Tempeh

This Indonesian speciality is made by fermenting cooked soya beans with a cultured starter. Tempeh is similar to tofu but has a nuttier, more savoury flavour. It can be used in the same way as firm tofu and also benefits from marinating. While some types of tofu are regarded as a dairy replacement, the firmer texture of tempeh means that it can be used instead of meat in pies and casseroles.

Beancurd skins and sticks

Made from soya "milk", dried beancurd skins and sticks, like fresh beancurd, have neither aroma nor flavour until they are cooked, when they will rapidly absorb the flavour of seasonings and other ingredients. Beancurd skins and sticks are used in Chinese cooking and need to be soaked until pliable before use. Beancurd skins should be soaked in cold water for an hour or two and can be used to wrap a variety of fillings.

Beancurd sticks need to be soaked for several hours or overnight. They can be chopped and added to soups, stir-fries and casseroles.

TVP

Textured vegetable protein, or TVP, is a useful meat replacement and is usually bought in dry chunks or as mince. Made from processed soya beans, TVP is very versatile and readily absorbs the strong flavours of ingredients such as herbs, spices and vegetable stock. It is inexpensive and is a convenient store-cupboard item. TVP needs to be rehydrated in boiling water or vegetable stock, and can be used in stews and curries, or as a filling for pies.

TOFU FRUIT FOOL

1 Place a packet of silken tofu in the bowl of a food processor. Add some soft fruit or berries – for example, strawberries, raspberries or blackberries.

2 Process the mixture to form a smooth purée, then sweeten to taste with a little honey, maple syrup or maize malt syrup.

Above, clockwise from left: Silken bean curd, bean curd skins, firm bean curd, and marinated bean curd. Tofu is a soya bean curd made from coagulated soya milk. It can be bought as silken tofu which is soft and creamy, or firm tofu which also comes smoked and marinated.

PASTA, RICE, GRAINS AND PULSES

These important staple ingredients are used as the basis of many healthy vegetarian meals. They may be added to hearty soups or vegetable stews such as tagines, used in salads as tabbouleh, or served as accompaniments to vegetarian dishes. They are versatile, healthy, nutritious and delicious – and above all naturally low in fat.

PASTA

Once considered a fattening food, pasta is now recognized as an important part of a healthy diet. The variety of shapes is almost endless, from the myriad tiny soup pastas to huge shells used for stuffing. Low in fat and high in complex carbohydrates, pasta provides plenty of long-term energy.

Durum wheat pasta

This is the most readily available type of pasta and can be made with or without egg. Plain wheat pasta is used for straight long shapes such as spaghetti, while long shapes made with egg pasta, because it is more delicate, are traditionally packed in nests or compressed into waves. Lasagne can be made with either plain or egg pasta. At one time, almost all short pasta shapes were made from plain pasta, but shapes made with egg pasta are becoming increasingly available. Pasta made with egg has several advantages over plain pasta: it is more nutritious, many people consider it to have a superior flavour, and it is more difficult to overcook.

Wholemeal (whole-wheat) pasta

This substantial pasta is made using wholemeal flour and it contains more fibre than plain durum wheat pasta. It has a slightly chewy texture and nutty flavour and it does takes longer to cook. Wholemeal (whole-wheat) spaghetti, called bigoli, is a traditional Italian variety that comes from the area around Venice known as the Veneto and can be found in good Italian delicatessens, as well as in health food shops and supermarkets. There is a growing range of tempting wholemeal shapes, from tiny soup pastas to rotelle (wheels) and lasagne.

Buckwheat pasta

Pasta made from buckwheat flour has a nutty taste and is darker in colour than wholemeal (whole-wheat) pasta. Pizzoccheri from Lombardy is the classic shape. These thin, flat noodles are traditionally sold in nests like tagliatelle (although pizzoccheri are about half the length), but they are also available cut into short strips.

Corn pasta

This pasta is made with corn or maize flour, is gluten-free and is a good alternative pasta for people who cannot tolerate gluten or wheat. It is made in a wide range of shapes, including spaghetti, fusilli (spirals) and conchiglie (shells), as well as more unusual varieties. Plain corn pasta is a sunshine-yellow colour, and may be flavoured with spinach or tomato.

PASTA SHAPES

From capellini (meaning 'angel hair') to thicker pasta shapes, such as fettucine, pasta comes in all sorts of shapes and sizes. As a general rule thin spaghetti goes well with light, thin sauces, while heavier sauces mix well with the thicker tagliatelles.

Long pasta

Dried long pasta in the form of spaghetti is probably the best known, but there are many other varieties, from fine vermicelli to pappardelle – broad ribbon noodles. Tagliatelle, the most common form of ribbon noodles, is usually sold coiled into nests. Long pasta is best served with a thin sauce, made with olive oil, butter, cream, eggs, grated cheese or chopped fresh herbs. When vegetables are added to the sauce, they should be finely chopped. Fresh spaghetti, tagliatelle and fettucine are widely available.

Short pasta

There are hundreds of different short dried pasta shapes, which may be made with plain pasta dough or the more nutritious yellow, egg pasta. Short pasta isn't often sold fresh because most shapes are difficult to produce.

Above: Pasta has very little fat but plenty of "complex" carbohydrates to keep one feeling satisfied after a meal.

Conchiglie (shells) are one of the most useful shapes because they are concave and trap the sauce. Fusilli (spirals) are good with thick tomato-based sauces and farfalle (butterflies) can be served with creamy sauces, but are very versatile and work equally well with tomato- or olive oil-based sauces. Macaroni used to be the most common short shape, and being hollow, it is good for most sauces and baked dishes. However, penne (quills) have become more popular, perhaps because the hollow tubes with diagonally cut ends go particularly well with chunky vegetable sauces.

Flat pasta

Lasagne is designed to be baked between layers of sauce, or cooked in boiling water, then layered, or rolled around a filling to make cannelloni. Lasagne is made from plain or egg pasta and both fresh and dried versions are available. The pasta sheets may be flavoured with tomato or spinach, or made with wholemeal (whole-wheat) flour.

Stuffed pasta

The most common stuffed pasta shapes are ravioli, tortellini (little pies) and cappelletti (little hats). Plain, spinach and tomato doughs are the most usual, and there is a wide range of vegetarian fillings.

RICE

For over half the world's population rice is a staple food. In Italy, there are at least four different short-grained types such as arborio and carnaroli, used for risotto. In Spain, Valencia rice is the preferred variety for paella. In Thailand fragrant jasmine rice is often used. This valuable low-fat food provides a good source of vitamins and minerals, and creates an ideal basis for a wide variety of nutritious, low-fat vegetarian dishes.

Long grain rice

The most widely used type of rice is long grain rice, where the grain is five times as long as it is wide. Long grain brown rice has had its outer husk removed, leaving the bran and germ intact, which gives it a chewy nutty flavour. It takes longer to cook than white rice but contains more fibre, vitamins and minerals. Long grain white rice has had its husk, bran and germ removed, taking most of the nutrients with them and leaving a bland-flavoured rice that is light and fluffy when cooked. It is often whitened with chalk, talc or other preservatives, so rinsing is essential. Easy-cook long grain white rice, sometimes called parboiled or converted rice, has been steamed under pressure. This process hardens the grain and makes it difficult to overcook, and some nutrients are transferred from the bran and germ into the kernel during this process. Easy-cook brown rice cooks more quickly than normal brown rice.

Basmati rice

This is a slender, long grain rice, which is grown in the foothills of the Himalayas. It is aged for a year after harvest, giving it a characteristic light, fluffy texture and aromatic flavour. Its name means "fragrant".

Both white and brown types of basmati rice are available. Brown basmati contains more nutrients, and has a slightly nuttier flavour than the white variety. Widely used in Indian cooking, basmati rice has a cooling effect on hot and spicy curries. It is also excellent for biryanis and rice salads.

Wild rice

This is not a true rice but an aquatic grass grown in North America. It has dramatic, long, slender brown-black grains that have a nutty flavour and chewy texture. It takes longer to cook than most types of rice – from 35–60 minutes, depending on whether you like it chewy or tender – but you can reduce the cooking time by soaking it in water overnight. Wild rice is extremely nutritious. It contains all eight essential amino acids and is particularly rich in lysine. It is a good source of fibre, low in calories and gluten free. Use in stuffings, serve plain or mix with other rices in pilaffs and rice salads.

Risotto rice

To make Italian risotto, it is essential that you use a special, fat, short grain rice. Arborio rice, which originates from the Po Valley region in Italy, is the most widely sold variety. When cooked, most rice absorbs around three times its weight in water, but risotto rice can absorb nearly five times its weight, and the result is a creamy grain that still retains a slight bite.

OTHER GRAINS

There are other grains besides wheat and rice that provide variety in our diet and are packed with nutrients. Amongst them are oats, rye, corn, barley, quinoa

Above: Basmati makes an excellent long grain rice. Boil, steam or bake for healthiest results and fuller flavour. It stores well in sealed containers.

(originally from the high Andes this ivory coloured nutrient-rich grain cooks like regular rice but takes half the time), and spelt (an ancient wheat variety useful for those with wheat allergies). Grains come in many forms, from wholegrains to flour and are used for baking, breakfast cereals and cooked dishes.

Oats

Available rolled, flaked, as oatmeal or oatbran, oats are warming and sustaining when cooked. Like rye, oats are a popular grain in northern Europe, particularly Scotland, where they are turned into porridge and oatcakes.

Whole oats are unprocessed with the nutritious bran and germ remaining intact. Oat groats are the hulled, whole kernel, while rolled oats are made from groats that have been heated and pressed flat. Quick cooking rolled oats have been pre-cooked in water and then dried, which diminishes their nutritional value. Medium oatmeal is best in cakes and breads, while fine is ideal in pancakes and fruit and milk drinks. Oat bran can be sprinkled over breakfast cereals and mixed into natural (plain) or fruit yogurt.

Rye

The most popular grain for bread-making in Eastern Europe, Scandinavia and Russia, rye flour produces a dark, dense and dry loaf that keeps well. The wholegrain can be soaked overnight, then cooked in boiling water until tender, but the flour, with its robust, full flavour and greyish colour, is the most commonly used form. The flour ranges from dark to light, depending on whether the bran and germ have been removed. Rye is low in gluten and is a good source of vitamin E and some B vitamins, as well as protein, calcium, iron, phosphorus and potassium. It is also high in fibre.

Corn

We are most familiar with yellow corn or maize and in its ground form it remains an essential store-cupboard ingredient in the USA, the Caribbean and Italy.

Cornmeal

The main culinary uses for cornmeal are cornbread, a classic, southern American bread, and polenta, which confusingly is both the Italian name for cornmeal and a dish made with the grain. Polenta (the cooked dish) is a thick, golden porridge, which is often flavoured with butter and cheese or chopped herbs. Once cooked, polenta can also be left to cool, then cut into slabs and fried, barbecued or griddled until golden brown. It is delicious with roasted vegetables.

Cornflour (cornstarch)

This fine white powder is a useful thickening agent for sauces, soups and casseroles. It can also be added to cakes.

Above: Cornmeal, a grainy yellow flour, comes in many forms, such as polenta.

Barley

Believed to be the oldest cultivated grain, barley is a fundamental part of everyday Eastern and Asian cooking. Pearl barley, the most usual form, is husked, steamed and then polished to give it its characteristic ivory-coloured appearance. It has a mild, sweet flavour and chewy texture, and can be added to soups, stews and bakes. It is also used to make old-fashioned barley water. Barley flakes make a satisfying porridge, and barley flour is also available.

Buckwheat

In spite of its name, buckwheat is not a type of wheat, but is actually related to the rhubarb family. Available plain or toasted, it has a nutty, earthy flavour. It is a staple food in Eastern Europe where it is milled to make blini. The flour is also used in Japan for soba noodles and in Italy for pasta.

Couscous

This tiny yellowish grain is a form of pasta made from semolina. It is a staple of North African cooking and widely available in packaged form in most supermarkets. Couscous is a good low-fat source of complex carbohydrates. The grains are rolled, dampened and cooked with fine wheat flour. Couscous simply needs soaking, although it can also be steamed or baked. It has a light and fluffy texture and a fairly bland flavour, which makes it a good foil for spicy dishes, such as low-fat vegetable stews. Couscous is also ideal for salads.

Quinoa

From the ancient Incas, this amazing grain has protein at least equivalent to that in milk and is stuffed full of potassium and riboflavin, as well as vitamin B6. Among other uses quinoa can be used in soups, salads and desserts or in pilaf recipes.

PULSES

Pulses are the edible seeds from plants belonging to the legume family. They include chickpeas and a vast range of beans and are packed with protein, vitamins, minerals and fibre. They are extremely low in fat. For the cook, their ability to absorb the flavours of other foods means that pulses can be used as the base for an infinite number of

dishes. Dried pulses require soaking overnight in cold water before use.

Lentils

These low-fat nutritious pulses come in different sizes and can be yellow, red, brown or green. The tiny green Puy lentils are favoured in France, whereas the brown and red ones are more popular in the Middle East, where they are often cooked with spices. They do not need soaking before cooking.

Aduki beans

Also known as adzuki beans, these tiny, deep-red beans have a sweet, nutty flavour and are popular in Oriental dishes. In Chinese cooking, they form the base of red bean paste. Known as the "king of beans" in Japan, the aduki bean is reputed to be good for the liver and kidneys. They cook quickly and can be used in casseroles and bakes.

Black beans

These shiny, black, kidney-shaped beans are often used in Caribbean cooking. They have a sweetish flavour, and their distinctive colour adds a dramatic touch to soups, mixed bean salads or casseroles.

Black-eyed beans (peas)

Known as black-eyed peas or cow peas in the USA, black-eyed beans are an essential ingredient in Creole cooking and some spicy Indian curries. The small, creamy-coloured bean is characterized by the black spot on its side where it was once attached to the

Above: Red lentils become very soft when cooked and are ideal for purées. Green or brown lentils are firmer and retain more texture. The finest flavoured are Puy lentils.

PREPARING PULSES

1 Rinse well, pick out any small stones, then put the pulses in a bowl of cold water. Soak for 4–8 hours.

2 Drain the pulses, rinse them under cold water and drain them again. Tip them into a pan. Add plenty of cold water but no salt. Bring to boil, boil hard for 10 minutes, then simmer until tender. Drain and season.

pod. Good in soups and salads, they can also be added to savoury bakes and casseroles, and can be used in place of haricot (navy) or flageolet or cannellini beans in a wide variety of dishes.

Borlotti beans

These oval beans have red-streaked, pinkish-brown skin and a bitter-sweet flavour. When cooked, they have a tender, moist texture, which is good in Italian bean and pasta soups, as well as hearty vegetable stews. In most recipes, they are interchangeable with red kidney beans.

Broad (fava) beans

These large beans were first cultivated by the ancient Egyptians. Usually eaten in their fresh form, broad beans change in colour from green to brown when dried, making them difficult to recognize in their dried state. The outer skin can be very tough and chewy, and some people prefer to remove it after cooking. They can also be bought ready-skinned.

Butter (wax) beans and lima beans

Similar in flavour and appearance, both butter beans and lima beans are characterized by their flattish, kidney shape and soft, floury texture. Cream-coloured butter beans are familiar in Britain and Greece, while lima beans are popular in the USA. Butter and lima beans are good with creamy herb sauces. Care should be taken not to overcook butter and lima beans as they tend to become pulpy and mushy in texture.

Cannellini beans

These small, white, kidney-shaped beans have a soft, creamy texture when cooked and are popular in Italian cooking. They can be used in place of haricot (navy) beans and, when dressed with olive oil, lemon juice, crushed garlic and fresh chopped parsley, make an excellent warm salad.

Chickpeas

Also known as garbanzo beans, robust and hearty chickpeas resemble shelled hazelnuts and have a delicious nutty flavour and creamy texture. They need lengthy cooking and are much used in Mediterranean and Middle Eastern cooking. In India, they are known as gram and are ground into flour to make fritters and flat breads. Gram flour, also called besan, can be found in health food shops and Asian grocery stores.

Flageolet beans

These young haricot (navy) beans are removed from the pod before they are fully ripe, hence their fresh delicate flavour. A pretty, mint-green colour, they are the most expensive bean to buy and are best treated simply. Cook them until they are tender, then season and drizzle with a little olive oil and lemon juice.

Haricot (navy) beans

Most commonly used for canned baked beans, these versatile, ivory-coloured beans are small and oval in shape. Called navy or Boston beans in the USA, they suit slow-cooked dishes, such as casseroles and bakes.

Pinto beans

A smaller, paler version of the borlotti bean, the savoury-tasting pinto has an attractive speckled skin – it is aptly called the painted bean. One of the many relatives of the kidney bean, pinto beans feature extensively in Mexican cooking, most familiarly in refried beans,

Above: Quick and convenient, choose canned beans that do not have any added sugar or salt. Store in a cool, dry place and use within a year of purchase for best flavour and texture. Drain and rinse under cold running water before use.

when they are cooked until tender and fried with garlic, chilli and tomatoes. The beans are then mashed, resulting in a wonderful, spicy, rough purée that is usually served with warm tortillas. Soured cream and garlic-flavoured guacamole are good accompaniments.

Red kidney beans

Glossy, mahogany-red kidney beans retain their colour and shape when cooked. They have a soft, "mealy" texture and are much used in South American cooking. An essential ingredient in spicy chillies, they can also be used to make refried beans (although this dish is traditionally made from pinto beans). Cooked kidney beans can be used to make a variety of salads, but they are especially good combined with red onion and chopped flat leaf parsley and mint, then tossed in an olive oil dressing.

Mung beans

Instantly recognizable in their sprouted form as beansprouts, mung or moong beans are small, olive-coloured beans native to India. They are soft and sweet when cooked, and are used in the spicy curry, moong dahl. Soaking is not essential, but if they are soaked overnight this will reduce the usual 40 minutes cooking time by about half.

HERBS AND SPICES

In many vegetarian dishes, some ingredients are added to dishes to give essential extra flavour or to enhance those already present. Flavours provided by herbs and spices are naturally low in fat, and they contribute a lot of taste and colour, without extra fat, making them ideal for creating a wide range of delicious and nutritious low-fat vegetarian dishes.

Basil

One of the most popular herbs, basil has a wonderful intense aroma, sweet flavour and bright green colour. The sweet, tender leaves have a natural affinity with tomatoes, aubergines (eggplants), (bell) peppers, courgettes (zucchini) and cheese. Basil is perhaps best known as the basis of the Italian sauce pesto, but a handful of torn leaves will also enliven a green salad. Tear the leaves rather than chop them, as they bruise easily, and add basil to dishes towards the end of the cooking time.

Bay leaves

Picked from the hardy bay shrub or tree, bay leaves are widely used to flavour slow-cooked recipes such as low-fat stocks, soups and vegetable stews. They are invariably included in a bouquet garni. They are also threaded on to mixed vegetable kebab skewers or thrown on the barbecue to invigorate the smoky flavour.

Below: Bay leaves have a distinctively strong, aromatic, spicy flavour.

Chillies

These are the small fiery relatives of the sweet (bell) pepper family and are commonly used in vegetarian cooking. Chillies, both fresh and dried, may be used in spicy vegetable stews, as well as in stir-fries, curries and other hot dishes.

Chives

A member of the onion family, chives have a milder flavour and are best used as a garnish, snipped over egg or potato dishes, or added to salads or low-fat flans.

Coriander (cilantro)

Fresh coriander leaves impart a distinctive flavour to low-fat soups, vegetable stews, sauces and spicy dishes when added towards the end of cooking. Coriander is also used in salads and yogurt dishes.

Cumin seeds

These dark, spindly seeds play a major role in Indian, Mexican, Thai and Vietnamese cuisines. Cumin is a crucial ingredient of chilli powder. Cumin has a strong, spicy, sweet aroma with a slightly bitter, pungent taste. Cumin seeds are crushed or used whole.

Below: Chillies add intense heat and a crunchy texture to all dishes.

Above: Mixed herbs of lemon balm, marjoram, mint and oregano.

Dill

The mild, yet distinctive, aniseed flavour of the herb dill goes well with potatoes, courgettes (zucchini) and cucumber. It makes a good addition to sauces and can be added to a wide variety of egg dishes. It can also be used as a flavouring for low-fat dressings and marinades and is a good partner for mustard. Add to dishes just prior to serving as its mild flavour diminishes with cooking.

Below: Oregano is a wild form of marjoram and has a distinct aroma.

Above: Nutmeg makes a good addition to many sweet and savoury dishes.

Lemon balm

This herb makes a refreshing tea and is good in any sweet or savoury dish that uses lemon juice.

Marjoram

Closely related to oregano, marjoram has a slightly sweeter flavour. It goes well in Mediterranean-style vegetable dishes, such as ratatouille, or in vegetable casseroles and tomato sauces, but should be added at the last minute as its flavour diminishes when heated. It also goes well in marinades.

Mint

Chopped mint accompanies other herbs to enhance stuffed vegetables in countries such as Greece and in countries in the Middle East. Finely chopped mint adds a cooling tang to low-fat yogurt dishes as well as teas and iced drinks.

Nutmeg

The sweet, warm aroma of nutmeg makes a good addition to many sweet and savoury dishes, particularly those containing spinach, cheese and eggs. For the best flavour, buy whole nutmegs and grate them freshly as required.

Oregano

This herb is a wild form of marjoram, and has a slightly stronger flavour. It is a very popular herb, widely used in vegetarian cooking and is a classic addition to pizza-based recipes.

Parsley

Both flat leaf parsley and the tightly curled variety are widely used in vegetarian cooking. Parsley is commonly used to add flavour and colour, and it also makes an attractive garnish.

Pepper

This is one of the most versatile of all spices. There are several types of peppercorns, all of which are picked from the pepper vine. Black peppercorns have the strongest flavour, which is rich, earthy and pungent. Green peppercorns are the fresh unripe berries that are bottled while soft.

Rosemary

Wonderfully aromatic, rosemary is traditionally used in meat dishes, but it can also add a smoky flavour to hearty bean and vegetable dishes.

Sage

The leaves of this herb, which may be silver-grey or purple, have a potent aroma and only a small amount is needed. Sage is commonly added to meat dishes but used discreetly, it is delicious with beans, cheese, lentils and in stuffings.

Thyme

There are many types of thyme, from lemon thyme to plain garden thyme, ranging in colour from yellow to grey-green. A few sprigs will add a warm earthy flavour to vegetable soups, marinades and other vegetarian dishes. This robustly flavoured aromatic herb is good in tomato-based recipes, and with roasted vegetables, lentils and beans. It is also essential in a bouquet garni.

Above: Thyme

Tarragon

With its distinctive grey-green leaves, tarragon is a popular herb in French cooking. Tarragon has an affinity with all egg- and cheese-based dishes. The short slender-leafed French variety has a warm, aniseed flavour. Tarragon also makes a zesty addition to salads and vinaigrettes.

BUYING AND STORING FRESH HERBS

Fresh herbs are widely available, sold loose, in packets or growing in pots. Herbs in packets do not keep for as long and should be stored in the refrigerator. Place stems of fresh herbs in a half-filled jar of water and cover with a plastic bag. Sealed with an elastic band, the herbs should keep in the refrigerator for a week. Growing herbs should be kept on a sunny windowsill. If watered regularly, and not cut too often, they will keep for months.

Above: Rosemary (left) and sage (right).

NUTS AND DRIED FRUIT

When it comes to nuts, eat sparingly, as they have high levels of mono-unsaturated and polyunsaturated fats, but they are also low in saturated fats and have no cholesterol. They contain plant protein, which makes them a good meat-substitute. Nuts are also a great source of vitamins E, B6, niacin, folic acid and minerals. Here are just a few of the many types available.

Almonds

Widely used in the Middle East, almonds are an important ingredient in sweet pastries as well as savoury dishes. Almonds are sold fresh in their green velvety shells in many Mediterranean markets. Due to their high-fat content, almonds should be used sparingly in low-fat cooking.

Chestnuts

Raw chestnuts are not recommended as they are not only unpleasant to eat but also contain tannic acid, which inhibits the absorption of iron. Most chestnuts originate from France and Spain and they are excellent after roasting – it complements their soft, floury texture. Unlike other nuts, they contain very little fat. Out of season, chestnuts can be bought dried, canned or puréed. Add whole chestnuts to winter stews, soups, stuffings or pies. The sweetened purée is delicious in desserts.

Coconuts

This versatile nut grows all over the tropics. The white dense meat, or flesh, is made into desiccated (dry, unsweetened shredded)

DRIED FRUIT AND VINE FRUIT

A useful source of energy, dried fruit is higher in calories than fresh fruit, and packed with vitamins and minerals. The drying process boosts the levels of vitamin C, beta carotene, potassium and iron. Apricots and prunes are the most popular types, but many other types such as dried apple rings, cherries and peaches are also available (*below left*).

Currants, sultanas and raisins are the most popular dried fruits. Traditionally, these vine fruits are used for fruit cakes and breads, but currants and raisins are also good in savoury vegetarian dishes. In Indian and North African cookery they are frequently used for their sweetness. Figs and dates are also popular – chopped or puréed (*below right*) – as an ingredient in low-fat cakes and tea breads.

It takes about 1.75–2.25kg/4–5lb fresh grapes to produce 450g/1lb sultanas, raisins or currants, while 1.5kg/3lb fresh figs and dates produces just 450g/1lb dried fruit. Although high in natural sugars, dried fruit is a concentrated source of nutrients, including iron, potassium, calcium, phosphorus, vitamin C, beta carotene and some B vitamins.

coconut, blocks of creamed coconut and a thick and creamy milk. A popular curry ingredient, coconut lends a sweet, creamy flavour to desserts, curries, soups and casseroles. Use coconut in moderation, as it is particularly high in fat.

Peanuts

Not strictly a nut but a member of the pulse family, peanuts bury themselves just below the earth after flowering – hence their alternative name, groundnuts. They are widely used in South-east Asia, notably for satay sauce, and in African cuisines, where they are used as an ingredient in stews.

Use sparingly – like olive oil, peanut oil is a monounsaturated fat and helps lower LDL (bad) cholesterol.

Walnuts

When picked young, walnuts are referred to as "wet" and have fresh, milky-white kernels, which can be eaten raw, but are often pickled. Dried walnuts have a delicious bitter-sweet flavour and can be bought shelled, chopped or ground. They can be used to make excellent cakes and biscuits, but are also good added to savoury dishes such as stir-fries and salads – a low-fat Waldorf salad combines kernels with sliced celery and apples in a low-fat mayonnaise dressing.

Left: Blanched, whole and shelled almonds; shelled cashews (in bowl); and shelled and whole Brazil nuts.

OILS AND VINEGARS

Oils have positive health benefits – olive oil for example is heart-protective, because it is rich in monounsaturated fats – but use such oils sparingly because they can increase the fat content of your diet. Vinegars make excellent low-fat additions to sauces and salad dressings.

OILS

There is a wide variety of cooking oils and they are produced from a number of different sources: from cereals such as corn; from fruits such as olives; from nuts such as walnuts, almonds and hazelnuts; and from seeds such as rapeseed, safflower and sunflower.

Olive oil

This is one of the most popular oils, but should be used in moderation in low-fat cooking because of its high-fat content. Unlike other oils, which are extracted from the seeds or dried fruits of plants, olive oil is pressed from the pulp of ripe olives, which gives it an inimitable richness and flavour. Besides being high in monounsaturated fat and low in saturated fat, making it a healthy alternative to many other fats, olive oil is valued for its fine, nutty flavour. Different countries and regions produce distinctively different oils. The richest and best oil comes from the first cold pressing of the olives, with no further processing, producing a rich green 'extra virgin' oil. Virgin olive oil is pressed in the same way, but is usually from a second pressing. Extra virgin olive oil is ideal used 'raw' in salad dressings, uncooked sauces and for drizzling lightly over vegetables. Virgin olive oil is used for cooking and baking.

Extra virgin olive oil

This premium olive oil has a superior flavour. It comes from the first cold pressing of the olives and has a low acidity – less than 1 per cent. Extra virgin olive oil is not recommended for frying, as heat impairs its flavour, but it is good in salad dressings, especially when combined with lighter oils. It is delicious as a sauce on its own, stirred into pasta with chopped garlic and black pepper, or drizzled over steamed vegetables.

Corn oil

One of the most economical and widely used vegetable oils, corn oil has a deep golden colour and a fairly strong flavour. It is suitable for cooking and frying, but should not be used for salad dressings. Corn is rich in omega-6 (linoleic) fatty acids, which are believed to reduce harmful cholesterol in the body.

Safflower oil

This is a light, all-purpose oil, which comes from the seeds of the safflower. It can be used in place of sunflower and groundnut oils, but is a little thicker with a slightly stronger flavour. It is best used with other more strongly flavoured ingredients, and is ideal for cooking spicy foods. Safflower oil contains more polyunsaturated fat than any other type of oil and it is low in saturated fat.

Sunflower oil

Perhaps the best all-purpose oil, sunflower oil is very light and almost tasteless. It is very versatile, and can be used for cooking, or to make salad dressings, when it can be combined with a stronger flavoured oil such as olive oil or walnut oil. Sunflower oil is extracted from the seeds of the sunflower. It is very high in polyunsaturated fat and low in saturated fat.

Soya oil

This neutral flavoured, all-purpose oil, which is extracted from soya beans, is probably the most widely used oil in the world. It is useful for frying because it has a high smoking point, and remains stable at high temperatures. It is also widely used in margarines. It is rich in polyunsaturated and monounsaturated fats and low in saturates.

VINEGARS

One of our oldest condiments, vinegar is made by acetic fermentation, a process that occurs when a liquid containing less than 18 per cent alcohol is exposed to the air. Most countries produce their own type of vinegar, usually based on their most popular alcoholic drink – wine in France and Italy; sherry in Spain; rice wine in Asia; and beer and cider in Great

Britain. Commonly used as a preservative in pickles and chutneys, it is also an ingredient in marinades and salad dressings. A spoonful or two of a good-quality vinegar can really add flavour to cooked dishes and sauces.

Balsamic vinegar

This is a rich, dark, mellow vinegar, which has become hugely popular. Traditionally made in Modena in northern Italy, balsamic vinegar is made from grape juice (predominantly from Trebbiano grapes), which is fermented in vast wooden barrels for a minimum of four to five years and up to 40 or more years, resulting in an intensely rich vinegar with a concentrated flavour. Balsamic vinegar is delicious in dressings or sprinkled over roasted vegetables.

Raspberry vinegar

Any soft fruit can be used to enhance the flavour of white wine vinegar but raspberries are the most popular. Raspberry vinegar can be made by macerating fresh raspberries in good-quality wine vinegar for 2–3 weeks. Once the mixture is strained, the vinegar is delicious as part of a salad dressing, or in sauces. It can be mixed with sparkling mineral water to make a refreshing drink.

Above: Make salad dressings with vinegars or predominantly unsaturated oils.

FAT AND CALORIE CONTENTS OF FOOD

The figures show the weight of fat (g) and the energy content per 100g (3½oz) of each foods used in low-fat cooking.

	Fat (g)	Energy
VEGETABLES		
Asparagus	0	15kcals/63kJ
Aubergines (eggplants)	0.4	15kcal/63kJ
Beetroot (beets), cooked	0.1	36kcal/151kJ
Bell peppers	0.4	32kcal/128kJ
Broad (fava) beans	0.8	48kcal/204kJ
Broccoli	0.9	33kcal/138kJ
Cabbage	0.4	26kcal/109kJ
Carrots	0.3	35kcal/146kJ
Cauliflower	0.9	34kcal/146kJ
Celery, raw	0.2	33kcal/142kJ
Courgettes (zucchini)	0.4	18kcal/74kJ
Cucumber	0.1	10kcal/40kJ
Fennel	0	14kcal/56kJ
Globe artichoke	0	9kcal/35kJ
Green beans	0	22kcal/92kJ
Jerusalem artichoke	0	41kcal/207kJ
Mushrooms	0.5	13kcal/55kJ
Okra	0	26kcal/110kJ
Onions	0.2	36kcal/151kJ
Peas	1.5	83kcal/344kJ
Potatoes	0.2	75kcal/318kJ
Chips (French fries), home-made	6.7	189kcal/796kJ
Chips, retail	12.4	239kcal/1001kJ
Oven-chips, frozen, baked	4.2	162kcal/687kJ
Potato crisps (potato chips)	34.2	530kcal/1924kJ
Spinach (fresh, cooked)	0	21kcal/84kJ
Tomatoes	0.3	17kcal/73kJ
FRUITS AND NUTS		
Apples, eating	0.1	47kcal/199kJ
Avocados	19.5	190kcal/784kJ
Bananas	0.3	95kcal/403kJ
Dates	0	226/kcal/970kJ

	Fat (g)	Energy
Dried mixed fruit	0.4	268kcal/1114kJ
Figs	0	43kcal/185kJ
Grapefruit	0.1	30kcal/126kJ
Grapes	0	63kcal/265kJ
Lemons, with peel	0.2	9kcal/38kJ
Melon	0	32kcal/135kJ
Olives (green)	11	112kcal/422kJ
Oranges	0.1	37kcal/158kJ
Peaches/nectarines	0.1	33kcal/142kJ
Pears	0.1	40kcal/169kJ
Pomegranate	0.2	51kcal/218kJ
Almonds	55.8	612kcal/2534kJ
Brazil nuts	68.2	682kcal/2813kJ
Hazelnuts	63.5	650kcal/2685kJ
Peanut butter, smooth	53.7	623kcal/2581kJ
Pine nuts	68.6	688kcal/2840kJ
Pistachio nuts	58.3	632kcal/2650kJ
Walnuts	68.5	688kcal/2840kJ
BEANS, RICE, GRAINS AND PASTA		
Black-eyed beans (peas), cooked	1.8	116kcal/494kJ
Brown rice, raw	2.8	357kcal/1518kJ
Bulgur (cracked wheat)	2.5	319kcal/1340kJ
Butter beans, canned	0.5	77kcal/327kJ
Chickpeas, canned	2.9	115kcal/487kJ
Couscous (cooked)	0	112kcal/470kJ
Hummus	12.6	187kcal/781kJ
Pasta, white, raw	1.8	342kcal/1456kJ
Pasta, wholemeal (whole-wheat), uncooked	2.5	324kcal/1379kJ
Polenta	1.6	330kcal/1383kJ
Red kidney beans, canned	0.6	100kcal/424kJ
Red lentils, cooked	0.4	100kcal/424kJ
White rice, raw	3.6	383kcal/1630kJ

Below: Vegetables are very low in fat. Eat them raw for a filling snack; steam them to retain maximum nutrition value.

Below: Vegetables contain plenty of dietary fibre and are valuable sources of vitamins, especially A, C and E.

BAKING AND SPREADS

	Fat (g)	Energy
Bread, brown	2.0	218kcal/927kJ
Bread, white	1.9	235kcal/1002kJ
Bread, wholemeal (whole-wheat)	2.5	215kcal/914kJ
Chocolate, milk	30.7	520kcal/2157kJ
Chocolate, plain (semisweet)	28.0	510kcal/2116kJ
Croissant	20.3	360kcal/1505kJ
Digestive biscuit (plain)	20.9	471kcal/1978kJ
Reduced-fat digestive biscuits	16.4	467kcal/1965kJ
Doughnut, jam	14.5	336kcal/1414kJ
Fatless sponge cake	6.1	294kcal/1245kJ
Flapjack	26.6	484kcal/2028kJ
Flour, plain (all-purpose) white	1.3	341kcal/1450kJ
Flour, self-raising (self-rising)	1.2	330kcal/1407kJ
Flour, wholemeal (whole-wheat)	2.2	310kcal/1318kJ
Fruit jam	0.26	268kcal/1114kJ
Honey	0	288kcal/1229kJ
Madeira cake	16.9	393kcal/1652kJ
Shortbread	26.1	498kcal/2087kJ
Sugar, white	0.3	94kcal/1680kJ

FATS, OILS AND EGGS

	Fat (g)	Energy
Butter	81.7	737kcal/3031kJ
Margarine	81.6	739kcal/3039kJ
Low-fat spread	40.5	390kcal/1605kJ
Very low-fat spread	25.0	273kcal/1128kJ
Cooking oil	99.9	899kcal/3696kJ
Corn oil	99.9	899kcal/3696kJ
Olive oil	99.9	899kcal/3696kJ
Safflower oil	99.9	899kcal/3696kJ
Eggs	10.8	147kcal/612kJ
Egg yolk	30.5	399kcal/1402kJ
Egg white	Trace	36kcal/153kJ
French dressing	49.4	462kcal/1902kJ
Fat-free dressing	1.2	67kcal/282kJ
Mayonnaise	75.6	691kcal/2843kJ
Mayonnaise, reduced calorie	28.1	288kcal/1188kJ

CREAM, MILK AND CHEESE

	Fat (g)	Energy
Cream, double (heavy)	48.0	449kcal/1849kJ
Reduced-fat double (heavy) cream	24.0	243kcal/1002kJ
Cream, single (light)	19.1	198kcal/817kJ
Cream, whipping	39.3	373kcal/1539kJ
Crème fraîche	40.0	379kcal/156kJ
Reduced-fat crème fraîche	15.0	165kcal/683kJ
Milk, skimmed	0.1	33kcal/130kJ
Milk, semi-skimmed (low-fat)	1.7	49kcal/204kJ
Milk, full cream (whole)	3.9	66kcal/275kJ
Brie	26.9	319kcal/1323kJ
Cheddar cheese	34.4	412kcal/1708kJ
Cheddar-type, reduced fat	15.0	261kcal/1091kJ
Cottage cheese	3.9	98kcal/413kJ
Cream cheese	47.4	439kcal/1807kJ
Curd cheese (medium fat)	11.7	173kcal/723kJ
Edam cheese	25.4	333kcal/1382kJ
Feta cheese	20.2	250kcal/1037kJ
Fromage frais, plain	7.1	113kcal/469kJ
Fromage frais, very low-fat	0.2	58kcal/247kJ
Mozzarella cheese	21.0	289kcal/1204kJ
Parmesan cheese	32.7	452kcal/1880kJ
Ricotta cheese	10	150kcal/625kJ
Skimmed-milk soft cheese	trace	74kcal/313kJ
Low-fat yogurt, natural (plain)	0.8	56kcal/236kJ
Greek (US strained plain) yogurt	9.1	115kcal/477kJ
Reduced-fat Greek yogurt	5.0	80kcal/335k

Below: Pasta, rice and beans play a key role in maintaining a healthy, low-fat, vegetarian diet.

Below: Exotic fruits, with a few notable exceptions like avocado, have a very low fat content.

SOUPS

*Vegetarian soups are ideal served as a light
starter, but many also provide a tasty, low-fat
vegetarian lunch, supper or more substantial
meal served with fresh crusty bread. In this
chapter, there is a tempting selection of recipes
for chilled soups to keep you cool in summer, as
well as many hot, more hearty low-fat soups
to warm you on those chilly winter days.*

CHILLED TOMATO AND SWEET PEPPER SOUP ★

A LOW-FAT SOUP RECIPE INSPIRED BY THE CLASSICALLY COOL SPANISH GAZPACHO, WHERE RAW INGREDIENTS ARE COMBINED TO MAKE A REFRESHING CHILLED SOUP. IN THIS MODERN VARIATION THE PEPPERS, ONION, TOMATOES AND OTHER INGREDIENTS ARE COOKED FIRST AND THEN CHILLED.

SERVES FOUR

INGREDIENTS
  2 red (bell) peppers, halved
  10ml/2 tsp olive oil
  1 onion, finely chopped
  2 garlic cloves, crushed
  675g/1½lb ripe well-flavoured
    tomatoes
  150ml/¼ pint/⅔ cup red wine
  600ml/1 pint/2½ cups vegetable stock
  salt and ground black pepper
  chopped fresh chives, to garnish
For the croûtons
  2 slices day-old white bread,
    crusts removed
  10ml/2 tsp olive oil

COOK'S TIP
Any juice that accumulates in the pan after grilling (broiling) the peppers, or in the bowl, should be stirred into the soup. It will add a delectable flavour.

1 Cut each pepper half into quarters and seed. Place skin-side up on a grill (broiling) rack and grill (broil) until the skins have charred. Transfer to a bowl and cover with a plate.

2 Heat the oil in a large non-stick pan. Add the onion and garlic, and cook until soft. Meanwhile, remove the skin from the peppers and roughly chop them. Cut the tomatoes into chunks.

3 Add the peppers and tomatoes to the pan, then cover and cook gently for 10 minutes. Add the wine and cook for a further 5 minutes, then add the stock and salt and pepper, and simmer for 20 minutes.

4 Meanwhile, make the croûtons. Cut the bread into cubes. Heat the oil in a small non-stick frying pan, add the bread and fry until golden brown and crisp. Drain on kitchen paper, cool, then store in an airtight box.

5 Process the soup in a blender or food processor until smooth. Pour into a clean glass or ceramic bowl and leave to cool thoroughly before chilling for at least 3 hours. When the soup is cold, season to taste with salt and pepper.

6 Serve in bowls, topped with croûtons and garnished with chopped chives.

Energy 103Kcal/433kJ; Protein 2.4g; Carbohydrate 12.2g, of which sugars 11.5g; Fat 2.5g, of which saturates 0.5g; Cholesterol 0mg; Calcium 26mg; Fibre 3.3g; Sodium 148mg.

GAZPACHO ★

THIS CLASSIC CHILLED SOUP IS DEEPLY ROOTED IN ANDALUSIA. THE SOOTHING BLEND OF TOMATOES, SWEET PEPPERS AND GARLIC IS SHARPENED WITH SHERRY VINEGAR. SERVE IT WITH TRADITIONAL SMALL DISHES OF GARNISHES, IF YOU LIKE, BUT REMEMBER THESE WILL ADD EXTRA FAT AND CALORIES TO THE RECIPE.

SERVES FOUR

INGREDIENTS
1.3–1.6kg/3–3½lb ripe tomatoes
1 green (bell) pepper, seeded and
    roughly chopped
2 garlic cloves, finely chopped
2 slices stale bread, crusts removed
20ml/4 tsp extra virgin olive oil
60ml/4 tbsp sherry vinegar
175ml/6fl oz/¾ cup tomato juice
300ml/½ pint/1¼ cups iced water
salt and ground black pepper
ice cubes, to serve (optional)
For the garnishes
10ml/2 tsp olive oil
2–3 slices stale bread, diced
1 small cucumber, peeled
    and finely diced
1 small onion, finely chopped
1 red (bell) and 1 green (bell)
    pepper, seeded and finely diced
2 hard-boiled eggs, chopped
    (optional)

COOK'S TIP
In Spain, ripe tomatoes are used for salads and very ripe ones for sauces and soups. No further flavouring ingredients are needed. If you cannot find really ripe tomatoes, add a pinch of sugar to sweeten the soup slightly.

1 Skin the tomatoes, then quarter them and remove the cores and seeds, saving the juices. Put the pepper in a food processor and process for a few seconds. Add the tomatoes, reserved juices, garlic, bread, oil and vinegar and process. Add the tomato juice and process to combine.

2 Season the soup, then pour into a large bowl, cover with clear film (plastic wrap) and chill for at least 12 hours.

3 Prepare the garnishes. Heat the olive oil in a non-stick frying pan and lightly fry the bread cubes for 4–5 minutes until golden brown and crisp. Drain well on kitchen paper, then arrange in a small dish. Place each of the remaining garnishes in separate small dishes.

4 Just before serving, dilute the soup with the ice-cold water. The consistency should be thick but not too stodgy. If you like, stir a few ice cubes into the soup, then spoon into serving bowls and serve with the garnishes.

Energy 134Kcal/569kJ; Protein 4.2g; Carbohydrate 20.9g, of which sugars 14.4g; Fat 4.4g, of which saturates 0.8g; Cholesterol 0mg; Calcium 46mg; Fibre 4.4g; Sodium 202mg.

SPICED MANGO SOUP WITH YOGURT ★

THE RECIPE FOR DELICIOUS, LIGHT MANGO SOUP COMES FROM CHUTNEY MARY, THE FAMOUS ANGLO-INDIAN RESTAURANT IN LONDON. IT IS BEST WHEN SERVED LIGHTLY CHILLED.

SERVES FOUR

INGREDIENTS
2 ripe mangoes
15ml/1 tbsp gram flour
120ml/4fl oz/½ cup low-fat natural
  (plain) yogurt
900ml/1½ pints/3¾ cups cold water
2.5ml/½ tsp grated fresh root ginger
2 red chillies, seeded and
  finely chopped
10ml/2 tsp olive oil
2.5ml/½ tsp mustard seeds
2.5ml/½ tsp cumin seeds
8 curry leaves
salt and ground black pepper
fresh mint leaves, shredded,
  to garnish
low-fat natural (plain) yogurt, to serve

1 Peel the mangoes, remove the stones and cut the flesh into chunks. Purée the mango flesh in a blender or food processor until smooth. Pour the mango purée into a saucepan and gently stir in the gram flour, yogurt, water, ginger and chillies.

2 Bring slowly to the boil, stirring occasionally. Simmer for 4–5 minutes until thickened slightly, then remove the pan from the heat and set aside.

3 Heat the oil in a non-stick frying pan. Add the mustard seeds and cook for a few seconds until they begin to pop, then add the cumin seeds.

4 Add the curry leaves and cook gently for 5 minutes. Stir the spice mixture into the soup, return the soup to the heat and cook for 10 minutes.

5 Press the soup through a sieve (strainer), if you like, then season to taste with salt and pepper. Leave the soup to cool completely, then chill for at least 1 hour.

6 Ladle the soup into bowls, and top each with a dollop of yogurt. Garnish with shredded mint leaves and serve.

COOK'S TIP
Gram flour, also known as besan flour, is often used in Indian cooking and is made from ground chickpeas (*chana dhal*).

Energy 83Kcal/354kJ; Protein 3g; Carbohydrate 14.4g, of which sugars 12.7g; Fat 2g, of which saturates 0.5g; Cholesterol 0mg; Calcium 72mg; Fibre 2g; Sodium 28mg.

ROASTED TOMATO AND PASTA SOUP ★

*WHEN THE ONLY TOMATOES YOU CAN BUY ARE NOT PARTICULARLY FLAVOURSOME, MAKE THIS TASTY
LOW-FAT SOUP. THE OVEN-ROASTING GIVES THE TOMATOES A BIT OF ADDED PIQUANCY.*

SERVES FOUR

INGREDIENTS

450g/1lb ripe Italian plum tomatoes,
  halved lengthways
1 large red (bell) pepper, quartered
  lengthways and deseeded
1 large red onion, quartered
  lengthways
2 garlic cloves, unpeeled
10ml/2 tsp olive oil
1.2 litres/2 pints/5 cups vegetable
  stock or water
a good pinch of sugar
90g/3½oz/scant 1 cup dried small
  pasta shapes, such as tubetti or
  small macaroni
salt and ground black pepper
fresh basil leaves, to garnish

1 Preheat the oven to 190°C/375°F/
Gas 5. Spread out the tomatoes, red
pepper, onion and garlic in a roasting
pan and drizzle with the olive oil. Roast
in the oven for 30–40 minutes, or until
the vegetables are soft and charred,
stirring and turning them halfway
through the cooking time.

2 Tip the vegetables into a blender or
food processor, add about 250ml/8fl oz/
1 cup of the stock or water and process
until puréed. Scrape the vegetable
mixture into a sieve (strainer) placed
over a large pan and press the purée
through the sieve into the pan. Discard
the contents of the sieve.

3 Add the remaining stock or water to
the pan, then add the sugar, salt and
pepper to taste. Bring to the boil, stirring.

4 Add the pasta to the pan, return to
the boil, then simmer, stirring frequently
for 7–8 minutes, or according to the
packet instructions, until the pasta is
tender or *al dente*. Adjust the seasoning
to taste. Serve hot in soup bowls,
garnished with fresh basil leaves.

COOK'S TIP
The soup can be frozen without the
pasta. Thaw the soup and bring it gently
to the boil before adding the pasta, then
continue to cook as directed above.

Energy 142Kcal/599kJ; Protein 4.5g; Carbohydrate 26.9g, of which sugars 9.7g; Fat 2.5g, of which saturates 0.4g; Cholesterol 0mg; Calcium 30mg; Fibre 3.2g; Sodium 14mg.

TOMATO AND FRESH BASIL SOUP ★

A LIGHT SOUP IDEAL FOR LATE SUMMER, WHEN FRESH PLUM TOMATOES ARE AT THEIR MOST SUCCULENT, THIS FRESH TOMATO SOUP FLAVOURED WITH BASIL CREATES A TASTY SUPPER DISH.

SERVES FOUR

INGREDIENTS
  10ml/2 tsp olive oil
  1 onion, finely chopped
  900g/2lb ripe Italian plum tomatoes,
    roughly chopped
  1 garlic clove, roughly chopped
  about 750ml/1¼ pints/3 cups
    vegetable stock
  120ml/4fl oz/½ cup dry white wine
  30ml/2 tbsp sun-dried tomato
    purée (paste)
  30ml/2 tbsp shredded fresh basil,
    plus a few whole leaves to garnish
  30ml/2 tbsp single (light) cream
  salt and ground black pepper

1 Heat the olive oil in a large non-stick pan over a medium heat. Add the onion and cook gently for about 5 minutes, until it is softened but not brown, stirring frequently.

2 Stir in the chopped tomatoes and garlic, then add the stock, white wine and tomato purée, with salt and pepper to taste. Bring to the boil, then reduce the heat, half-cover the pan and simmer gently for 20 minutes, stirring the mixture occasionally to stop the tomatoes sticking to the base of the pan.

COOK'S TIP
When buying garlic, choose plump garlic with tightly packed cloves and dry skin. Avoid bulbs with soft, shrivelled cloves or green sprouting shoots.

3 Process the soup with the shredded basil in a blender or food processor until smooth, then press the mixture through a sieve (strainer) into a clean pan. Discard the contents of the sieve.

4 Add the cream to the soup in the pan and heat through gently, stirring. Do not allow the soup to boil. Check the consistency of the soup and add more hot stock if necessary, then adjust the seasoning to taste. Pour into soup bowls and garnish with whole basil leaves. Serve immediately.

Energy 97Kcal/409kJ; Protein 2.4g; Carbohydrate 9.6g, of which sugars 9.2g; Fat 3.7g, of which saturates 1.4g; Cholesterol 4mg; Calcium 32mg; Fibre 2.7g; Sodium 42mg.

FARMHOUSE SOUP ★

ROOT VEGETABLES FORM THE BASIS OF THIS DELICIOUS LOW-FAT, CHUNKY, MINESTRONE-STYLE SOUP. FOR A MORE SUBSTANTIAL MEAL, SERVE IT WITH FRESH CRUSTY BREAD.

SERVES SIX

INGREDIENTS

15 ml/1 tbsp olive oil
1 onion, roughly chopped
3 carrots, cut into large chunks
175–200g/6–7oz turnips, cut into
    large chunks
175g/6oz swede (rutabaga), cut into
    large chunks
400g/14oz can chopped tomatoes
15ml/1 tbsp tomato purée (paste)
5ml/1 tsp mixed dried herbs
5ml/1 tsp dried oregano
50g/2oz/½ cup dried peppers,
    washed and thinly sliced (optional)
1.5 litres/2½ pints/6¼ cups
    vegetable stock or water
50g/2oz/½ cup dried small macaroni
    or conchiglie
400g/14oz can red kidney beans,
    rinsed and drained
30ml/2 tbsp chopped fresh
    flat leaf parsley
salt and ground black pepper
15ml/1 tbsp grated fresh Parmesan
    cheese, to serve

COOK'S TIP
Dried Italian peppers are piquant and firm with a "meaty" bite, which makes them ideal for adding substance to vegetarian soups.

VARIATIONS
Use 1 red onion in place of standard onion. Use parsnips in place of turnips or swede.

1 Heat the oil in a large non-stick pan, add the onion and cook over a low heat for about 5 minutes, until softened. Add the prepared fresh vegetables, canned tomatoes, tomato purée, dried herbs and dried peppers, if using. Stir in salt and pepper to taste. Pour in the stock or water and bring to the boil. Stir well, then reduce the heat, cover and simmer for 30 minutes, stirring occasionally.

2 Add the pasta and bring to the boil, stirring, then simmer, uncovered, for about 5 minutes or according to the packet instructions, until the pasta is just tender or *al dente*. Stir frequently.

3 Stir in the beans. Heat through for 2–3 minutes, then remove from the heat and stir in the parsley. Adjust the seasoning to taste. Serve hot, sprinkled with a little grated Parmesan.

Energy 161Kcal/678kJ; Protein 7.1g; Carbohydrate 28.2g, of which sugars 12.3g; Fat 3g, of which saturates 0.5g; Cholesterol 0mg; Calcium 100mg; Fibre 7.8g; Sodium 294mg.

SHIITAKE MUSHROOM AND RED ONION LAKSA ★

"NOODLES" OF THINLY SLICED RED ONIONS ENHANCE THE TRADITIONAL FLOUR NOODLES IN THIS TASTY, LOW-FAT SOUP, WHICH IS BASED ON THE CLASSIC SOUP, PENANG LAKSA.

SERVES SIX

INGREDIENTS

150g/5oz/2½ cups dried shiitake
  mushrooms
1.2 litres/2 pints/5 cups boiling
  vegetable stock
30ml/2 tbsp tamarind paste
250ml/8fl oz/1 cup hot water
6 large dried red chillies, stems
  removed and seeded
2 lemon grass stalks, thinly sliced
5ml/1 tsp ground turmeric
15ml/1 tbsp grated fresh galangal
1 onion, chopped
15ml/1 tbsp sunflower oil
10ml/2 tsp palm sugar
175g/6oz rice vermicelli
1 red onion, very thinly sliced
1 small cucumber, seeded and cut
  into strips
a handful of fresh mint leaves,
  to garnish

1 Place the dried shiitake mushrooms in a bowl and pour in enough boiling vegetable stock to cover them, then leave to soak for about 30 minutes. Put the tamarind paste into a bowl and pour in the hot water. Mash the paste against the side of the bowl with a fork to extract as much flavour as possible, then strain and reserve the liquid, discarding the pulp.

2 Soak the chillies in enough hot water to cover for 5 minutes, then drain, reserving the liquid and soaked chillies separately.

3 Process the lemon grass, turmeric, galangal, onion and soaked chillies in a blender or food processor, adding a little soaking water from the chillies to form a paste.

4 Heat the oil in a large, heavy, non-stick pan and cook the paste over a low heat for 4–5 minutes until fragrant. Add the tamarind liquid and bring to the boil, then simmer for 5 minutes. Remove the pan from the heat.

5 Drain the mushrooms and reserve the stock. Discard the stems, then halve or quarter the mushrooms, if large. Add the mushrooms to the pan with their soaking liquid, the remaining stock and the palm sugar. Bring to the boil, then reduce the heat and simmer for 25–30 minutes, or until the mushrooms are tender.

6 Put the rice vermicelli into a large bowl and cover with boiling water, then leave to soak for 4 minutes or according to the packet instructions. Drain well, then divide among six bowls. Top with onion and cucumber, then ladle in the boiling shiitake soup. Add a small bunch of mint leaves to each bowl and serve immediately.

Energy 146Kcal/611kJ; Protein 4.4g; Carbohydrate 27.1g, of which sugars 3.7g; Fat 2.3g, of which saturates 0.3g; Cholesterol 4mg; Calcium 27mg; Fibre 1g; Sodium 54mg.

WILD MUSHROOM SOUP ★

*DRIED PORCINI MUSHROOMS — THE KING OF MUSHROOMS IN ITALIAN COOKING — ARE PRICY BUT HAVE
AN INTENSE FLAVOUR SO ONLY A SMALL QUANTITY IS NEEDED FOR THIS DELICIOUS LIGHT SOUP.*

SERVES FOUR

INGREDIENTS

25g/1oz/½ cup dried porcini
   mushrooms
10ml/2 tsp olive oil
2 leeks, thinly sliced
2 shallots, roughly chopped
1 garlic clove, roughly chopped
225g/8oz/3 cups fresh wild
   mushrooms
about 1.2 litres/2 pints/5 cups
   vegetable stock
2.5ml/½ tsp dried thyme
30ml/2 tbsp single (light) cream
salt and ground black pepper
fresh thyme sprigs, to garnish

1 Put the dried porcini mushrooms in a bowl, add 250ml/8fl oz/1 cup warm water and leave to soak for 20–30 minutes. Lift the mushrooms out of the liquid and squeeze over the bowl to remove as much of the soaking liquid as possible. Strain all the liquid and reserve to use later. Finely chop the porcini and set aside.

2 Heat the olive oil in a large, non-stick pan. Add the leeks, shallots and garlic and cook gently for about 5 minutes, stirring the mixture frequently, until softened but not coloured.

COOK'S TIP
Store dried herbs, such as dried thyme, in airtight glass containers, and keep them in a cool, dark place.

3 Chop or slice the fresh mushrooms and add to the pan. Stir over a medium heat for a few minutes until they begin to soften. Pour in the stock and bring to the boil. Add the chopped porcini, reserved soaking liquid, dried thyme and salt and pepper to taste. Reduce the heat, half-cover the pan and simmer gently for 30 minutes, stirring occasionally.

4 Pour about three-quarters of the soup into a blender or food processor and process until smooth. Return to the soup left in the pan, stir in the cream and heat through gently, stirring. Check the consistency and add more hot stock if the soup is too thick. Adjust the seasoning to taste. Serve hot in soup bowls, garnished with fresh thyme sprigs.

Energy 62Kcal/257kJ; Protein 3.1g; Carbohydrate 4.2g, of which sugars 3.1g; Fat 3.8g, of which saturates 1.3g; Cholesterol 4mg; Calcium 36mg; Fibre 2.9g; Sodium 8mg.

ROASTED VEGETABLE SOUP ★

ROASTING THE VEGETABLES, ESPECIALLY THE BUTTERNUT SQUASH, GIVES THIS HEARTY LOW-FAT WINTER SOUP A WONDERFUL DEPTH OF FLAVOUR AND A BEAUTIFUL RICH COLOUR. THE FILLING ROOT VEGETABLES MAKE THIS EITHER A SATISFYING LUNCH OR SUPPER DISH.

SERVES SIX

INGREDIENTS
   30ml/2 tbsp olive oil
   1 small butternut squash, peeled,
      seeded and cubed
   2 carrots, cut into thick rounds
   1 large parsnip, cubed
   1 small swede (rutabaga), cubed
   2 leeks, washed and thickly sliced
   1 onion, quartered
   3 bay leaves
   4 fresh thyme sprigs, plus extra
      to garnish
   3 fresh rosemary sprigs
   1.2 litres/2 pints/5 cups
      vegetable stock
   salt and ground black pepper
   sour cream, to serve

1 Preheat the oven to 200°C/400°F/ Gas 6. Pour the oil into a large bowl, add all the prepared vegetables and toss until well coated.

2 Spread out the vegetables in a single layer on one large or two small baking sheets. Tuck the bay leaves, thyme and rosemary sprigs among the vegetables.

COOK'S TIP
To make sure you remove all the dirt and grit from between the leaves of leeks, slit the leeks lengthways, almost to the root end. Hold the leeks under running cold water, fanning out the leaves to wash them well.

3 Roast the vegetables in the oven for about 50 minutes, turning them occasionally to make sure that they brown evenly. Remove from the oven, discard the herbs and transfer the vegetables to a large pan.

4 Pour the stock into the pan and bring to the boil. Reduce the heat, season to taste with salt and pepper, then simmer for 10 minutes. Transfer the soup to a blender or food processor and process until thick and smooth.

5 Return the soup to the rinsed out pan and heat through gently, stirring. Serve in heated bowls, adding a swirl of sour cream to each portion. Garnish with the extra thyme sprigs.

VARIATION
For the buttenut squash you might substitute an acorn squash with its sweet flavour but slightly dryer texture, or even a pumpkin which is ideal for soups.

Energy 113Kcal/474kJ; Protein 3.1g; Carbohydrate 15.1g, of which sugars 10.4g; Fat 4.9g, of which saturates 0.8g; Cholesterol 0mg; Calcium 105mg; Fibre 6g; Sodium 18mg.

RIBOLLITA ★

SEEMING VERY SIMILAR TO MINESTRONE AT FIRST GLANCE, RIBOLLITA INCLUDES BEANS INSTEAD OF PASTA. IN ITALY IT IS TRADITIONALLY SERVED LADLED OVER BREAD AND A RICH GREEN VEGETABLE, MAKING IT A DELICIOUS AND WHOLESOME LOW-FAT SOUP.

SERVES EIGHT

INGREDIENTS
15ml/1 tbsp olive oil
2 onions, chopped
2 carrots, sliced
4 garlic cloves, crushed
2 celery sticks, thinly sliced
1 fennel bulb, trimmed and chopped
2 large courgettes (zucchini), thinly sliced
400g/14oz can chopped tomatoes
15ml/1 tbsp homemade or bought green pesto
900ml/1½ pints/3¾ cups vegetable stock
400g/14oz can white or borlotti beans, rinsed and drained
salt and ground black pepper
To finish
450g/1lb young spinach
10ml/2 tsp extra virgin olive oil
8 small slices of white bread
15ml/1 tbsp shaved fresh Parmesan cheese (optional)

1 Heat the oil in a large, non-stick pan. Add the onions, carrots, garlic, celery and fennel and cook gently for 10 minutes, stirring occasionally. Add the courgettes and cook for another 2 minutes.

VARIATION
Use other dark greens, such as chard or cabbage, instead of the spinach; simply shred and cook until tender, then ladle the soup over the top.

COOK'S TIP
When using a garlic press, leave the peel on the garlic clove. The soft garlic flesh will be pushed through the mesh, leaving the skin behind, and the garlic press will be easy to clean out after use.

2 Add the chopped tomatoes, pesto, stock and beans and bring to the boil. Reduce the heat, cover and simmer gently for 25–30 minutes, or until the vegetables are completely tender, stirring occasionally. Season to taste.

3 Cook the spinach or greens in a non-stick pan in the oil for 2 minutes, or until wilted. Spoon onto the bread in soup bowls, then ladle in the soup and serve. Serve with Parmesan cheese shavings sprinkled on top.

Energy 104Kcal/436kJ; Protein 5.6g; Carbohydrate 14.5g, of which sugars 6.9g; Fat 3g, of which saturates 0.5g; Cholesterol 0mg; Calcium 78mg; Fibre 5.9g; Sodium 218mg.

SUMMER VEGETABLE SOUP ★

THIS BRIGHTLY COLOURED, FRESH-TASTING, LIGHT TOMATO SOUP MAKES THE MOST OF SUMMER VEGETABLES IN SEASON. ADD LOTS OF RED AND YELLOW PEPPERS TO MAKE A SWEETER VERSION.

SERVES FOUR

INGREDIENTS

450g/1lb ripe plum tomatoes
225g/8oz ripe yellow tomatoes
10ml/2 tsp olive oil
1 large onion, finely chopped
15ml/1 tbsp sun-dried tomato
  purée (paste)
225g/8oz green courgettes (zucchini),
  trimmed and roughly chopped
225g/8oz yellow courgettes (summer
  squash), trimmed and roughly
  chopped
3 waxy new potatoes, diced
2 garlic cloves, crushed
about 1.2 litres/2 pints/5 cups
  vegetable stock or water
60ml/4 tbsp shredded fresh basil
25g/1oz/⅓ cup grated
  fresh Parmesan cheese
salt and ground black pepper

1 Plunge all the tomatoes in boiling water for 30 seconds, refresh in cold water, then skin and chop finely. Heat the oil in a large non-stick pan, add the onion and cook gently for 5 minutes, until softened, stirring constantly. Stir in the sun-dried tomato purée, chopped tomatoes, courgettes, potatoes and garlic. Mix well and cook gently for 10 minutes, shaking the pan often.

2 Pour in the stock or water. Bring to the boil, reduce the heat, half-cover the pan and simmer gently for 15 minutes or until the vegetables are just tender. Add more stock or water, if necessary.

3 Remove the pan from the heat and stir in the basil and half the cheese. Add seasoning to taste. Serve hot, sprinkled with the remaining cheese.

Energy 146Kcal/615kJ; Protein 7.1g; Carbohydrate 19.9g, of which sugars 8.7g; Fat 4.7g, of which saturates 1.9g; Cholesterol 6mg; Calcium 121mg; Fibre 3.6g; Sodium 102mg.

HERB SOUP WITH CHARGRILLED RADICCHIO ★

THE SWEETNESS OF SHALLOTS AND LEEKS IN THIS TASTY, LOW-FAT SOUP IS BALANCED BEAUTIFULLY BY THE SLIGHTLY ACIDIC SORREL WITH ITS HINT OF LEMON, AND A BOUQUET OF SUMMER HERBS.

SERVES SIX

INGREDIENTS

30ml/2 tbsp dry white wine
2 shallots, finely chopped
1 garlic clove, crushed
2 leeks, sliced
1 large potato, about 225g/8oz,
    roughly chopped
2 courgettes (zucchini), chopped
600ml/1 pint/2½ cups water
115g/4oz sorrel, torn
a large handful of fresh chervil
a large handful of fresh
    flat leaf parsley
a large handful of fresh mint
1 round (butterhead) lettuce,
    separated into leaves
600ml/1 pint/2½ cups
    vegetable stock
1 small head of radicchio
5ml/1 tsp groundnut (peanut) oil
salt and ground black pepper

1 Put the wine, shallots and garlic into a heavy pan and bring to the boil. Cook for 2–3 minutes, until softened. Add the leeks, potato and courgettes with enough of the water to come about halfway up the vegetables.

2 Lay a wetted piece of greaseproof paper over the vegetables and put a lid on the pan, then cook gently for 10–15 minutes, or until softened. Remove and discard the paper and add the fresh herbs and lettuce. Cook for 1–2 minutes, or until wilted.

3 Pour in the remaining water and vegetable stock and bring to the boil, then reduce the heat and simmer for 10–12 minutes. Cool the soup slightly, then process it in a blender or food processor until smooth. Return the soup to the rinsed-out pan. Season well to taste with salt and pepper.

4 Cut the radicchio into thin wedges that hold together, then brush the cut sides with the oil. Heat a ridged griddle or frying pan until very hot and add the radicchio wedges.

5 Cook the radicchio wedges for 1 minute on each side, or until slightly charred. Reheat the soup over a low heat, stirring, then ladle it into warmed shallow bowls. Serve a wedge of charred radicchio on top of each portion.

COOK'S TIP
Radicchio is a ruby-leaved Italian chicory that is now grown in Britain as well as imported. Radicchio has a firm texture, a bitter but pleasant flavour, and adds an attractive colour to many dishes. It is often used raw, but may also be lightly cooked, as with this recipe.

Energy 75Kcal/314kJ; Protein 3.8g; Carbohydrate 11g, of which sugars 4.7g; Fat 1.6g, of which saturates 0.3g; Cholesterol 0mg; Calcium 85mg; Fibre 3.2g; Sodium 35mg.

TUSCAN BEAN SOUP ★

CAVOLO NERO IS A VERY DARK GREEN CABBAGE WITH A NUTTY FLAVOUR FROM ITALY. IT'S AVAILABLE IN MOST LARGE SUPERMARKETS, BUT IF YOU CAN'T GET IT, TRY SAVOY CABBAGE. SERVE WITH CIABATTA BREAD.

SERVES FOUR

INGREDIENTS

2 x 400g/14oz cans chopped
  tomatoes with herbs
250g/9oz cavolo nero leaves
400g/14oz can cannellini beans
10ml/2 tsp extra virgin olive oil
salt and ground black pepper

1 Pour the tomatoes into a large pan and add a can of cold water. Season to taste with salt and pepper. Bring to the boil, then reduce the heat to a simmer.

2 Roughly shred the cabbage leaves and add them to the pan. Half-cover the pan and simmer gently for about 15 minutes, or until the cabbage is tender.

3 Drain and rinse the cannellini beans, then add them to the pan and heat through for a few minutes until hot. Check and adjust the seasoning to taste, then ladle the soup into bowls. Drizzle each portion with a little olive oil and serve.

Energy 164Kcal/696kJ; Protein 9.2g; Carbohydrate 27.1g, of which sugars 12.9g; Fat 2.8g, of which saturates 0.5g; Cholesterol 0mg; Calcium 116mg; Fibre 9.5g; Sodium 413mg.

PASTA, BEAN AND VEGETABLE SOUP ★★

THIS TASTY SOUP IS A SPECIALITY FROM THE CALABRIAN REGION OF ITALY. THE COMBINATION OF PULSES, PASTA AND VEGETABLES CREATES A FILLING LOW-FAT SOUP.

SERVES SIX

INGREDIENTS
75g/3oz/scant ½ cup brown lentils
15g/½oz/¼ cup dried mushrooms
15ml/1 tbsp olive oil
1 carrot, diced
1 celery stick, diced
1 onion, finely chopped
1 garlic clove, finely chopped
a little chopped fresh flat leaf parsley
a good pinch of dried crushed
  red chillies (optional)
1.5 litres/2½ pints/6¼ cups
  vegetable stock
150g/5oz/scant 1 cup each canned
  red kidney beans, cannellini beans
  and chickpeas, rinsed and drained
115g/4oz/1 cup dried small pasta
  shapes, such as rigatoni or penne
salt and ground black pepper
chopped fresh flat parsley to garnish
30ml/2 tbsp grated fresh Pecorino
  cheese, to serve

1 Put the lentils in a medium pan, add 475ml/16fl oz/2 cups water and bring to the boil over a high heat. Reduce the heat to a gentle simmer and cook, for 15–20 minutes, or until just tender, stirring occasionally. Meanwhile, soak the dried mushrooms in 175ml/6fl oz/¾ cup warm water for 15–20 minutes.

2 Tip the lentils into a sieve (strainer) to drain, then rinse under the cold tap. Drain the soaked mushrooms and reserve the soaking liquid. Finely chop the mushrooms and set aside.

3 Heat the oil in a large, non-stick pan and add the carrot, celery, onion, garlic, parsley and chillies, if using. Cook over a low heat for 5–7 minutes, stirring occasionally. Add the stock, then the mushrooms and their soaking liquid.

4 Bring to the boil, then add the beans, chickpeas and lentils. Season to taste with salt and pepper. Cover and simmer gently for 20 minutes.

5 Add the pasta and bring the soup back to the boil, stirring. Reduce the heat, then simmer, for 7–8 minutes, or according to the packet instructions, until the pasta is tender or *al dente*, stirring frequently. Adjust the seasoning to taste, then serve hot, sprinkled with chopped parsley and grated Pecorino.

VARIATIONS
Use 3–4 shallots in place of onion. Use grated fresh Parmesan cheese in place of Pecorino.

Energy 205Kcal/869kJ; Protein 10.7g; Carbohydrate 36.4g, of which sugars 5.2g; Fat 2.9g, of which saturates 0.4g; Cholesterol 0mg; Calcium 72mg; Fibre 6.3g; Sodium 304mg.

CLASSIC PEA AND BASIL SOUP ★

THE PUNGENT FLAVOUR OF BASIL LIFTS THIS APPETIZING LOW-FAT ITALIAN SOUP OF PETITS POIS, WHILE THE ONION AND GARLIC GIVE DEPTH. SERVE IT WITH GOOD CRUSTY BREAD TO ENJOY IT AT ITS BEST.

2 Add the petits pois and stock to the pan and bring to the boil. Reduce the heat, add the basil and seasoning, then simmer for 10 minutes.

3 Spoon the soup into a blender or food processor (you may have to do this in batches) and process until the soup is smooth.

4 Return the soup to the rinsed out pan and reheat gently until piping hot, stirring. Ladle into warm bowls, sprinkle with shaved Parmesan and garnish with basil.

SERVES SIX

INGREDIENTS
    75ml/5 tbsp olive oil
    2 large onions, chopped
    1 celery stick, chopped
    1 carrot, chopped
    1 garlic clove, finely chopped
    400g/14oz/3½ cups frozen
        petits pois (baby peas)
    900ml/1½ pints/3¾ cups
        vegetable stock
    25g/1oz/1 cup fresh basil leaves,
        roughly torn, plus extra to garnish
    salt and ground black pepper
    shaved fresh Parmesan cheese,
        to serve

1 Heat the oil in a large, non-stick pan and add the onions, celery, carrot and garlic. Cover the pan and cook over a low heat for 45 minutes, or until the vegetables are soft, stirring occasionally to prevent the vegetables sticking.

COOK'S TIP
Remove the pan from the heat and allow the mixture to cool slightly before processing it in a blender or food processor.

VARIATIONS
You can also use mint or a mixture of parsley, mint and chives in place of the basil, if you like. Use frozen peas in place of petits pois (baby peas).

Energy 106Kcal/439kJ; Protein 5.6g; Carbohydrate 13.6g, of which sugars 6g; Fat 3.7g, of which saturates 0.6g; Cholesterol 0mg; Calcium 40mg; Fibre 4.5g; Sodium 9mg.

BROAD BEAN AND MANGETOUT MINESTRONE ★

THE CLASSIC, WINTRY ITALIAN MINESTRONE SOUP TAKES ON A SUMMER-FRESH IMAGE IN THIS LIGHT AND TASTY RECIPE. ANY SMALL PASTA SHAPES CAN BE USED INSTEAD OF THE SPAGHETTINI IF YOU PREFER.

SERVES SIX

INGREDIENTS

15ml/1 tbsp olive oil
2 onions, finely chopped
2 garlic cloves, finely chopped
2 carrots, very finely chopped
1 celery stick, very finely chopped
1.27 litres/2¼ pints/5⅔ cups
   boiling water
450g/1lb shelled fresh broad
   (fava) beans
225g/8oz mangetouts (snow peas),
   cut into thin strips
3 tomatoes, skinned and chopped
5ml/1 tsp tomato purée (paste)
50g/2oz spaghettini, broken into
   4cm/1½in lengths
225g/8oz baby spinach
30ml/2 tbsp chopped fresh parsley
handful of fresh basil leaves
salt and ground black pepper
basil sprigs, to garnish
grated fresh Parmesan cheese,
   to serve

1 Heat the oil in a non-stick pan and add the onions and garlic. Cook for 4–5 minutes, until softened. Add the carrots and celery, and cook for 2–3 minutes. Add the boiling water and bring to the boil, then reduce the heat and simmer for 15 minutes, or until the vegetables are tender.

2 Cook the broad beans in pan of salted boiling water for 4–5 minutes. Remove with a slotted spoon, refresh under cold water and set aside.

3 Bring the pan of water back to the boil, add the mangetouts and cook for 1 minute, or until just tender. Drain, refresh under cold water, then set aside.

4 Add the tomatoes and tomato purée to the soup. Cook for 1 minute. Purée two or three large ladlefuls of the soup and a quarter of the broad beans in a blender or food processor until smooth. Set aside.

5 Add the spaghettini to the remaining soup in the pan and cook for 6–8 minutes, until tender. Stir in the purée and spinach and cook for 2–3 minutes. Add the rest of the broad beans, the mangetouts and parsley, and season well.

6 Heat gently until hot, then stir in the basil leaves. Ladle the soup into deep cups or bowls and garnish with sprigs of basil. Serve a little grated Parmesan with each portion of soup.

167Kcal/705kJ; Protein 10.7g; Carbohydrate 25.5g, of which sugars 9.8g; Fat 3.2g, of which saturates 0.5g; Cholesterol 0mg; Calcium 156mg; Fibre 8.8g; Sodium 76mg.

ITALIAN PASTA AND CHICKPEA SOUP ★

A SIMPLE, NOURISHING SOUP, IDEAL FOR AN APPEALING, LOW-FAT STARTER. YOU CAN USE OTHER PASTA SHAPES, BUT CONCHIGLIE ARE IDEAL BECAUSE THEY SCOOP UP THE CHICKPEAS AND BEANS.

SERVES SIX

INGREDIENTS
   1 onion
   2 carrots
   2 celery sticks
   15ml/1 tbsp olive oil
   400g/14oz can chickpeas, rinsed
      and drained
   200g/7oz can cannellini beans,
      rinsed and drained
   150ml/¼ pint/⅔ cup passata
      (bottled strained tomatoes)
   120ml/4fl oz/½ cup water
   1.5 litres/2½ pints/6¼ cups
      vegetable stock
   1 fresh or dried rosemary sprig
   200g/7oz/scant 2 cups dried
      conchiglie
   salt and ground black pepper
   fresh rosemary leaves, to garnish
   15ml/1 tbsp grated fresh Parmesan
      cheese, to serve

1 Chop the onion, carrots and celery sticks finely, either in a food processor or by hand.

2 Heat the olive oil in a large, non-stick pan, add the chopped vegetables and cook over a low heat, for 5–7 minutes, stirring frequently.

3 Add the chickpeas and cannellini beans, stir well to mix, then cook for 5 minutes. Stir in the passata and water. Cook for 2–3 minutes, stirring.

4 Add 475ml/16fl oz/2 cups of the stock, the rosemary sprig and salt and pepper to taste. Bring to the boil, then reduce the heat, cover and simmer gently for 1 hour, stirring occasionally.

5 Pour in the remaining stock, add the pasta and bring to the boil, stirring. Reduce the heat and simmer for 7–8 minutes, or according to the packet instructions, until the pasta is tender or *al dente*, stirring frequently. Adjust the seasoning. Remove and discard the rosemary sprig, then serve the hot soup in soup bowls, topped with a few rosemary leaves and a little grated Parmesan.

VARIATIONS
Use red kidney beans in place of cannellini beans. Use fresh thyme in place of rosemary.

COOK'S TIP
Choose beans or chickpeas canned in water, rather than in brine, if you like. Otherwise, rinse canned beans or chickpeas thoroughly under cold running water and drain well before use.

Energy 271Kcal/1151kJ; Protein 13.9g; Carbohydrate 50.3g, of which sugars 6.4g; Fat 3g, of which saturates 0.4g; Cholesterol 0mg; Calcium 98mg; Fibre 8.6g; Sodium 476mg.

BROWN LENTIL AND PASTA SOUP

THIS RUSTIC VEGETARIAN SOUP MAKES A WARMING WINTER MEAL. IT GOES WELL WITH GRANARY OR CRUSTY ITALIAN BREAD TO CREATE A HEALTHY, LOW-FAT SUPPER DISH.

SERVES SIX

INGREDIENTS
175g/6oz/¾ cup brown lentils
3 garlic cloves
1 litre/1¾ pints/4 cups water
15ml/1 tbsp olive oil
1 onion, finely chopped
2 celery sticks, finely chopped
30ml/2 tbsp sun-dried tomato
  purée (paste)
1.75 litres/3 pints/7½ cups
  vegetable stock
a few fresh marjoram leaves
a few fresh basil leaves
leaves from 1 fresh thyme sprig
50g/2oz/½ cup dried small pasta
  shapes, such as tubetti
salt and ground black pepper
tiny fresh herb leaves, to garnish

COOK'S TIP
Use green lentils instead of brown if you
like, but don't use the orange or red ones
as they will go mushy.

1 Put the lentils in a large pan. Smash 1 garlic clove (there's no need to peel it first) and add it to the lentils. Pour in the water and bring to the boil. Reduce the heat to a gentle simmer and cook, for about 20 minutes, or until the lentils are just tender, stirring occasionally. Tip the lentils into a sieve (strainer), remove the garlic and set it aside. Rinse the lentils under the cold tap, then leave them to drain.

2 Heat the oil in a large, non-stick pan. Add the onion and celery and cook over a low heat for 5–7 minutes, or until softened, stirring frequently.

3 Crush the remaining garlic, then peel and mash the reserved garlic. Add to the vegetables with the tomato purée and the lentils. Stir, then add the stock, the fresh herbs and salt and pepper to taste. Bring to the boil, then reduce the heat and simmer for 30 minutes, stirring occasionally.

4 Add the pasta to the pan and bring back to the boil, stirring. Simmer for 7–8 minutes, or according to the packet instructions, until the pasta is tender or *al dente*, stirring frequently. Adjust the seasoning to taste. Serve hot, sprinkled with the herb leaves.

Energy 140Kcal/592kJ; Protein 7g; Carbohydrate 24.4g, of which sugars 0.8g; Fat 2.3g, of which saturates 0.3g; Cholesterol 0mg; Calcium 20mg; Fibre 1.6g; Sodium 17mg.

FRESH BROAD BEAN AND POTATO SOUP ★

THIS LIGHT SOUP USES FRESH MEDITERRANEAN FAVA BEANS MIXED WITH CORIANDER TO GIVE AN INVIGORATING FLAVOUR TO A HEARTY DISH. FRESH BEANS NEED TO BE SHELLED FIRST.

SERVES FOUR

INGREDIENTS
10ml/2 tsp olive oil
2 onions, chopped
3 large floury potatoes
450g/1lb fresh shelled broad
    (fava) beans
1.75 litres/3 pints/7½ cups
    vegetable stock
a bunch of fresh coriander (cilantro),
    roughly chopped
150ml/¼ pint/⅔ cup semi-skimmed
    (low-fat) milk
salt and ground black pepper
single (light) cream, to garnish

1 Heat the oil in a large, non-stick pan and cook the onions for 5 minutes until soft, stirring. Add the potatoes, most of the beans (reserving a few for the garnish) and the stock, and bring to the boil. Simmer for 5 minutes, then add the coriander and simmer for a further 10 minutes.

2 Process the soup in batches in a blender or food processor, then return to the rinsed out pan.

3 Stir in the milk and seasoning. Heat gently until almost boiling, stirring. Serve garnished with coriander, beans and cream.

Energy 263Kcal/1113kJ; Protein 13.9g; Carbohydrate 47g, of which sugars 10.8g; Fat 3.5g, of which saturates 0.9g; Cholesterol 2mg; Calcium 142mg; Fibre 10.2g; Sodium 45mg.

CREAMY CORN AND POTATO CHOWDER ★

THIS CHUNKY LOW-FAT SOUP IS RICH WITH THE SWEET TASTE OF CORN. IT'S EXCELLENT SERVED WITH THICK CRUSTY BREAD AND TOPPED WITH A LITTLE MELTED, REDUCED-FAT CHEDDAR CHEESE.

SERVES SIX

INGREDIENTS
- 1 onion, chopped
- 1 garlic clove, crushed
- 1 medium baking potato, chopped
- 2 celery sticks, sliced
- 1 small green (bell) pepper, seeded, halved and sliced
- 15ml/1 tbsp sunflower oil
- 600ml/1 pint/2½ cups vegetable stock or water
- 300ml/½ pint/1¼ cups semi-skimmed (low-fat) milk
- 200g/7oz can flageolet or small cannellini beans
- 300g/11oz can corn kernels
- a good pinch of dried sage
- salt and ground black pepper
- reduced-fat Cheddar cheese, grated, to serve (optional)

1 Put the fresh vegetables into a large, non-stick pan with the oil.

2 Heat the pan until the vegetables are sizzling, then reduce the heat to low. Cover and cook gently for about 10 minutes, shaking the pan occasionally.

3 Pour in the stock or water, season to taste with salt and pepper and bring to the boil. Reduce the heat, cover again and simmer gently for about 15 minutes, or until the vegetables are tender.

4 Add the milk, the beans and corn kernels (including their liquids) and the sage. Simmer, uncovered, for 5 minutes. Adjust the seasoning and serve hot, sprinkled with cheese, if you like.

Energy 181Kcal/766kJ; Protein 6.8g; Carbohydrate 32.1g, of which sugars 12.7g; Fat 3.8g, of which saturates 0.9g; Cholesterol 3mg; Calcium 106mg; Fibre 4.2g; Sodium 298mg.

CREAMED SPINACH AND POTATO SOUP ★

THIS IS A DELICIOUS LOW-FAT CREAMY SOUP. THIS RECIPE USES SPINACH BUT OTHER VEGETABLES SUCH AS CABBAGE OR SWISS CHARD WOULD WORK JUST AS WELL. SERVE IT WITH FRESH CRUSTY BREAD.

SERVES FOUR

INGREDIENTS
1 large onion, finely chopped
1 garlic clove, crushed
900g/2lb floury potatoes, diced
2 celery sticks, chopped
1.2 litres/2 pints/5 cups
  vegetable stock
250g/9oz fresh spinach leaves
115g/4oz/½ cup low-fat
  soft cheese
300ml/½ pint/1¼ cups
  semi-skimmed (low-fat milk)
a dash of dry sherry
salt and ground black pepper
chopped fresh parsley, to garnish

1 Place the onion, garlic, potatoes, celery and stock in a large pan. Bring to the boil, then reduce the heat and simmer for 20 minutes.

2 Season the soup, add the spinach and cook for a further 10 minutes.

3 Process the soup in batches in a blender or food processor, then return the soup to the rinsed-out pan.

4 Stir or whisk in the soft cheese and milk, then reheat gently, stirring. Add a dash of sherry and adjust the seasoning to taste. Serve garnished with parsley.

Energy 274kcal/1157kJ; Protein 15.3g; Carbohydrate 46.2g, of which sugars 11.6g; Fat 5g, of which saturates 2.7g; Cholesterol 13mg; Calcium 281mg; Fibre 4.4g; Sodium 348mg.

POTATO AND GARLIC BROTH ★

ALTHOUGH THERE IS PLENTY OF GARLIC IN THIS SOUP, THE END RESULT IS NOT OVERPOWERING. SERVE PIPING HOT WITH BREAD, AS A PERFECT LOW-FAT, WINTER-WARMING DISH.

SERVES FOUR

INGREDIENTS
2 small or 1 large whole head of
  garlic (about 20 cloves)
4 medium potatoes, diced
1.75 litres/3 pints/7½ cups
  vegetable stock
salt and ground black pepper
chopped fresh flat leaf parsley,
  to garnish

VARIATION
Make the soup more substantial by placing in each bowl a slice of French bread which has been toasted and topped with a little reduced-fat melted cheese. Pour the soup over so that the bread soaks it up. Remember this will increase the calorie and fat content of this recipe.

1 Preheat the oven to 190°C/375°F/ Gas 5. Place the unpeeled garlic bulbs or bulb in a small roasting pan and bake in the oven for 30 minutes, or until they are soft in the centre.

2 Meanwhile, par-boil the potatoes in a large pan of lightly salted boiling water for 10 minutes. Drain well.

3 Simmer the stock in a separate pan for 5 minutes. Add the potatoes to the stock.

4 Squeeze the garlic pulp into the soup, reserving a few cloves to garnish, stir and season to taste with salt and pepper. Simmer for 15 minutes. Serve garnished with whole garlic cloves and parsley.

Energy 203Kcal/861kJ; Protein 6.4g; Carbohydrate 44.5g, of which sugars 3.7g; Fat 1.1g, of which saturates 0.3g; Cholesterol 0mg; Calcium 20mg; Fibre 3.5g; Sodium 239mg.

CARROT AND ORANGE SOUP ★

THIS TRADITIONAL, BRIGHT AND SUMMERY LOW-FAT SOUP IS ALWAYS POPULAR FOR ITS WONDERFULLY CREAMY CONSISTENCY AND VIBRANTLY FRESH CITRUS FLAVOUR. USE A GOOD, HOME-MADE, LOW-FAT VEGETABLE STOCK IF YOU CAN FOR THE BEST RESULTS.

SERVES SIX

INGREDIENTS
    25g/1oz/2 tbsp butter
    3 leeks, thinly sliced
    450g/1lb carrots, sliced
    1.2 litres/2 pints/5 cups
        vegetable stock
    grated rind and juice of 2 oranges
    2.5ml/½ tsp freshly grated nutmeg
    150ml/¼ pint/⅔ cup reduced-fat
        Greek (US strained plain) yogurt
    salt and ground black pepper
    fresh sprigs of coriander (cilantro),
        to garnish

1 Melt the butter in a large, non-stick pan. Add the leeks and carrots and stir well, lightly coating the vegetables with the butter. Cover and cook for about 10 minutes, until the vegetables are beginning to soften but not colour.

2 Pour in the stock and the orange rind and juice. Add the nutmeg and season to taste with salt and pepper. Bring to the boil then reduce the heat, cover and simmer for about 40 minutes, or until the vegetables are tender.

3 Leave to cool slightly, then process the soup in a blender or food processor until smooth.

4 Return the soup to the rinsed-out pan and add 30ml/2 tbsp of the yogurt, then adjust the seasoning to taste, if necessary. Reheat gently, stirring.

5 Ladle the soup into warm individual bowls and put a swirl of yogurt in the centre of each. Sprinkle the fresh sprigs of coriander over each bowl to garnish, and serve immediately.

Energy 93Kcal/389kJ; Protein 3.4g; Carbohydrate 10.7g, of which sugars 9.7g; Fat 4.4g, of which saturates 2.5g; Cholesterol 9mg; Calcium 91mg; Fibre 4g; Sodium 67mg.

BORSCHT ★

BEETROOT IS THE MAIN INGREDIENT OF BORSCHT, AND ITS FLAVOUR AND COLOUR DOMINATE THIS WELL-KNOWN LOW-FAT RUSSIAN OR POLISH SOUP. FOR THIS VEGETARIAN VERSION, THE USUAL BEEF STOCK HAS BEEN REPLACED WITH VEGETABLE STOCK.

SERVES SIX

INGREDIENTS

900g/2lb uncooked beetroot, peeled
2 carrots, peeled
2 celery sticks
25g/1oz/2 tbsp butter
2 onions, sliced
2 garlic cloves, crushed
4 tomatoes, skinned, seeded
  and chopped
1 bay leaf
1 large fresh parsley sprig
2 cloves
4 whole black peppercorns
1.2 litres/2 pints/5 cups
  well-flavoured vegetable stock
150ml/¼ pint/⅔ cup beetroot *kvas*
  (see Cook's Tip) or the liquid from
  pickled beetroot
salt and ground black pepper
sour cream, garnished with chopped
  fresh chives or sprigs of fresh dill,
  to serve

1 Cut the beetroot, carrots and celery into fairly thick strips. Set aside. Melt the butter in a large, non-stick pan and cook the onions over a low heat for 5 minutes, stirring occasionally.

2 Add the beetroot, carrots and celery and cook for a further 5 minutes, stirring occasionally.

3 Add the garlic and chopped tomatoes to the pan and cook for a further 2 minutes, stirring.

COOK'S TIP
Beetroot *kvas*, fermented beetroot juice, adds an intense colour and a slight tartness. If unavailable, peel and grate 1 beetroot, add 150ml/¼ pint/⅔ cup stock and 10ml/2 tsp lemon juice. Bring to the boil, then remove the pan from the heat, cover and leave for 30 minutes. Strain before using.

4 Place the bay leaf, parsley, cloves and peppercorns in a piece of muslin (cheesecloth) and tie with string.

5 Add the muslin bag to the pan with the stock. Bring to the boil, then reduce the heat, cover and simmer for 1¼ hours, or until the vegetables are very tender. Discard the muslin bag. Stir in the beetroot *kvas* and season to taste with salt and pepper. Bring back to the boil. Ladle the soup into bowls and serve with sour cream, garnished with chives or dill.

VARIATION
Use 6–8 shallots in place of onions.

Energy 127Kcal/535kJ; Protein 4g; Carbohydrate 20.2g, of which sugars 17.7g; Fat 4g, of which saturates 2.3g; Cholesterol 9mg; Calcium 60mg; Fibre 5g; Sodium 143mg.

CORN AND SWEET POTATO SOUP ★

THE COMBINATION OF CORN AND SWEET POTATO GIVES THIS LIGHT VEGETARIAN SOUP A REAL DEPTH OF FLAVOUR, AS WELL AS MAKING IT LOOK VERY COLOURFUL.

<u>SERVES SIX</u>

INGREDIENTS
  15ml/1 tbsp olive oil
  1 onion, finely chopped
  2 garlic cloves, crushed
  1 small red chilli, seeded and
    finely chopped
  1.75 litres/3 pints/7½ cups
    vegetable stock
  10ml/2 tsp ground cumin
  1 medium sweet potato, diced
  ½ red (bell) pepper, seeded and
    finely chopped
  450g/1lb corn kernels
  salt and ground black pepper
  lime wedges, to serve

COOK'S TIP
Use frozen or canned (drained weight) corn kernels for this recipe.

1 Heat the oil in a non-stick pan, add the onion and cook for 5 minutes, until softened, stirring occasionally. Add the garlic and chilli and cook for a further 2 minutes.

2 Add 300ml/½ pint/1¼ cups of the stock to the pan, then bring to the boil, reduce the heat and simmer for 10 minutes.

3 In a small bowl, mix the cumin with a little stock to form a paste, then stir this into the soup. Add the sweet potato, stir, then simmer for 10 minutes. Add salt and pepper to taste.

4 Add the red pepper, corn and remaining stock. Simmer for 10 minutes. Process half of the soup in a blender until smooth, then stir the purée into the chunky soup. Reheat gently. Serve with lime wedges.

Energy 127Kcal/535kJ; Protein 4g; Carbohydrate 20.2g, of which sugars 17.7g; Fat 4g, of which saturates 2.3g; Cholesterol 9mg; Calcium 60mg; Fibre 5g; Sodium 143mg.

GENOESE MINESTRONE ★

THE VARIATIONS ON THIS SOUP ARE ENDLESS. THIS LIGHT, PASTA-FREE VEGETARIAN VERSION IS PACKED WITH HEAPS OF VEGETABLES TO MAKE A SUBSTANTIAL, HEARTY LUNCH — IDEAL SERVED WITH CRUSTY BREAD.

<u>SERVES SIX</u>

INGREDIENTS
  1.75 litres/3 pints/7½ cups
    vegetable stock
  1 large onion, chopped
  3 celery sticks, chopped
  2 carrots, finely diced
  2 large floury potatoes, finely diced
  ½ head of cabbage, very finely diced
  225g/8oz runner (green) beans,
    sliced diagonally
  2 x 400g/14oz cans cannellini beans,
    rinsed and drained
  30ml/2 tbsp ready-made pesto sauce
  salt and ground black pepper
  crusty bread, to serve
  grated fresh Parmesan cheese,
    to serve

1 Pour the stock into a large pan. Add the onion, celery and carrots. Simmer for 10 minutes.

2 Add the potatoes, cabbage, and beans and simmer for 10–12 minutes, or until the potatoes are tender.

3 Stir in the cannellini beans and pesto, then return the mixture to the boil. Season to taste with salt and pepper and serve hot with crusty bread and a sprinkling of grated fresh Parmesan cheese.

Energy 233Kcal/983kJ; Protein 12.1g; Carbohydrate 40.1g, of which sugars 10.7g; Fat 3.7g, of which saturates 0.6g; Cholesterol 1mg; Calcium 151mg; Fibre 10.9g; Sodium 556mg.

CURRIED CAULIFLOWER SOUP ★

THIS SPICY, CREAMY LOW-FAT SOUP IS PERFECT FOR LUNCH ON A COLD WINTER'S DAY SERVED WITH FLATBREAD SUCH A PITTA AND GARNISHED WITH FRESH CORIANDER.

SERVES FOUR

INGREDIENTS
   750ml/1¼ pints/3 cups
      semi-skimmed (low-fat) milk
   1 large cauliflower
   15ml/1 tbsp garam masala
   salt and ground black pepper

1 Pour the milk into a large pan and place over a medium heat. Cut the cauliflower into florets and add to the milk with the garam masala. Season to taste with salt and pepper.

2 Bring the milk to the boil, then reduce the heat, half-cover the pan and simmer for about 20 minutes, or until the cauliflower is tender, stirring occasionally.

3 Remove the pan from the heat and allow the mixture to cool for a few minutes, then transfer to a blender or food processor and process until smooth (you may have to do this in two batches). Return the purée to the rinsed-out pan and reheat gently, stirring. Adjust the seasoning to taste, and serve immediately.

Energy 151Kcal/636kJ; Protein 12.9g; Carbohydrate 14.7g, of which sugars 13.2g; Fat 5g, of which saturates 2.4g; Cholesterol 11mg; Calcium 276mg; Fibre 3.7g; Sodium 107mg.

CREAMY CAULIFLOWER SOUP ★

*THIS SOUP IS LIGHT IN FLAVOUR AND FAT YET SATISFYING ENOUGH FOR A LUNCHTIME SNACK.
YOU CAN TRY GREEN CAULIFLOWER FOR A COLOURFUL CHANGE.*

SERVES SIX

INGREDIENTS

15ml/1 tbsp olive oil
2 large onions, finely chopped
1 garlic clove, crushed
3 large floury potatoes, finely diced
3 celery sticks, finely diced
1.75 litres/3 pints/7½ cups
   vegetable stock
2 carrots, finely diced
1 medium cauliflower, chopped
15ml/1 tbsp chopped fresh dill
15ml/1 tbsp lemon juice
5ml/1 tsp mustard powder
1.5ml/¼ tsp caraway seeds
300ml/½ pint/1¼ cups
   semi-skimmed (low-fat) milk
salt and ground black pepper
shredded spring onions (scallions),
   to garnish

3 Add the cauliflower, dill, lemon juice, mustard powder and caraway seeds and simmer for a further 20 minutes.

4 Process the soup in a blender or food processor until smooth, then return the soup to the rinsed-out pan and stir in the milk. Reheat gently, stirring. Season to taste with salt and pepper, and serve garnished with shredded spring onions.

1 Heat the oil in a large, non-stick pan, add the onions and garlic and cook for a few minutes until they soften. Add the potatoes, celery and stock and bring to the boil, then reduce the heat and simmer for 10 minutes, stirring occasionally.

2 Add the carrots and simmer for a further 10 minutes, stirring occasionally.

COOK'S TIP
For a special treat, use single cream in place of some or all of the milk, but remember this will add both calories and fat to this recipe.

Energy 169Kcal/711kJ; Protein 7.4g; Carbohydrate 27.7g, of which sugars 10.8g; Fat 4g, of which saturates 1.1g; Cholesterol 3mg; Calcium 111mg; Fibre 4g; Sodium 55mg.

CHICKPEA, LEMON AND PARSLEY SOUP ★

LEMON ENHANCES THE FLAVOUR OF FRESH PARSLEY IN THIS TASTY NORTH AFRICAN INSPIRED LOW-FAT SOUP, WHICH MAKES A SUBSTANTIAL VEGETARIAN LUNCH SERVED WITH CRUSTY BREAD.

2 Place the onion and parsley in a blender or food processor and process until finely chopped.

3 Heat the mixed oils in a large, non-stick frying pan and gently cook the onion mixture over a low heat for about 4 minutes, or until slightly softened.

4 Add the chickpeas, cook gently for about 2 minutes, then add the stock. Season well. Bring the soup to the boil, then reduce the heat, cover and simmer for 20 minutes, or until the chickpeas are very tender.

5 Leave the soup to cool a little and then part-purée it in a blender or food processor, or mash the chickpeas fairly coarsely with a fork, so that the soup is thick, but still quite chunky.

SERVES SIX

INGREDIENTS
   225g/8oz/1¼ cups chickpeas,
     soaked overnight
   1 small onion, coarsely chopped
   1 bunch fresh parsley (about
     40g/1½oz/¾ cup)
   15ml/1 tbsp olive oil and sunflower
     oil, mixed
   1.2 litres/2 pints/5 cups
     vegetable stock
juice of ½ lemon
salt and ground black pepper
lemon wedges and thinly pared
   and shredded lemon rind,
   to garnish
crusty bread, to serve

1 Drain the chickpeas and rinse well under cold running water. Cook them in a pan of rapidly boiling water for 10 minutes, then simmer for 1–1½ hours, or until tender. Drain, then, using your fingertips, gently peel away the skins.

6 Return the soup to the rinsed-out pan, stir in the lemon juice, then adjust the seasoning to taste. Heat it through gently, then serve, garnished with lemon wedges and shredded lemon rind, and accompanied by crusty bread.

Energy 140Kcal/591kJ; Protein 8.1g; Carbohydrate 19.4g, of which sugars 1.5g; Fat 3.9g, of which saturates 0.5g; Cholesterol 0mg; Calcium 63mg; Fibre 4.2g; Sodium 15mg.

CURRIED PARSNIP SOUP ★

THE MILD SWEETNESS OF PARSNIPS WITH SWEET MANGO CHUTNEY IS GIVEN AN EXCITING LIFT WITH A BLEND OF SPICES IN THIS DELICIOUS, SIMPLE, LIGHT VEGETARIAN SOUP.

SERVES FOUR

INGREDIENTS

10ml/2 tsp olive oil
1 onion, chopped
1 garlic clove, crushed
1 small green chilli, seeded and
   finely chopped
15ml/1 tbsp grated fresh root ginger
5 large parsnips, diced
5ml/1 tsp cumin seeds
5ml/1 tsp ground coriander
2.5ml/½ tsp ground turmeric
30ml/2 tbsp sweet mango chutney
1.2 litres/2 pints/5 cups water
juice of 1 lime
salt and ground black pepper
60ml/4 tbsp low-fat natural (plain)
   yogurt and sweet mango chutney,
   to serve
chopped fresh coriander (cilantro),
   to garnish (optional)
For the sesame naan croûtons (to serve)
15ml/1 tbsp olive oil
1 large naan bread, cut into
   small dice
15ml/1 tbsp sesame seeds

1 Heat the oil in a large, non-stick pan and add the onion, garlic, chilli and ginger. Cook for 4–5 minutes, until the onion has softened, stirring occasionally. Add the parsnips and cook for 2–3 minutes. Sprinkle in the cumin seeds, ground coriander and turmeric, and cook for 1 minute, stirring constantly.

2 Add the chutney and the water. Season well and bring to the boil. Reduce the heat and simmer for 15 minutes, until the parsnips are soft.

3 Cool the soup slightly, then process it in a blender or food processor until smooth, then return it to the rinsed-out pan. Stir in the lime juice.

4 To make the naan croûtons, heat the oil in a large, non-stick frying pan and cook the diced naan bread for 3–4 minutes, until golden all over, stirring. Remove the pan from the heat and drain off any excess oil. Add the sesame seeds and return to the heat for 30 seconds, until the seeds are pale golden.

5 Ladle the soup into bowls. Spoon a little yogurt into each portion, then top with a little mango chutney and some of the sesame naan croûton mixture. Garnish with chopped coriander, if you like.

Energy 58Kcal/244kJ; Protein 3.3g; Carbohydrate 3.8g, of which sugars 0.3g; Fat 3.6g, of which saturates 0.9g; Cholesterol 95mg; Calcium 16mg; Fibre 0g; Sodium 304mg.

EGG FLOWER SOUP ★

THIS SIMPLE, HEALTHY SOUP IS FLAVOURED WITH FRESH ROOT GINGER AND CHINESE FIVE-SPICE POWDER. IT IS QUICK AND DELICIOUS AND CAN EASILY BE MADE AT THE LAST MINUTE.

SERVES FOUR

INGREDIENTS
    1.2 litres/2 pints/5 cups fresh
      vegetable stock
    10ml/2 tsp grated fresh root ginger
    10ml/2 tsp light soy sauce
    5ml/1 tsp sesame oil
    5ml/1 tsp Chinese five-spice powder
    15–30ml/1–2 tbsp cornflour
      (cornstarch)
    2 eggs
    salt and ground black pepper
    1 spring onion (scallion), very thinly
      sliced diagonally and 15ml/1 tbsp
      roughly chopped fresh coriander
      (cilantro) or fresh flat leaf parsley,
      to garnish

COOK'S TIP

This soup is a good way of using up leftover egg yolks or whites, which have been stored in the freezer.

1 Put the vegetable stock into a large pan with the ginger, soy sauce, sesame oil and five-spice powder. Bring to the boil and allow to simmer gently for about 10 minutes.

2 Blend the cornflour in a measuring jug (cup) with 60–75ml/4–5 tbsp water and stir into the stock. Cook until slightly thickened, stirring constantly. Season to taste with salt and pepper.

3 In a jug, beat the eggs together with 30ml/2 tbsp cold water, until the mixture becomes frothy.

4 Bring the soup just back to the boil and drizzle in the egg mixture, stirring vigorously with chopsticks. Choose a jug with a fine spout to form a very thin drizzle. Serve the soup immediately, sprinkled with the sliced spring onion and chopped coriander or parsley.

Energy 118Kcal/497kJ; Protein 3.2g; Carbohydrate 19.8g, of which sugars 10.9g; Fat 3.5g, of which saturates 0.6g; Cholesterol 0mg; Calcium 84mg; Fibre 6g; Sodium 66mg.

MISO BROTH WITH TOFU ★

THIS VEGETARIAN BROTH IS HIGHLY NUTRITIOUS AND MAKES A GOOD APPETIZER OR LIGHT LUNCH.
A STAPLE IN JAPAN, MISO IS A RICH, SALTY CONDIMENT; TOFU IS A SOFT CHEESE-LIKE FOOD.

SERVES FOUR

INGREDIENTS
1 bunch of spring onions (scallions)
  or 5 baby leeks
15g/½oz fresh coriander (cilantro)
3 thin slices fresh root ginger
2 star anise
1 small dried red chilli
1.2 litres/2 pints/5 cups
  vegetable stock
225g/8oz pak choi (bok choy) or
  other Asian greens, thickly sliced
200g/7oz firm tofu, cut into 2.5cm/
  1in cubes
60ml/4 tbsp red miso
30–45ml/2–3 tbsp Japanese
  soy sauce
1 fresh red chilli, seeded and
  shredded (optional)

1 Cut the coarse green tops off the spring onions or baby leeks and slice the rest of the spring onions or leeks finely on the diagonal.

2 Place the coarse green tops in a large pan with the stalks from the coriander, the fresh root ginger, star anise, dried chilli and vegetable stock.

3 Heat the mixture over a low heat until boiling, then reduce the heat and simmer for about 10 minutes. Strain the broth, return it to the pan and reheat until simmering. Add the green portion of the sliced spring onions or leeks to the soup with the pak choi or Asian greens and tofu. Cook for 2 minutes.

4 In a small bowl, combine the miso with a little soup, then stir the mixture into the pan. Add soy sauce to taste.

5 Coarsely chop the coriander leaves and stir most of them into the soup with the white part of the spring onions or leeks. Cook for 1 minute, then ladle the soup into warmed bowls. Sprinkle with the remaining chopped coriander and the shredded fresh red chilli, if using, and serve immediately.

Energy 25Kcal/103kJ; Protein 2.4g; Carbohydrate 2.6g, of which sugars 2.4g; Fat 0.6g, of which saturates 0.1g; Cholesterol 0mg; Calcium 107mg; Fibre 1.6g; Sodium 882mg.

APPETIZERS
AND SNACKS

There are many low-fat options when it comes to starters or snacks — all of which can be prepared and eaten at any time of day. From tempting cold dishes such as Tzatziki or Artichoke and Cumin Dip, to popular warm delights such as Peperonata or Vegetable Samosas, these dishes combine satisfying fillers while staying below the low-fat threshold.

SPICED YOGURT AND CUCUMBER RAITA ★

THESE SLIGHTLY SOUR, YOGURT-BASED DISHES HAVE A COOLING EFFECT ON THE PALATE WHEN EATEN WITH SPICY, LOW-FAT INDIAN FOODS. THEY CREATE A TASTY LOW-FAT SNACK.

SERVES FOUR

INGREDIENTS
FOR THE SPICED YOGURT
450ml/¾ pint/scant 2 cups low-fat
    natural (plain) yogurt
2.5ml/½ tsp freshly ground
    fennel seeds
2.5ml/½ tsp granulated sugar
25ml/5 tsp vegetable oil
1 dried red chilli
1.5ml/¼ tsp mustard seeds
1.5ml/¼ tsp cumin seeds
4–6 curry leaves
a pinch each of asafoetida and
    ground turmeric
salt

1 In a bowl, mix together the yogurt, fennel and sugar, and add salt to taste. Chill in the refrigerator.

2 Heat the oil in a non-stick pan and fry the remaining ingredients. When the chilli turns dark, pour the oil and spices over the yogurt and mix. Chill before serving.

SERVES SIX

INGREDIENTS
FOR THE CUCUMBER RAITI
½ cucumber
1 fresh green chilli, seeded
    and chopped
300ml/½ pint/1¼ cups low-fat
    natural (plain) yogurt
1.5ml/¼ tsp salt
1.5ml/¼ tsp ground cumin

1 Dice the cucumber finely and place in a large mixing bowl. Add the chilli.

2 Beat the yogurt with a fork until smooth, then stir into the cucumber and chilli mixture.

3 Stir in the salt and cumin. Cover the bowl with clear film (plastic wrap) and chill before serving.

VARIATION
Instead of using cucumber, try two skinned, seeded and chopped tomatoes and 15ml/1 tbsp chopped fresh coriander (cilantro).

Yogurt: Energy 36Kcal/149kJ; Protein 6.6g; Carbohydrate 1.8g, of which sugars 1.8g; Fat 2.6g, of which saturates 0.4g; Cholesterol 2mg; Calcium 244mg; Fibre 0g; Sodium 236mg.
Raita: Energy 98kcal/408kJ; Protein 6.6g; Carbohydrate 10.3g, of which sugars 10.3g; Fat 3.8g, of which saturates 0.9g; Cholesterol 2mg; Calcium 244mg; Fibre 0.2g; Sodium 236mg.

TZATZIKI

A Greek cucumber salad dressed with yogurt, mint and garlic, Tzatziki makes a refreshing low-fat vegetarian starter. It's best served with fresh vegetable crudités.

SERVES FOUR

INGREDIENTS

1 cucumber
5ml/1 tsp salt
45ml/3 tbsp finely chopped fresh
   mint, plus a few sprigs to garnish
1 garlic clove, crushed
5ml/1 tsp caster (superfine) sugar
200ml/7fl oz/scant 1 cup reduced fat
   Greek (US strained plain) yogurt
a cucumber flower, to garnish
   (optional)

1 Peel the cucumber. Reserve a little of the cucumber to use as a garnish if you wish and cut the rest in half lengthways. Remove the seeds with a teaspoon and discard. Slice the cucumber thinly and combine with the salt in a bowl. Leave for approximately 15–20 minutes. Salt will soften the cucumber and draw out any bitter juices.

2 Combine the mint, garlic, sugar and yogurt in a separate bowl, reserving a few sprigs of mint as decoration.

3 Rinse the cucumber in a sieve (strainer) under cold running water to flush away the salt. Drain well and combine with the yogurt. Serve cold.

COOK'S TIPS
• If you want to prepare Tzatziki in a hurry, then leave out the method for salting the cucumber at the end of Step 1. The cucumber will have a more crunchy texture, and will be slightly less sweet.
• Wash fresh herbs, such as mint, before use. Simply wash the herbs by shaking them quickly under cold running water. Drain well and dry on kitchen paper, then chop or use as required.

Energy 41Kcal/170kJ; Protein 3.2g; Carbohydrate 6.1g, of which sugars 5.9g; Fat 0.6g, of which saturates 0.3g; Cholesterol 1mg; Calcium 110mg; Fibre 0.5g; Sodium 535mg.

PEPERONATA ★

THIS RICHLY FLAVOURED LOW-FAT DIP COMBINES SPICY TOMATO WITH SWEET RED PEPPER. BEST COMPLEMENTED WITH CRISP ITALIAN-STYLE BREADSTICKS, IT IS DELICIOUS SERVED HOT, COLD OR AT ROOM TEMPERATURE AND CAN BE STORED IN THE REFRIGERATOR FOR SEVERAL DAYS.

SERVES SIX

INGREDIENTS
    30ml/2 tbsp garlic-infused olive oil
    2 large red (bell) peppers, halved,
        seeded and sliced
    a pinch of dried chilli flakes
    400g/14oz can pomodorino tomatoes
    salt and ground black pepper

COOK'S TIP
Long, slow cooking helps to bring out
the sweetness of the peppers and
tomatoes, so don't be tempted to cheat
on the cooking time by cooking over a
higher heat.

1 Heat the oil in a large, non-stick pan
over a low heat and add the sliced
peppers. Cook very gently for
3–4 minutes, stirring occasionally.

2 Add the chilli flakes to the pan and
cook for 1 minute, then stir in the
tomatoes. Season with salt and pepper.
Cook gently for 50 minutes to 1 hour,
stirring occasionally.

Energy 66Kcal/274kJ; Protein 1.1g; Carbohydrate 6.3g, of which sugars 6.1g; Fat 4.1g, of which saturates 0.7g; Cholesterol 0mg; Calcium 10mg; Fibre 1.7g; Sodium 9mg.

ARTICHOKE AND CUMIN DIP ★

THIS LOW-FAT VEGETARIAN DIP IS SO EASY TO MAKE AND IS REALLY TASTY. SERVE WITH OLIVES, LOW-FAT HUMMUS AND WEDGES OF PITTA BREAD AS A SUMMERY SNACK SELECTION. GRILLED ARTICHOKES BOTTLED IN OIL HAVE A FABULOUS FLAVOUR AND CAN BE USED INSTEAD OF CANNED ARTICHOKES BUT REMEMBER TO DRAIN THEM WELL BEFORE USE. YOU CAN ALSO VARY THE FLAVOURINGS — TRY ADDING CHILLI POWDER IN PLACE OF THE CUMIN AND ADD A HANDFUL OF FRESH BASIL LEAVES TO THE ARTICHOKES BEFORE PROCESSING.

SERVES SIX

INGREDIENTS
    2 x 400g/14oz cans artichoke hearts,
        drained
    2 garlic cloves, peeled
    2.5ml/½ tsp ground cumin
    30ml/2 tbsp olive oil
    salt and ground black pepper

COOK'S TIP
Canned artichoke hearts tend to be
preserved in brine; rinse and drain them
before serving to reduce their high
sodium content.

1 Put the artichoke hearts in a food
processor with the garlic and ground
cumin, and a generous drizzle of olive
oil. Process to a smooth purée and
season to taste with plenty of salt and
ground black pepper.

2 Spoon the purée into a serving bowl
and serve with an extra drizzle of olive
oil swirled on the top and slices of warm
pitta bread for dipping.

Energy 42Kcal/172kJ; Protein 0.6g; Carbohydrate 1.2g, of which sugars 0.9g; Fat 3.9g, of which saturates 0.5g; Cholesterol 0mg; Calcium 41mg; Fibre 1.2g; Sodium 60mg.

ROASTED VEGETABLE LAVASH WRAPS ★

*MIDDLE-EASTERN FLATBREADS ARE PERFECT FOR SNACK-TIME LOW-FAT WRAPS. TEAR OFF SUITABLY
SIZED PIECES TO WRAP, FOLD OR ROLL UP FRAGRANT ROASTED VEGETABLES.*

SERVES SIX

INGREDIENTS

    3 courgettes (zucchini), trimmed and
       sliced lengthways
    1 large fennel bulb, cut into wedges
    450g/1lb butternut squash, seeded
       and cut into 2cm/¾in chunks
    12 shallots
    2 red (bell) peppers, seeded and
       cut lengthways into thick slices
    4 plum tomatoes, halved and seeded
    30ml/2 tbsp extra virgin olive oil
    2 garlic cloves, crushed
    5ml/1 tsp balsamic vinegar
    salt and ground black pepper
To serve
    lavash or other flat bread
    a little fresh or good quality bottled pesto
    chopped fresh mint
    low-fat Greek (US strained plain) yogurt
    a little feta cheese, diced

1 Preheat the oven to 220°C/425°F/
Gas 7. Place the courgettes, fennel,
butternut squash, shallots, red peppers
and tomatoes in a large bowl. Add the
olive oil, garlic and balsamic vinegar
and toss until all the ingredients are
thoroughly coated in the mixture. Set
aside for about 10 minutes to allow the
flavours to mingle.

2 Using a slotted spoon, lift just the
tomatoes and butternut squash out of
the mixture and set them aside on a
plate. Use the spoon to transfer all the
remaining vegetables to a large roasting
pan. Brush with half the oil and vinegar
mixture remaining in the bowl, season
with salt and pepper and roast in the
oven for 25 minutes.

3 Remove the pan from the oven and
turn the vegetables over. Brush with the
remaining oil and vinegar mixture, add
the squash and tomatoes and roast for
a further 20–25 minutes, or until all the
vegetables are tender and have begun
to char around the edges.

4 Put the bread on the table, with the
pesto, mint, yogurt and feta cheese in
separate bowls. Spoon the roasted
vegetables on to a large platter and
invite everyone to tuck in.

VARIATION
Use vine-ripened tomatoes in place of
plum tomatoes.

Energy 109Kcal/453kJ; Protein 4.1g; Carbohydrate 13g, of which sugars 11.5g; Fat 4.8g, of which saturates 0.8g; Cholesterol 0mg; Calcium 72mg; Fibre 4.6g; Sodium 14mg.

VEGETABLE PANCAKES WITH TOMATO SALSA ★

THESE DELICIOUS SPINACH AND EGG PANCAKES MAKE A GREAT LOW-FAT VEGETARIAN STARTER OR SNACK, IDEAL SERVED WITH A TASTY TOMATO SALSA.

MAKES TEN

INGREDIENTS
    225g/8oz fresh spinach leaves
    1 small leek
    a few sprigs of fresh coriander
      (cilantro) or fresh parsley
    3 large (US extra large) eggs
    50g/2oz/½ cup plain (all-purpose)
      flour, sifted
    15ml/1 tbsp sunflower oil
    25g/1oz/⅓ cup grated fresh
      Parmesan cheese
    salt, ground black pepper and freshly
      grated nutmeg
For the salsa
    2 tomatoes, skinned and chopped
    ¼ fresh red chilli, finely chopped
    2 pieces sun-dried tomato in oil,
      drained and chopped
    1 small red onion, finely chopped
    1 garlic clove, crushed
    60ml/4 tbsp tomato juice
    30ml/2 tbsp sherry
    2.5ml/½ tsp soft light brown sugar

1 Prepare the tomato salsa: place all the ingredients in a bowl and toss together to combine. Cover and leave to stand in a cool place for 2–3 hours.

2 To make the pancakes, finely shred or chop the spinach, leek and coriander or parsley. If you prefer, chop them in a food processor, but do not overprocess. Place the chopped vegetables in a bowl and beat in the eggs and seasoning. Blend in the flour and 30–45ml/ 2–3 tbsp water, then leave to stand for 20 minutes.

3 To cook the pancakes, drop spoonfuls of the batter into a lightly oiled frying pan and cook until golden underneath. Using a fish slice or metal spatula, turn the pancakes over and cook briefly on the other side.

4 Carefully lift the pancakes out of the pan, drain on kitchen paper and keep warm while you cook the remaining mixture in the same way. Sprinkle the pancakes with grated Parmesan cheese and serve with the salsa.

VARIATION
Use 3–4 spring onions (scallions) in place of leek.

COOK'S TIP
Try to find sun-ripened tomatoes for the salsa, as these have the best and sweetest flavour and are much superior to those ripened under glass.

Energy 70Kcal/294kJ; Protein 4.5g; Carbohydrate 6.2g, of which sugars 2.1g; Fat 2.9g, of which saturates 1.1g; Cholesterol 60mg; Calcium 91mg; Fibre 1.3g; Sodium 96mg.

ROASTED RED PEPPER AND TOMATO SALAD ★

THIS IS ONE OF THOSE LOVELY RECIPES THAT BRINGS TOGETHER PERFECTLY THE COLOURS, FLAVOURS AND TEXTURES OF SOUTHERN ITALIAN FOOD. EAT THIS LOW-FAT STARTER OR SNACK AT ROOM TEMPERATURE.

SERVES FOUR

INGREDIENTS
   3 red (bell) peppers
   6 large plum tomatoes, halved
   2.5ml/½ tsp dried red chilli flakes
   1 red onion, finely sliced
   3 garlic cloves, thinly chopped
   finely grated rind and juice
     of 1 lemon
   45ml/3 tbsp chopped fresh flat
     leaf parsley
   15ml/1 tbsp extra virgin olive oil
   salt
   black and green olives and extra
     chopped flat leaf parsley, to garnish

COOK'S TIP
These peppers will keep for several weeks if the peeled pepper pieces are placed in a jar of olive oil, with a tight-fitting lid. Store in the refrigerator.

1 Preheat the oven to 220°C/425°F/ Gas 7. Place the peppers on a baking sheet and roast for 10 minutes until the skins are slightly blackened. Add the tomatoes and bake for 5 minutes more.

2 Place the peppers in a plastic bag. Close the top loosely, trapping in the steam, and then set them aside, with the tomatoes, until they are cool.

3 Skin and seed the peppers. Chop the peppers and tomatoes roughly and place them both in a mixing bowl.

4 Add the chilli flakes, onion, garlic and lemon rind and juice. Sprinkle over the parsley. Mix well, then transfer to a serving dish. Season with salt, drizzle over the olive oil and sprinkle the olives and extra parsley over the top. Serve.

Energy 96Kcal/400kJ; Protein 2.7g; Carbohydrate 13.4g, of which sugars 12.6g; Fat 3.8g, of which saturates 0.7g; Cholesterol 0mg; Calcium 46mg; Fibre 4.1g; Sodium 22mg.

MUSHROOM CAVIAR ★

THE NAME CAVIAR REFERS TO THE DARK COLOUR AND TEXTURE OF THIS LOW-FAT VEGETARIAN DISH OF CHOPPED MUSHROOMS. SERVE WITH TOASTED RYE BREAD RUBBED WITH CUT GARLIC CLOVES.

SERVES FOUR

INGREDIENTS

15ml/1 tbsp olive or vegetable oil
450g/1lb mushrooms,
  coarsely chopped
5–10 shallots, chopped
4 garlic cloves, chopped
salt

VARIATION

For a rich wild mushroom caviar, soak 10–15g/¼–½oz dried porcini in about 120ml/4fl oz/½ cup water for about 30 minutes. Add the porcini and their soaking liquid to the browned mushrooms in Step 2. Continue as in the recipe. Serve with wedges of lemon, for their tangy juice.

1 Heat the oil in a large, non-stick pan, add the mushrooms, shallots and garlic, and cook until browned, stirring occasionally. Season with salt, then continue cooking until the mushrooms give up their liquor.

2 Continue cooking until the liquor has evaporated and the mushrooms are brown and dry, stirring frequently.

3 Put the mixture in a blender or food processor and process briefly until a chunky paste is formed. Spoon the mushroom caviar into dishes and serve.

Energy 68Kcal/283kJ; Protein 3.3g; Carbohydrate 6.4g, of which sugars 3.8g; Fat 3.5g, of which saturates 0.5g; Cholesterol 0mg; Calcium 24mg; Fibre 2.4g; Sodium 8mg.

BABY SPINACH WITH TOASTED SESAME SEEDS ★

BASED ON A JAPANESE SPECIALITY — O-HITASHI — SEASONAL GREEN VEGETABLES ARE SIMPLY BLANCHED AND COOLED AND FORMED INTO LITTLE TOWERS. WITH A LITTLE HELP FROM SOY SAUCE AND SESAME SEEDS, THEY WRAP UP A SUPERB ORIENTAL FLAVOUR.

SERVES FOUR

INGREDIENTS
450g/1lb fresh young or baby
   spinach leaves
30ml/2 tbsp shoyu or soy sauce
30ml/2 tbsp water
15ml/1 tbsp sesame seeds
salt

VARIATION
Japanese spinach, the long-leaf type
with the stalks and pink root intact, is
best, but you can use ordinary young
spinach leaves, or any soft and deep-
green salad leaves – such as watercress,
rocket (arugula) or lamb's lettuce.

1 Blanch the spinach leaves in a pan
of lightly salted, boiling water for
15 seconds. For Japanese-type spinach,
hold the leafy part and slip the stems
into the pan. After 15 seconds, drop in
the leaves and cook for 20 seconds.

2 Drain immediately and place the
spinach under cold running water.
Squeeze out all the excess water by
hand. Now what looked like a large
amount of spinach has become a ball,
roughly the size of an orange. Mix the
shoyu or soy sauce and water in a small
bowl, then pour it on to the spinach.
Mix well and leave to cool.

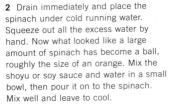

3 Meanwhile, put the sesame seeds in
a dry frying pan and stir or toss over a
low heat until they start to pop. Remove
the pan from the heat and leave to cool.

4 Drain the spinach and squeeze
out the excess sauce with your hands.
Form the spinach into a log shape
about 4cm/1½in in diameter on a
chopping board. Squeeze again to
make it firm. With a sharp knife, cut
it across into four cylinders.

5 Place the spinach cylinders on a
large plate or individual serving dishes.
Sprinkle with the toasted sesame seeds
and a little salt and serve.

Energy 54Kcal/222kJ; Protein 4.1g; Carbohydrate 2.5g, of which sugars 2.3g; Fat 3.1g, of which saturates 0.4g; Cholesterol 0mg; Calcium 218mg; Fibre 2.7g; Sodium 692mg.

VEGETABLE SAMOSAS ★

A SELECTION OF HIGHLY SPICED VEGETABLES IN A LIGHT, CRISPY PASTRY CASING MAKES THESE SAMOSAS A TASTY VEGETARIAN SNACK AT ANY TIME OF THE DAY. SERVE THESE DELICIOUS PASTRIES FRESHLY BAKED AND HOT FROM THE OVEN.

MAKES TWENTY-EIGHT

INGREDIENTS
14 sheets filo pastry, thawed and wrapped in a damp dish towel
45ml/3 tbsp sunflower oil
For the filling
3 large potatoes, boiled and coarsely mashed
75g/3oz/¾ cup frozen peas, thawed
50g/2oz/⅓ cup canned corn kernels, drained
5ml/1 tsp ground coriander
5ml/1 tsp ground cumin
5ml/1 tsp dry mango powder (amchur)
1 small onion, finely chopped
2 fresh green chillies, seeded and finely chopped
30ml/2 tbsp chopped fresh coriander (cilantro) leaves
30ml/2 tbsp chopped fresh mint leaves
juice of 1 lemon
salt

1 Preheat the oven to 200°C/400°F/ Gas 6. Cut each sheet of filo pastry in half lengthways and fold each piece in half lengthways to give 28 thin strips. Lightly brush with oil.

VARIATIONS
Use sweet potatoes in place of standard potatoes. Use 2 shallots in place of onion.

COOK'S TIP
Work with one or two sheets of filo pastry at a time and keep the rest covered with a damp dish towel to prevent it drying out.

2 Toss all the filling ingredients together in a large mixing bowl until they are well blended. Adjust the seasoning with salt and lemon juice, if necessary.

3 Using one strip of the pastry at a time, place about 15ml/1 tbsp of the filling mixture at one end of the strip and diagonally fold the pastry up to form a triangle shape. Brush the samosas with oil, place on a baking sheet and bake in the oven for 10–15 minutes, or until cooked and golden brown. Serve.

Energy 56Kcal/235kJ; Protein 1.3g; Carbohydrate 10g, of which sugars 0.8g; Fat 1.4g, of which saturates 0.2g; Cholesterol 0mg; Calcium 16mg; Fibre 0.7g; Sodium 8mg.

STUFFED VINE LEAVES ★

THIS POPULAR LOW-FAT GREEK DISH, DOLMADES, KEEPS MOIST WHEN COOKED SLOWLY IN A CLAY POT. FRESH VINE LEAVES GIVE THE BEST FLAVOUR, BUT PRESERVED OR CANNED ONES WILL ALSO WORK WELL.

SERVES FOUR

INGREDIENTS
    12 fresh vine leaves
    10ml/2 tsp olive oil
    1 small onion, chopped
    15g/½oz pine nuts
    1 garlic clove, crushed
    115g/4oz/1 cup cooked long
      grain rice
    2 tomatoes, skinned, seeded and
      finely chopped
    15ml/1 tbsp chopped fresh mint
    1 lemon, sliced
    150ml/¼ pint/⅔ cup dry white wine
    200ml/7fl oz/scant 1 cup
      vegetable stock
    salt and ground black pepper
    lemon wedges and fresh mint sprigs,
      to garnish

COOK'S TIPS
• You can use preserved vine leaves; do
not rinse, but blanch them before use.
• A lidded clay pot, or "brick", is a useful
piece of equipment for sealing in the
juices of food while it cooks. It must be
thoroughly soaked in water before use.
• This delicious dish can be served as a
starter or as part of a meze table.

2 Heat the oil in a non-stick frying pan,
add the onion and cook for 5–6 minutes
until softened, stirring frequently. Add
the pine nuts and garlic and cook
until the onions and pine nuts are
golden, stirring constantly.

3 Stir the onion mixture into the rice,
then add and stir in the tomatoes and
chopped mint. Season to taste with salt
and pepper.

5 Place the stuffed vine leaves close
together, seam-side down, in the clay
pot. Place the lemon slices on top and
in between the stuffed vine leaves. Pour
over the white wine and sufficient stock
just to cover the stuffed vine leaves and
lemon slices.

6 Cover the dish with the lid and place
in an unheated oven. Set the oven to
200°C/400°F/Gas 6 and cook for 30
minutes. Reduce the oven temperature
to 160°C/325°F/Gas 3 and cook for a
further 30 minutes.

7 Serve hot or cold, and drizzle with a
little fruity extra virgin olive oil, if you
like. Garnish with lemon wedges and a
few sprigs of fresh mint.

1 Soak the clay pot in cold water for
20 minutes, then drain. Blanch the
vine leaves in a pan of boiling water for
about 2 minutes, or until they darken
and soften. Rinse the leaves under cold
running water and leave to drain.

4 Place a spoonful of the rice mixture at
the stalk end of each vine leaf. Fold the
sides over the filling and roll up tightly.

Energy 131Kcal/549kJ; Protein 2.6g; Carbohydrate 14.5g, of which sugars 5.2g; Fat 4.7g, of which saturates 0.5g; Cholesterol 0mg; Calcium 41mg; Fibre 1.9g; Sodium 10mg.

CHINESE-STYLE BRAISED TOFU
<u>WITH</u> MUSHROOMS ★

FOUR DIFFERENT KINDS OF MUSHROOMS COMBINE SUCCULENTLY WITH TOFU IN THIS ROBUST LOW-FAT RECIPE. CHINESE FLAVOURINGS ENHANCE ALL THE INGREDIENTS TO MAKE THIS AN INTERESTING VEGETARIAN VARIATION TO TRY OUT.

SERVES SIX

INGREDIENTS
    350g/12oz firm tofu
    2.5ml/½ tsp sesame oil
    10ml/2 tsp light soy sauce
    15ml/1 tbsp vegetable oil
    2 garlic cloves, finely chopped
    2.5ml/½ tsp grated fresh root ginger
    115g/4oz/scant 2 cups fresh shiitake
        mushrooms, stalks removed
    175g/6oz/scant 2 cups fresh oyster
        mushrooms
    115g/4oz/scant 2 cups drained,
        canned straw mushrooms
    115g/4oz/scant 2 cups button (white)
        mushrooms, halved
    15ml/1 tbsp Chinese rice wine or
        dry sherry
    15ml/1 tbsp dark soy sauce
    90ml/6 tbsp vegetable stock
    5ml/1 tsp cornflour (cornstarch)
    15ml/1 tbsp cold water
    salt and ground white pepper
    2 shredded spring onions (scallions),
        to garnish

1 Put the tofu in a dish or bowl and sprinkle with the sesame oil, light soy sauce and a large pinch of pepper. Leave to marinate for 10 minutes, then drain and cut into 2.5 x 1cm/1 x ½in pieces using a sharp knife.

2 Heat the vegetable oil in a large non-stick frying pan or wok. When the oil is very hot, add the garlic and ginger and stir-fry for a few seconds. Add all the mushrooms and stir-fry for a further 2 minutes.

3 Stir in the Chinese rice wine or dry sherry, dark soy sauce and stock. Season to taste with salt, if necessary, and white pepper. Reduce the heat and simmer gently for 4 minutes.

4 Place the cornflour in a bowl with the water. Mix to make a smooth paste. Stir the cornflour mixture into the pan or wok and cook until thickened, stirring constantly to prevent lumps forming.

VARIATIONS
Use galangal instead of root ginger. Stir-fry 1–2 seeded and chopped fresh red chillies with the garlic and garnish with chopped coriander (cilantro).

5 Carefully add the pieces of tofu, toss gently to coat thoroughly in the sauce and simmer for 2 minutes.

6 Sprinkle the shredded spring onions over the top of the mixture to garnish, transfer to a warm serving dish or individual plates, and serve immediately.

COOK'S TIPS
• If fresh shiitake mushrooms are not available, use dried Chinese mushrooms. Soak them in hot water for about 20–30 minutes, then drain. Use the soaking liquid instead of vegetable stock for a more intense flavour.
• Straw mushrooms, so called because they are grown on beds of straw, are rarely available fresh in the West. However, they are widely available canned. Their main contribution to this dish – and to Chinese cooking in general – is their slippery texture rather than their flavour which is quite bland.

Energy 85Kcal/356kJ; Protein 6.4g; Carbohydrate 3.3g, of which sugars 0.6g; Fat 5g, of which saturates 0.6g; Cholesterol 0mg; Calcium 304mg; Fibre 1g; Sodium 186mg.

SALADS

Vegetarian salads offer plenty of scope for the cook's imagination. The selection here combines an extensive variety of fresh vegetables, fruit, herbs, beans, grains, seeds and other delights, such as tofu, to create delicious low-fat salads to have for lunchtime or evenings. Go easy on the dressings though, and choose low-fat or fat-free recipes (there are several given in the introduction). Tempting, light vegetarian salads include Garlicky Green Salad with Raspberry Vinaigrette, Baked Sweet Potato Salad and Lemony Couscous Salad.

GARLICKY GREEN SALAD WITH RASPBERRY VINAIGRETTE ★

ADDING A SPLASH OF RASPBERRY VINEGAR TO THE DRESSING ENLIVENS A SIMPLE GREEN SALAD, TRANSFORMING IT INTO THIS SOPHISTICATED LOW-FAT SIDE DISH.

SERVES SIX

INGREDIENTS
    30ml/2 tbsp olive oil
    2 garlic cloves, thinly sliced
    6 handfuls green salad leaves
    15ml/1 tbsp raspberry vinegar
    salt and ground black pepper

1 Heat the oil in a small, non-stick pan and add the garlic. Cook gently for 1–2 minutes, or until just golden, being careful not to burn the garlic. Remove the garlic with a slotted spoon and drain on kitchen paper. Pour the oil into a small bowl.

2 Arrange the salad leaves in a serving bowl. Whisk the raspberry vinegar into the reserved oil and season to taste with salt and pepper.

3 Pour the garlic dressing over the salad leaves and toss to combine. Sprinkle over the fried garlic slices and serve immediately.

Energy 45Kcal/185kJ; Protein 0.7g; Carbohydrate 1.4g, of which sugars 1.4g; Fat 4.1g, of which saturates 0.6g; Cholesterol 0mg; Calcium 23mg; Fibre 0.8g; Sodium 3mg.

WILD ROCKET AND COS LETTUCE SALAD WITH HERBS ★

THIS AROMATIC SALAD FOLLOWS A GREEK RECIPE COMBINING A LEMONY FLAVOUR WITH THE STRONG SWEET TASTE OF COS LETTUCE. WILD ROCKET IS ADDED TO GIVE A SHARP NEW EDGE.

SERVES FOUR

INGREDIENTS
    a large handful of rocket
      (arugula) leaves
    2 cos or romaine lettuce hearts
    3 or 4 fresh flat leaf parsley sprigs,
      coarsely chopped
    30–45ml/2–3 tbsp finely
      chopped fresh dill
    90ml/6 tbsp low-fat French dressing
    salt and ground black pepper

COOK'S TIP
It is important to balance the bitterness of the rocket and the sweetness of the cos or romaine lettuce, and the best way to find this out is by taste.

1 If the rocket leaves are young and tender they can be left whole, but older ones should be trimmed of thick stalks and then sliced coarsely. Discard any tough stalks.

2 Slice the cos or romaine lettuce hearts into thin ribbons and place these in a bowl, then add the rocket and chopped parsley and dill.

3 Taste the dressing and adjust the seasoning to taste. Just before serving, pour the dressing over the salad and toss lightly to coat everything with the dressing. Serve the salad with crusty bread.

Energy 26Kcal/110kJ; Protein 1g; Carbohydrate 4.4g, of which sugars 4.2g; Fat 0.6g, of which saturates 0.1g; Cholesterol 0mg; Calcium 35mg; Fibre 1.2g; Sodium 341mg.

ASPARAGUS, TOMATO AND ORANGE SALAD ★

THIS LIGHT SALAD ORIGINATES FROM SPAIN, WHERE COOKS SIMPLY RELY ON THE WONDERFUL TASTE OF A GOOD-QUALITY OLIVE OIL. USE EXTRA VIRGIN OLIVE OIL TO BRING OUT THE BEST FLAVOUR.

SERVES SIX

INGREDIENTS

    350g/12oz asparagus, trimmed and
      cut into 5cm/2in pieces
    2 large oranges
    2 well-flavoured tomatoes, cut
      into eighths
    50g/2oz cos or romaine lettuce
      leaves, shredded
    30ml/2 tbsp extra virgin olive oil
    2.5ml/½ tsp sherry vinegar
    salt and ground black pepper

VARIATIONS
• Little Gem (Bibb) lettuce can be used in place of cos lettuce.
• Grapefruit segments also work well in this salad. Use 1 ruby grapefruit instead of the oranges.

1 Cook the asparagus in a pan of salted boiling water for 3–4 minutes, or until just tender. Drain and refresh under cold water. Set aside.

2 Grate the rind from half an orange and reserve. Peel both the oranges and cut the flesh into segments. Squeeze out the juice from the membrane and reserve it.

3 Put the asparagus, orange segments, tomatoes and lettuce into a salad bowl. Make the dressing by whisking together the oil and vinegar and adding 15ml/ 1 tbsp of the reserved orange juice and 5ml/1 tsp of the grated rind. Season to taste with salt and pepper. Just before serving, pour the dressing over the salad and toss gently to coat.

Energy 73Kcal/304kJ; Protein 2.6g; Carbohydrate 6.6g, of which sugars 6.5g; Fat 4.2g, of which saturates 0.6g; Cholesterol 0mg; Calcium 44mg; Fibre 2.3g; Sodium 6mg.

ROCKET, PEAR AND PARMESAN SALAD ★

FOR A SOPHISTICATED SALAD TRY THIS SIMPLE ITALIAN-STYLE COMBINATION OF FRESH, RIPE PEARS, TASTY PARMESAN AND AROMATIC LEAVES OF ROCKET. SERVE WITH FRESH ITALIAN BREAD OR CRISPBREADS.

SERVES FOUR

INGREDIENTS

3 ripe pears, such as Williams
  or Packhams
10ml/2 tsp lemon juice
15ml/1 tbsp hazelnut or walnut oil
115g/4oz rocket (arugula) leaves
25g/1oz/⅓ cup fresh
  Parmesan cheese
ground black pepper

1 Peel and core the pears and slice them thickly. Place in a bowl and toss gently with the lemon juice to keep the flesh white.

2 In a bowl, combine the nut oil with the pears. Add the rocket leaves and toss gently to mix.

COOK'S TIP
You can grow your own rocket (arugula) from early spring to late summer. You can also use watercress instead of rocket.

3 Divide the salad among four small plates and top each portion with shavings of Parmesan cheese. Season with pepper and serve immediately.

Energy 100Kcal/416kJ; Protein 3.1g; Carbohydrate 11.7g, of which sugars 11.7g; Fat 4.7g, of which saturates 1.3g; Cholesterol 5mg; Calcium 121mg; Fibre 3.1g; Sodium 98mg.

ORANGE AND RED ONION SALAD WITH CUMIN ★

IN THIS SPANISH-DERIVED DISH, JUICY ORANGES PERFECTLY PARTNER THINLY SLICED RED ONIONS AND BLACK OLIVES. CUMIN SEEDS AND MINT ARE ADDED TO COMPLETE THIS MOUTHWATERING SALAD.

SERVES SIX

INGREDIENTS
6 oranges
2 red onions
15ml/1 tbsp cumin seeds
5ml/1 tsp coarsely ground
  black pepper
15ml/1 tbsp chopped fresh mint
40ml/8 tsp olive oil
salt
fresh mint sprigs and whole black
  olives, to garnish

COOK'S TIP
It is important to let the salad stand before serving. This allows the flavours to develop and the pungent taste of the onion to soften slightly.

1 Using a sharp knife, slice the oranges thinly, working over a bowl to catch any juice. Then, holding each orange slice in turn over the bowl, cut round the middle fleshy section with scissors to remove the peel and pith. Reserve the juice. Slice the red onions thinly and separate the rings.

2 Arrange the orange and onion slices in layers in a shallow dish, sprinkling each layer with cumin seeds, pepper, mint, olive oil and salt. Pour in the reserved orange juice. Leave to marinate in a cool place for about 2 hours. Just before serving, scatter with the mint sprigs and black olives.

Energy 110Kcal/460kJ; Protein 2.3g; Carbohydrate 16.7g, of which sugars 15.6g; Fat 4.3g, of which saturates 0.6g; Cholesterol 0mg; Calcium 83mg; Fibre 3.3g; Sodium 9mg.

SPANISH MIXED SALAD WITH OLIVES AND CAPERS ★

THIS COLOURFUL LOW-FAT VEGETARIAN SALAD ORIGINATES FROM SPAIN WHERE, TYPICALLY, THE BOWL OF SALAD IS PUT IN THE CENTRE OF THE TABLE FOR EVERYONE TO HELP THEMSELVES WITH A FORK.

SERVES FOUR

INGREDIENTS
4 large tomatoes
½ cucumber
1 bunch spring onions (scallions)
1 bunch watercress or rocket
  (arugula), washed
8 pimiento-stuffed olives
30ml/2 tbsp drained pickled capers
For the dressing
1 garlic clove, finely chopped
105ml/7 tbsp low-fat French dressing
5ml/1 tsp paprika
2.5ml/½ tsp ground cumin
salt and ground black pepper

COOK'S TIP
Scallions, or "green onions" are immature onions and and have a mild flavour for soups and stews. They can be eaten raw.

1 To skin the tomatoes, place them in a heatproof bowl, pour over boiling water to cover and leave to stand for 1 minute. Lift out the tomatoes with a slotted spoon and plunge them into a bowl of cold water. Leave for 1 minute, then drain. Slip off the skins and chop the flesh finely. Put in a salad bowl.

2 Peel the cucumber, finely dice and add it to the tomatoes. Trim and chop half the spring onions, then add them to the bowl.

3 Toss the vegetables together, then break the watercress or rocket into small sprigs. Add the olives and capers to the tomato mixture.

4 Make the dressing. Crush the garlic to a paste with a little salt, using the flat of a knife. Put in a bowl and mix in the French dressing and spices. Whisk together to mix well, then season to taste. Dress the salad, and serve garnished with the remaining spring onions.

Energy 42Kcal/177kJ; Protein 1.4g; Carbohydrate 6.7g, of which sugars 6.3g; Fat 1.3g, of which saturates 0.3g; Cholesterol 0mg; Calcium 22mg; Fibre 1.7g; Sodium 573mg.

COURGETTE AND FLAGEOLET BEAN SALAD ★

SERVE THIS MARINATED VEGETABLE DISH AS A DELICIOUS ACCOMPANIMENT TO A LIGHT VEGETARIAN MAIN MEAL OR AS A SUMMER LUNCH IN ITS OWN RIGHT.

SERVES SIX

INGREDIENTS

3 courgettes (zucchini), halved
   lengthways and sliced
400g/14oz can flageolet or cannellini
   beans, rinsed and drained
30ml/2 tbsp garlic-infused olive oil
finely grated rind and juice of
   1 unwaxed lemon
salt and ground black pepper

1 Cook the courgettes in a pan of salted boiling water for 2–3 minutes, or until just tender. Drain well and refresh under cold running water.

2 Transfer the drained courgettes to a bowl with the beans, then stir in the oil and lemon rind and juice. Season to taste with salt and pepper. Chill the salad in the refrigerator for 30 minutes before serving.

VARIATION

To add extra flavour to the salad, add 30ml/2 tbsp chopped fresh herbs before chilling. Basil and mint both have fresh, distinctive flavours that will work very well in this salad.

COOK'S TIP

When buying courgettes (zucchini), choose firm vegetables with unbroken skin and a good green colour. Avoid courgettes with soft or brown patches. Wrap loosely and store in the refrigerator.

Energy 106Kcal/445kJ; Protein 5.5g; Carbohydrate 11.9g, of which sugars 3.5g; Fat 4.4g, of which saturates 0.7g; Cholesterol 0mg; Calcium 62mg; Fibre 4.4g; Sodium 228mg.

ARTICHOKE SALAD WITH SALSA AGRODOLCE ★

AGRODOLCE IS AN ITALIAN SWEET-AND-SOUR SAUCE WHICH MAKES AN IDEAL ACCOMPANIMENT FOR THIS TASTY, LOW-FAT ARTICHOKE AND BEAN SALAD.

SERVES FOUR TO SIX

INGREDIENTS
    6 small globe artichokes
    juice of 1 lemon
    15ml/1 tbsp olive oil
    2 onions, roughly chopped
    175g/6oz/1 cup fresh or frozen broad
        (fava) beans (shelled weight)
    175g/6oz/1½ cups fresh or frozen
        peas (shelled weight)
    salt and ground black pepper
    fresh mint leaves, to garnish
For the salsa agrodolce
    120ml/4fl oz/½ cup white
        wine vinegar
    15ml/1 tbsp caster (superfine) sugar
    a handful of fresh mint leaves,
        roughly torn

1 Peel and discard the outer leaves from the artichokes and cut into quarters. Place the artichokes in a bowl of water with the lemon juice. Set aside.

2 Heat the oil in a large, non-stick pan and add the onions. Cook until the onions are golden, stirring occasionally. Add the broad beans and stir, then drain the artichokes and add to the pan. Pour in about 300ml/½ pint/ 1¼ cups of water and bring to the boil, then reduce the heat and cook, covered, for 10–15 minutes.

3 Add the peas, season to taste with salt and pepper and cook for a further 5 minutes until the vegetables are tender, stirring occasionally. Strain through a sieve (strainer), discard the liquid, then place all the vegetables in a bowl, leave to cool, cover and chill.

4 To make the salsa agrodolce, mix the vinegar, sugar and torn mint leaves in a small pan. Heat gently for 2–3 minutes, until the sugar has dissolved, then simmer for 5 minutes, stirring occasionally. Remove the pan from the heat and leave to cool. To serve, drizzle the salsa over the vegetables and garnish with mint leaves.

COOK'S TIP
Leave the root end intact when chopping or slicing an onion. This will prevent the release of the strong juices and fumes that can cause eyes to water.

VARIATION
Use 6–8 shallots in place of onions.

Energy 98Kcal/411kJ; Protein 5.4g; Carbohydrate 14g, of which sugars 7.2g; Fat 2.7g, of which saturates 0.4g; Cholesterol 0mg; Calcium 71mg; Fibre 4.9g; Sodium 54mg.

A V O C A D O <u>AND</u> P I N K   G R A P E F R U I T   S A L A D ★

ON ITS OWN OR SERVED AS A LIGHT VEGETARIAN SIDE DISH OR FIRST COURSE, THIS BITTER-SWEET
SALAD CAN BE PARTIALLY PREPARED IN ADVANCE, BUT DON'T LET THE AVOCADO DISCOLOUR.

2 Put the sugar and water in a small pan and heat gently until the sugar has dissolved. Add the shreds of orange rind, increase the heat and boil steadily for 5 minutes, or until the rind is tender. Using two forks, remove the orange rind from the syrup and spread it out on a wire rack to dry. Reserve the cooking syrup to add to the dressing, if you like.

3 Wash and dry the lettuce or other salad leaves and tear or chop them into bitesize pieces. Using a sharp knife, remove the pith from the oranges and the pith and peel from the grapefruit. Hold the citrus fruits over a bowl and cut out each segment leaving the membrane behind. Squeeze the remaining juice from the membrane into the bowl.

4 Put the French dressing into a screw-top jar with the garlic and mustard, if using. Add the reserved syrup, if using, put the lid on and shake well to combine. Adjust the seasoning to taste. Arrange the salad ingredients on plates with the cubed avocado. Spoon over the dressing and sprinkle with the caramelized peel. Serve.

SERVES EIGHT

INGREDIENTS
   mixed red and green lettuce or other
     salad leaves
   2 sweet pink grapefruit
   1 large or 2 small avocados, peeled,
     stoned (pitted) and cubed
   120ml/4fl oz/½ cup low-fat French
     dressing
   1 garlic clove, crushed
   5ml/1 tsp Dijon mustard (optional)
   salt and ground black pepper
For the caramelized peel
   4 oranges
   50g/2oz/¼ cup caster
     (superfine) sugar
   60ml/4 tbsp cold water

1 To make the caramelized peel, using a vegetable peeler, carefully remove the rind from the oranges in thin strips and reserve the fruit. Scrape away the white pith from the underside of the rind with a small, sharp knife, and cut the rind into fine shreds.

COOK'S TIP
To stop avocado flesh discolouring, brush with a citrus fruit – lemon, orange or lime juice – if you are not planning to eat your avocado at once.

Energy 43Kcal/180kJ; Protein 0.7g; Carbohydrate 4.7g, of which sugars 4.4g; Fat 2.5g, of which saturates 0.5g; Cholesterol 0mg; Calcium 14mg; Fibre 1.1g; Sodium 227mg.

ITALIAN THREE-COLOUR SALAD ★

THIS VIBRANT ITALIAN DISH, KNOWN AS INSALATA TRICOLORE, *CREATES AN APPETIZING AND COLOURFUL LIGHT STARTER OR SNACK. USE PLUM OR VINE-RIPENED TOMATOES FOR THE BEST FLAVOUR.*

SERVES SIX

INGREDIENTS
1 small red onion, thinly sliced
6 large well-flavoured tomatoes
50g/2oz/1 small bunch rocket (arugula)
  or watercress, roughly chopped
115g/4oz reduced-fat mozzarella
  cheese, thinly sliced or grated
20ml/4 tsp extra virgin olive oil
30ml/2 tbsp pine nuts (optional)
salt and ground black pepper

1 Soak the onion slices in a bowl of cold water for 30 minutes, then drain and pat dry. Set aside.

2 Prepare the tomatoes for skinning by slashing them with a sharp knife and dipping them briefly in boiling water.

VARIATIONS
Instead of the fresh rocket or watercress, use chopped fresh basil, which goes particularly well with the flavour of ripe tomatoes. To reduce the fat content even further, omit the oil and sprinkle the salad with a fat-free vinaigrette dressing.

3 Peel off and discard the skins, then thinly slice each tomato.

4 Arrange half the tomato slices on a large platter, or divide them among six small plates, if you prefer.

5 Layer with half the chopped rocket or watercress and half the onion slices, seasoning well with salt and pepper. Add half the mozzarella cheese, sprinkling over a little more seasoning as you go.

6 Repeat with the remaining tomato and onion slices, salad leaves and mozzarella cheese.

7 Season well to finish, then sprinkle the oil over the salad. Scatter the pine nuts over the top, if using. Cover the salad and chill for at least 2 hours before serving. Serve with fresh crusty bread.

Energy 66Kcal/277kJ; Protein 2.9g; Carbohydrate 4g, of which sugars 3.8g; Fat 4.4g, of which saturates 1.8g; Cholesterol 6mg; Calcium 60mg; Fibre 1.3g; Sodium 61mg.

CARROT AND ORANGE SALAD ★

THIS IS A WONDERFUL, FRESH-TASTING LOW-FAT SALAD WITH SUCH A FABULOUS COMBINATION OF CITRUS FRUIT AND VEGETABLES THAT IT IS DIFFICULT TO KNOW WHETHER IT IS A SALAD OR A DESSERT. IT MAKES A REFRESHING, LOW-FAT ACCOMPANIMENT TO VEGETARIAN MAIN DISHES.

2 Cut a thin slice of peel and pith from each end of the oranges. Place cut side down on a plate, then cut off the peel and pith in strips. Holding the oranges over a bowl, cut out each segment leaving the membrane behind. Squeeze the juice from the membrane.

3 Combine the oil, lemon juice and orange juice in a small bowl. Season with salt and pepper, and sugar, if you like.

SERVES FOUR

INGREDIENTS
    450g/1lb carrots
    2 large Navelina oranges, such as
      Washington or Bahia
    15ml/1 tbsp extra virgin
      olive oil
    30ml/2 tbsp freshly squeezed
      lemon juice
    pinch of granulated sugar (optional)
    30ml/2 tbsp chopped pistachio nuts
      or toasted pine nuts (optional)
    salt and ground black pepper

1 Peel the carrots and coarsely grate them into a large bowl.

4 Toss the oranges with the carrots and pour the dressing over. Sprinkle over the nuts, if using. Serve.

Energy 92Kcal/385kJ; Protein 1.5g; Carbohydrate 15.3g, of which sugars 14.7g; Fat 3.2g, of which saturates 0.5g; Cholesterol 0mg; Calcium 64mg; Fibre 4g; Sodium 32mg.

WATERMELON AND FETA SALAD WITH OLIVES ★

*THE COMBINATION OF SWEET WATERMELON WITH SALTY FETA CHEESE MAKES FOR A ZESTY
COMBINATION SALAD — ESPECIALLY WITH THE EXTRA INGREDIENTS OF LIGHTLY TOASTED PUMPKIN
SEEDS AND SUNFLOWER SEEDS FOR ADDED PIQUANCY.*

SERVES SIX

INGREDIENTS

  6 slices watermelon, chilled
  115g/4oz feta cheese, cut into
    bitesize pieces
  15–30ml/1–2 tbsp mixed seeds,
    such as pumpkin seeds and
    sunflower seeds, lightly toasted
  10 whole black olives

COOK'S TIP
The best choice of olives for this recipe
is plump black ones, such as *kalamata*,
dry-cured black olives or other shiny,
brined varieties.

1 Cut the rind off the watermelon and
remove as many seeds as possible.
The sweetest and juiciest part is right
in the core, and you may want to cut off
any whiter flesh just under the skin.

2 Cut the flesh into triangular chunks.
Mix the watermelon, feta cheese, mixed
seeds and olives in a bowl. Cover and
chill the salad in the refrigerator for 30
minutes before serving .

Energy 136Kcal/572kJ; Protein 4.9g; Carbohydrate 15g, of which sugars 14.6g; Fat 6.7g, of which saturates 3.4g; Cholesterol 15mg; Calcium 98mg; Fibre 0.5g; Sodium 429mg.

BEETROOT SALAD WITH ORANGES ★

THE COMBINATION OF SWEET BEETROOT, ZESTY ORANGE AND WARM CINNAMON IN THIS LOW-FAT SALAD IS SURPRISINGLY TASTY, AND PROVIDES A LOVELY BURST OF COLOUR IN A WINTER BUFFET SPREAD.

SERVES SIX

INGREDIENTS
    675g/1½lb beetroot (beets), steamed
      or boiled, then peeled
    1 orange, peeled and sliced
    30ml/2 tbsp orange flower water
    15ml/1 tbsp caster (superfine) sugar
    5ml/1 tsp ground cinnamon
    salt and ground black pepper

1 Quarter the cooked beetroot, then slice the quarters. Arrange the beetroot on a plate with the orange slices, or gently toss them together in a bowl.

2 Gently heat the orange flower water with the sugar in a small pan, then stir in the cinnamon and season to taste.

3 Pour the sweet mixture over the beetroot and orange salad, cool, then chill in the refrigerator for at least 1 hour before serving.

COOK'S TIP
You can use freshly steamed or pre-cooked beetroot. To cook raw beets, always leave the skin on, and trim off only the tops of the leaf stalks. Cook in a pan of boiling water or steam over rapidly boiling water for 1–2 hours, depending on size. Small beetroots are tender in about 1 hour, medium roots take 1–1½ hours, and larger roots can take up to 2 hours.

Energy 58Kcal/247kJ; Protein 2.2g; Carbohydrate 12.9g, of which sugars 12.2g; Fat 0.1g, of which saturates 0g; Cholesterol 0mg; Calcium 33mg; Fibre 2.5g; Sodium 75mg.

BEETROOT AND POTATO SALAD ★

THIS IS A BRIGHTLY COLOURED LOW-FAT VEGETARIAN SALAD WITH A LOVELY TEXTURE. THE SWEETNESS OF THE BEETROOT CONTRASTS PERFECTLY WITH THE TANGY DRESSING.

SERVES FOUR

INGREDIENTS

4 medium beetroot (beets)
4 potatoes, diced
1 red onion, finely chopped
150ml/¼ pint/⅔ cup low-fat natural (plain) yogurt
10ml/2 tsp cider vinegar
2 small sweet and sour cucumbers, finely chopped
10ml/2 tsp creamed horseradish
salt and ground black pepper
fresh parsley sprigs, to garnish

COOK'S TIP

To save yourself time and energy, buy ready-cooked and peeled beetroot. They are readily available in many supermarkets.

1 Place the beetroot in a large pan with plenty of water. Bring to the boil, then reduce the heat and simmer for 40 minutes, or until tender.

2 Meanwhile, cook the potatoes in a separate pan of boiling water for 20 minutes, or until just tender.

3 When the beetroot are cooked, rinse and pull the skins off, chop into rough pieces and place in a bowl. Drain the potatoes and add to the bowl with the onion. Mix the yogurt, vinegar, cucumbers, horseradish and seasoning together. Reserve a little for garnish. Pour the rest over the salad. Toss, then garnish with parsley and the reserved dressing.

Energy 143Kcal/607kJ; Protein 5.5g; Carbohydrate 30.1g, of which sugars 10.7g; Fat 1g, of which saturates 0.3g; Cholesterol 1mg; Calcium 98mg; Fibre 2.9g; Sodium 106mg.

BAKED SWEET POTATO SALAD ★

THIS DELICIOUS SALAD HAS A TRULY TROPICAL TASTE AND IS IDEAL SERVED WITH LOW-FAT VEGETARIAN ASIAN OR CARIBBEAN DISHES.

SERVES SIX

INGREDIENTS
 1kg/2¼lb sweet potatoes
For the dressing
 45ml/3 tbsp chopped fresh
  coriander (cilantro)
 juice of 1 lime
 150ml/¼ pint/⅔ cup low-fat natural
  (plain) yogurt
For the salad
 1 red (bell) pepper, seeded and
  finely chopped
 3 celery sticks, finely chopped
 ¼ red onion, finely chopped
 1 fresh red chilli, seeded and
  finely chopped
 salt and ground black pepper
 fresh coriander (cilantro) leaves,
  to garnish

1 Preheat the oven to 200°C/400°F/Gas 6. Wash and pierce the potatoes all over, then bake them in the oven for 40 minutes or until tender.

COOK'S TIP
Wash sweet potatoes well and cook them whole because most of the nutrients are next to the skin.

2 Meanwhile, mix the dressing ingredients together in a bowl. Season to taste with salt and pepper. Chill while you prepare the remaining ingredients.

3 In a large bowl, mix the red pepper, celery, onion and chilli together.

4 Remove the potatoes from the oven and when cool enough to handle, peel them. Cut the potatoes into cubes and add them to the bowl. Drizzle the dressing over the salad and toss carefully. Adjust the seasoning to taste and serve, garnished with coriander leaves.

Energy 173Kcal/739kJ; Protein 3.8g; Carbohydrate 40.2g, of which sugars 13.9g; Fat 0.9g, of which saturates 0.3g; Cholesterol 0mg; Calcium 101mg; Fibre 4.8g; Sodium 101mg.

SIMPLE MIXED VEGETABLE RICE SALAD ★

*IN THIS QUICK AND EASY SIDE DISH, RICE AND A SELECTION OF CHOPPED SALAD VEGETABLES ARE
SERVED IN A TASTY LOW-FAT DRESSING TO CREATE A PRETTY AND SATISFYING VEGETARIAN SALAD.*

SERVES SIX

INGREDIENTS

275g/10oz/scant 1½ cups long
   grain rice
1 bunch spring onions (scallions),
   thinly sliced
1 green (bell) pepper, seeded and
   finely chopped
1 yellow (bell) pepper, seeded and
   finely chopped
225g/8oz tomatoes, skinned, seeded
   and chopped
30ml/2 tbsp chopped fresh flat leaf
   parsley or coriander (cilantro)
For the dressing
90ml/6 tbsp low-fat French or Tomato
   dressing
5ml/1 tsp strong Dijon mustard
   (optional)
salt and ground black pepper

1 Cook the rice in a large pan of lightly
salted boiling water for 10–12 minutes,
or until tender but still *al dente*. Be
careful not to overcook it.

2 Drain the rice well in a sieve
(strainer), rinse thoroughly under cold
running water and drain again. Leave
the rice to cool completely.

3 Place the rice in a large serving bowl.
Add the spring onions, peppers,
tomatoes and parsley or coriander.

4 Make the dressing. Place the
dressing and mustard, if using, in a
screw-top jar, put the lid on and shake
vigorously until well mixed. Stir the
dressing into the rice, then adjust the
seasoning, to taste.

Energy 199Kcal/834kJ; Protein 4.6g; Carbohydrate 43.5g, of which sugars 6.6g; Fat 0.7g, of which saturates 0.1g; Cholesterol 0mg; Calcium 23mg; Fibre 1.6g; Sodium 232mg.

HERBY COUSCOUS SALAD ★

THIS IS A POPULAR SALAD OF OLIVES, ALMONDS AND COURGETTES MIXED WITH FLUFFY COUSCOUS AND TOSSED WITH A LIGHT, HERBY DRESSING. IT HAS A DELICATE FLAVOUR AND MAKES AN EXCELLENT ACCOMPANIMENT TO CHARGRILLED MIXED VEGETABLE KEBABS.

SERVES FOUR

INGREDIENTS

275g/10oz/1⅔ cups couscous
550ml/18fl oz/2½ cups boiling
   vegetable stock
2 small courgettes (zucchini)
16–20 whole black olives
25g/1oz/¼ cup flaked (sliced)
   almonds, toasted
75ml/5 tbsp low-fat French or tomato
   dressing (*see recipes on page 14*)
15ml/1 tbsp chopped fresh
   coriander (cilantro)
15ml/1 tbsp chopped fresh parsley
a good pinch of ground cumin
a good pinch of cayenne pepper

1 Place the couscous in a bowl and pour over the boiling stock. Stir with a fork, then set aside for 10 minutes to allow the stock to be absorbed. Fluff up with a fork.

2 Trim the courgettes at both ends then cut into pieces about 2.5cm/1in long. Slice into thin julienne strips. Halve the black olives, discarding the stones (pits).

3 Carefully mix the courgettes, olives and almonds into the couscous.

4 Whisk together the French or tomato dressing, coriander, parsley, cumin and cayenne in a small bowl. Stir into the salad, tossing gently to mix through. Transfer to a large serving dish and serve immediately.

Energy 211Kcal/879kJ; Protein 6g; Carbohydrate 38.4g, of which sugars 2.8g; Fat 4.5g, of which saturates 0.4g; Cholesterol 0mg; Calcium 42mg; Fibre 1.1g; Sodium 451mg.

TOFU AND WILD RICE SALAD ★

THE FLAVOURS IN THIS LIGHT, VEGETARIAN SALAD ARE INFLUENCED BY THE CUISINES OF NORTH AFRICA AND THE EASTERN SEABOARDS OF THE MEDITERRANEAN. IT GOES PARTICULARLY WELL WITH CHARGRILLED VEGETABLES SUCH AS RED ONIONS, TOMATOES, COURGETTES AND PEPPERS.

SERVES SIX

INGREDIENTS

175g/6oz/scant 1 cup basmati rice
50g/2oz/generous ¼ cup wild rice
250g/9oz firm tofu, drained and
  cubed
25g/1oz preserved lemon, finely
  chopped (see Cook's Tip)
20g/¾oz fresh parsley, chopped
For the dressing
1 garlic clove, crushed
10ml/2 tsp clear honey
10ml/2 tsp of the preserved lemon
  juice
15ml/1 tbsp balsamic vinegar
15ml/1 tbsp olive oil
1 small fresh red chilli, seeded and
  finely chopped
5ml/1 tsp harissa paste (optional)
salt and ground black pepper

1 Cook the basmati rice and the wild rice in separate pans until tender. The basmati rice will take about 10–15 minutes to cook, while the wild rice will take about 45–50 minutes. Drain both lots of rice, rinse under cold water and drain again, then place in a large bowl together.

2 Meanwhile, whisk together all the dressing ingredients in a small bowl. Add the tofu, stir to coat and leave to marinate while the rice cooks.

VARIATIONS

Keep an eye open for rose harissa paste, which is available from the special range in some large supermarkets or from delicatessens or food halls. It is exceptionally delicious in this recipe and still fiery hot.

3 Gently fold the tofu, dressing, preserved lemon and parsley into the rice, adjust the seasoning to taste and serve.

COOK'S TIP

Preserved lemons, packed in salt, are available from Middle Eastern delicatessens or from large food halls and some supermarkets.

Energy 183Kcal/766kJ; Protein 5.8g; Carbohydrate 31.5g, of which sugars 1.4g; Fat 3.6g, of which saturates 0.5g; Cholesterol 0mg; Calcium 199mg; Fibre 0g; Sodium 2mg.

SIDE DISHES

*Vegetarian side dishes provide a tasty anytime
snack in themselves or can be served to
accompany more hearty main courses such as
nut roasts and vegetarian sausage cutlets, or
pasta dishes such as risottos or pasta bakes. A
handy collection of low-fat side recipes is
presented here, including Vegetable Florets
Polonaise, Marinated Mushrooms and
Mixed Vegetables Monk-style, to complement
vegetarian meals.*

FENNEL GRATIN *

SWEET AND AROMATIC FENNEL MAKES A HEALTHY AND TASTY LOW-FAT LIGHT SNACK OR VEGETABLE ACCOMPANIMENT. MUCH USED IN MEDITERRANEAN COOKING IT IS A VERY VERSATILE STAND-BY.

SERVES SIX

INGREDIENTS

2 fennel bulbs, about 675g/
1½lb total
300ml/½ pint/1¼ cups semi-
skimmed (low-fat) milk
15g/½oz/1 tbsp butter
15ml/1 tbsp plain (all-purpose) flour
25g/1oz/scant ½ cup dry
white breadcrumbs
40g/1½oz Gruyère cheese, grated
salt and ground black pepper

1 Preheat the oven to 240°C/475°F/
Gas 9. Discard the fennel stalks and root
ends. Slice the fennel into quarters and
place in a large pan. Pour over the milk,
bring to boil; reduce the heat and simmer
for 10–15 minutes, or until tender.

2 Grease a small ovenproof dish.
Remove the fennel pieces with a slotted
spoon, reserving the milk. Arrange the
fennel pieces in the ovenproof dish.

3 Melt the butter in a small, non-stick
pan and add the flour. Stir well, then
gradually whisk in the reserved milk.

4 Cook the sauce until thickened,
stirring. Pour the sauce over the fennel
pieces, then sprinkle with the
breadcrumbs and Gruyère. Season to
taste with salt and pepper, then bake in
the oven for about 20 minutes, or until
browned. Serve.

VARIATIONS
• Instead of the Gruyère, fresh
Parmesan, Pecorino, mature Cheddar
or any other strong cheese would work
perfectly in this recipe.
• Use dry wholemeal (wholewheat)
breadcrumbs in place of
white breadcrumbs.

Energy 101Kcal/423kJ; Protein 5.4g; Carbohydrate 9.6g, of which sugars 4.4g; Fat 4.9g, of which saturates 2.9g; Cholesterol 13mg; Calcium 156mg; Fibre 2.9g; Sodium 135mg.

ITALIAN SWEET AND SOUR ONIONS *

ONIONS ARE NATURALLY SWEET, AND WHEN THEY ARE COOKED AT A HIGH TEMPERATURE THE SWEETNESS INTENSIFIES TO GIVE FANTASTIC LOW-FAT FLAVOURING TO MANY SAVOURY DISHES. SERVE THESE DELICIOUS ONIONS WITH A SELECTION OF COOKED FRESH VEGETABLES.

SERVES SIX

INGREDIENTS

25g/1oz/2 tbsp butter
75ml/5 tbsp granulated sugar
120ml/4fl oz/½ cup white wine
vinegar
30ml/2 tbsp balsamic vinegar
675g/1½lb small pickling (pearl)
onions, peeled
salt and ground black pepper

VARIATION
This recipe also looks and tastes
delicious when made with either yellow
or red onions, cut into slices. Cooking
times vary, depending on the size of
the pieces.

1 Melt the butter in a large pan over a
gentle heat. Add the sugar and cook
until it begins to dissolve. Stir constantly.

2 Add the vinegars to the pan with the
onions and heat gently. Season to taste,
then cover the pan and cook over a
medium heat for 20–25 minutes, until
the onions are soft when pierced with a
knife, stirring occasionally. Serve hot.

COOK'S TIP
When buying onions, choose firm onions
with a dry skin and no signs of blemishes
or discolouration. Avoid onions that are
showing signs of sprouting.

Energy 121Kcal/506kJ; Protein 1.4g; Carbohydrate 22g, of which sugars 19.4g; Fat 3.7g, of which saturates 2.2g; Cholesterol 9mg; Calcium 36mg; Fibre 1.6g; Sodium 29mg.

FRESH ASPARAGUS WITH LEMON SAUCE ★

FRESH ASPARAGUS CAN BE LIGHTLY STEAMED OR BOILED, AND IS A TASTY, LOW-FAT NUTRITIOUS SIDE DISH. THE SAUCE HAS A LIGHT, FRESH TASTE AND BRINGS OUT THE BEST IN ASPARAGUS.

2 Drain the asparagus well (reserving 200ml/7fl oz/scant 1 cup of the cooking liquid) and arrange the spears attractively in a serving dish. Set aside.

3 Blend the cornflour with the cooled, reserved cooking liquid and place in a small pan. Bring to the boil, stirring constantly with a wooden spoon, then cook over a gentle heat until the sauce thickens slightly. Stir in the sugar, then remove the pan from the heat and allow to cool slightly.

4 Beat the egg yolks thoroughly with the lemon juice and stir gradually into the cooled sauce. Cook the sauce over a very low heat until it thickens, stirring constantly. Be careful not to overheat the sauce or it may curdle. Once the sauce has thickened, remove the pan from the heat and continue stirring for 1 minute. Season to taste with salt or sugar, if necessary. Allow the sauce to cool slightly.

5 Stir the cooled lemon sauce, then pour a little over the cooked asparagus. Cover and chill for at least 2 hours, before serving the chilled asparagus accompanied by the remaining lemon sauce.

SERVES FOUR

INGREDIENTS

675g/1½lb asparagus, tough ends removed, and tied in a bundle
15ml/1 tbsp cornflour (cornstarch)
10ml/2 tsp unrefined granulated sugar
2 egg yolks
juice of 1½ lemons
salt

COOK'S TIP
Use tiny or baby asparagus spears for an elegant appetizer for a special dinner party.

1 Cook the bundle of asparagus in a pan of salted boiling water for 7–10 minutes.

COOK'S TIP
When buying asparagus, choose plump, even stalks with tightly-budded, compact heads.

Energy 96Kcal/399kJ; Protein 6.4g; Carbohydrate 9.5g, of which sugars 5.8g; Fat 3.8g, of which saturates 1g; Cholesterol 101mg; Calcium 59mg; Fibre 2.9g; Sodium 8mg.

COURGETTES ^{IN} TOMATO SAUCE ★

THIS RICHLY FLAVOURED MEDITERRANEAN DISH CAN BE SERVED HOT OR COLD AS A LIGHT SIDE DISH.
CUT THE COURGETTES INTO FAIRLY THICK SLICES, SO THAT THEY STAY SLIGHTLY CRUNCHY.

SERVES FOUR

INGREDIENTS

    15ml/1 tbsp extra virgin olive oil or
      sunflower oil
    1 onion, chopped
    1 garlic clove, chopped
    4 courgettes (zucchini), thickly sliced
    400g/14oz can tomatoes
    2 tomatoes, skinned, seeded
      and chopped
    5ml/1 tsp vegetable bouillon powder
    15ml/1 tbsp tomato purée (paste)
    salt and ground black pepper

1 Heat the oil in a heavy, non-stick pan, add the onion and garlic and cook for 5 minutes, until the onion is softened, stirring occasionally. Add the courgettes and cook for a further 5 minutes, stirring occasionally.

2 Add the canned and fresh tomatoes, bouillon powder and tomato purée. Stir well, then simmer for 10–15 minutes or until the sauce is thickened and the courgettes are just tender. Season to taste with salt and pepper and serve.

Energy 89Kcal/370kJ; Protein 4.3g; Carbohydrate 9.2g, of which sugars 8.6g; Fat 4.1g, of which saturates 0.7g; Cholesterol 0mg; Calcium 54mg; Fibre 3.2g; Sodium 235mg.

BRAISED LEEKS WITH CARROTS ★

SWEET CARROTS AND LEEKS GO WELL TOGETHER ESPECIALLY WHEN TOPPED WITH A LITTLE CHOPPED MINT OR CHERVIL. THIS IS AN EASY LOW-FAT ACCOMPANIMENT TO A VEGETARIAN NUT ROAST SUNDAY LUNCH.

SERVES SIX

INGREDIENTS

25g/1oz/2 tbsp butter or
  30ml/2 tbsp olive oil
675g/1½lb carrots, thickly sliced
2 fresh bay leaves
75ml/5 tbsp water
675g/1½lb leeks, cut into 5cm/
  2in lengths
120ml/4fl oz/½ cup white wine
30ml/2 tbsp chopped fresh mint
  or chervil
salt and ground black pepper

1 Heat 15g/½oz/1 tbsp of the butter or 15ml/1 tbsp of the oil in a non-stick pan and cook the carrots gently for 4–5 minutes.

2 Add the bay leaves, water and seasoning to the pan. Bring to the boil, cover loosely and cook for 10–15 minutes, until the carrots are tender. Uncover, then boil the cooking juices until they have all evaporated, leaving the carrots moist and glazed.

VARIATIONS
• Use chopped fresh tarragon in place of mint or chervil.
• Use shallots, sliced, in place of leeks.

3 Meanwhile, heat the remaining 15g/½oz/1 tbsp butter or 15ml/1 tbsp oil in a deep, non-stick frying pan or wide pan that will take the sliced leeks in a single layer. Add the leeks and cook them very gently in the melted butter or oil over a medium to low heat for 4–5 minutes, without allowing them to turn brown.

4 Add the wine, half the chopped herb and seasoning. Heat until simmering, then cover and cook gently for 5–8 minutes, until the leeks are tender, but not collapsed.

5 Uncover the leeks and turn them in the buttery juices. Increase the heat slightly, then boil the liquid rapidly until reduced to a few tablespoons.

6 Add the carrots to the leeks, toss together to mix, then reheat them gently. Adjust the seasoning to taste, if necessary. Transfer to a warmed serving dish and serve sprinkled with the remaining chopped herbs.

Energy 108Kcal/451kJ; Protein 2.5g; Carbohydrate 12.3g, of which sugars 11g; Fat 4.3g, of which saturates 2.4g; Cholesterol 9mg; Calcium 58mg; Fibre 5.2g; Sodium 57mg.

VEGETABLE FLORETS POLONAISE ★

SIMPLE STEAMED VEGETABLES BECOME SOMETHING SPECIAL WITH THIS PRETTY EGG TOPPING. THEY MAKE A PERFECT LOW-FAT DINNER PARTY SIDE DISH OR ARE GREAT WITH A WEEKDAY VEGETARIAN SUPPER.

SERVES SIX

INGREDIENTS
500g/1¼lb mixed vegetables, such
    as cauliflower, broccoli, romanesco
    and calabrese
25g/1oz/2 tbsp butter or 30ml/1 tbsp
    extra virgin olive oil
finely grated rind of ½ lemon
1 large garlic clove, crushed
25g/1oz/½ cup fresh breadcrumbs,
    lightly baked or grilled (broiled)
    until crisp
1 large (US extra large) egg,
    hard-boiled
salt and ground black pepper

VARIATION
Use wholemeal (whole-wheat) breadcrumbs
instead of the white crumbs. They will give
a nuttier flavour and crunchier texture.

1 Trim the vegetables and break into
equal size florets. Place the florets in a
steamer over a pan of boiling water and
steam for 5–7 minutes, until just tender.

2 Toss the steamed vegetables in
butter or oil, then transfer them to a
serving dish.

3 While the vegetables are cooking,
mix together the lemon rind, garlic,
baked or grilled (broiled) breadcrumbs
and seasoning. Finely chop the egg
and mix together with the breadcrumb
mixture. Sprinkle the chopped egg
combination over the cooked vegetables
and serve immediately.

Energy 71Kcal/297kJ; Protein 5.2g; Carbohydrate 4.7g, of which sugars 1.4g; Fat 3.6g, of which saturates 0.7g; Cholesterol 32mg; Calcium 57mg; Fibre 2.3g; Sodium 50mg.

ROASTED PLUM TOMATOES WITH GARLIC ★

THESE ARE SO SIMPLE TO PREPARE YET TASTE ABSOLUTELY WONDERFUL. USE A LARGE, SHALLOW EARTHENWARE DISH THAT WILL ALLOW THE TOMATOES TO SEAR AND CHAR IN A HOT OVEN.

SERVES FOUR

INGREDIENTS

8 plum tomatoes
12 garlic cloves
20ml/4 tsp extra virgin olive oil
3 bay leaves
salt and ground black pepper
45ml/3 tbsp fresh oregano leaves,
    to garnish

COOK'S TIPS

• Use ripe plum tomatoes for this recipe as they keep their shape and do not fall apart when roasted at such a high temperature. Leave the stalks on, if possible.
• To give the tomatoes a bit of extra zing, add a couple of dashes of hot pepper sauce to the olive oil.

1 Preheat the oven to 230°C/450°F/ Gas 8. Select an ovenproof dish that will hold all the tomatoes snugly in a single layer.

2 Cut the plum tomatoes in half lengthways. Place them in the dish, cut sides uppermost, and push the whole, unpeeled garlic cloves between them.

3 Brush the tomatoes with the oil, add the bay leaves and sprinkle pepper over the top. Roast in the oven for about 45 minutes, or until the tomatoes have softened and are sizzling in the dish. They should be charred around the edges. Season with salt and a little more pepper, if you like. Garnish with oregano leaves and serve.

Energy 65Kcal/272kJ; Protein 2.1g; Carbohydrate 6.7g, of which sugars 4.9g; Fat 3.5g, of which saturates 0.6g; Cholesterol 0mg; Calcium 13mg; Fibre 2g; Sodium 14mg.

GREEN BEANS WITH TOMATOES ★

THIS TASTY, LOW-FAT RECIPE IS FULL OF THE FLAVOURS OF SUMMER. IT RELIES ON FIRST-CLASS INGREDIENTS, SO USE ONLY THE BEST RIPE PLUM TOMATOES AND GREEN BEANS THAT YOU CAN BUY.

SERVES FOUR

INGREDIENTS

15ml/1 tbsp olive oil
1 large onion, thinly sliced
2 garlic cloves, finely chopped
6 large ripe plum tomatoes, skinned,
   seeded and coarsely chopped
150ml/¼ pint/⅔ cup dry white wine
450g/1lb green beans, sliced in
   half lengthways
16 pitted black olives
10ml/2 tsp lemon juice
salt and ground black pepper

COOK'S TIP
Green beans need little preparation, and now that many are grown without the string, you simply trim either end.

1 Heat the oil in a large, non-stick frying pan, then add the onion and garlic. Cook over a medium heat for about 5 minutes, until the onion has softened but not browned, stirring frequently, and reducing the heat, if necessary.

2 Add the tomatoes, white wine, green beans, olives and lemon juice, and cook over a gentle heat for a further 20 minutes, until the sauce has thickened and the beans are tender, stirring occasionally. Season to taste with salt and pepper and serve immediately.

Energy 130Kcal/543kJ; Protein 3.9g; Carbohydrate 12.4g, of which sugars 10.3g; Fat 5g, of which saturates 0.8g; Cholesterol 0mg; Calcium 73mg; Fibre 5g; Sodium 242mg.

MARINATED MUSHROOMS ★

A TOUCH OF SHERRY GIVES THIS LOW-FAT VEGETARIAN SIDE DISH A DELICATE PIQUANCY. SERVE WITH PLENTY OF CRUSTY BREAD TO MOP UP THE VELVETY JUICES.

SERVES FOUR

INGREDIENTS

15ml/1 tbsp olive oil
1 small onion, very finely chopped
1 garlic clove, finely chopped
15ml/1 tbsp tomato purée (paste)
50ml/2fl oz/¼ cup amontillado sherry
50ml/2fl oz/¼ cup water
2 cloves
225g/8oz/3 cups button (white)
  mushrooms, trimmed
salt and ground black pepper
chopped fresh parsley, to garnish

VARIATION

In Spain, wild mushrooms, known as *setas*, are served in this way.

1 Heat the oil in a non-stick pan. Add the onion and garlic and cook until soft. Stir in the tomato purée, sherry, water, cloves and seasoning. Bring to the boil, then reduce the heat, cover and simmer gently for 45 minutes, adding more water if it becomes too dry.

2 Add the mushrooms to the pan, then cover and simmer for about 5 minutes. Remove the pan from the heat and allow to cool, still covered. Chill in the refrigerator overnight. Serve the mushrooms cold, sprinkled with the chopped fresh parsley.

Energy 59Kcal/242kJ; Protein 1.5g; Carbohydrate 2.9g, of which sugars 2.2g; Fat 3.1g, of which saturates 0.5g; Cholesterol 0mg; Calcium 12mg; Fibre 1.1g; Sodium 14mg.

ORANGE CANDIED SWEET POTATOES ★

DICED SWEET POTATOES ARE TOSSED IN A SPICY SYRUP, THEN OVEN-BAKED, TO CREATE THIS SOFT TEXTURED SIDE DISH, IDEAL ACCOMPANIED WITH A STEAMED GREEN VEGETABLE.

SERVES EIGHT

INGREDIENTS

900g/2lb sweet potatoes
250ml/8fl oz/1 cup orange juice
50ml/2fl oz/¼ cup maple syrup
5ml/1 tsp grated fresh root ginger
7.5ml/1½ tsp ground cinnamon
6.5ml/1¼ tsp ground cardamom
2.5ml/½ tsp salt
ground black pepper
orange segments and ground
    cinnamon, to garnish

COOK'S TIP

This popular American dish is traditionally served at Thanksgiving and Christmas. Serve with extra orange segments to make it really special.

1 Preheat the oven to 180°C/350°F/ Gas 4. Peel and dice the potatoes into squares, then steam them for 5 minutes.

2 Meanwhile, stir the remaining ingredients together. Spread out on to a non-stick shallow baking tin (pan).

3 Scatter the potatoes over the baking tin, then bake for 1 hour, until they are tender and well coated in the spicy syrup, stirring every 15 minutes.

4 Serve garnished with orange segments and ground cinnamon.

Energy 40Kcal/169kJ; Protein 0.3g; Carbohydrate 10.1g, of which sugars 8.3g; Fat 0.1g, of which saturates 0g; Cholesterol 0mg; Calcium 7mg; Fibre 0.3g; Sodium 147mg.

ROASTED POTATOES, PEPPERS AND SHALLOTS ★

THESE POTATOES SOAK UP BOTH THE TASTE AND WONDERFUL AROMAS OF THE SHALLOTS AND ROSEMARY, TO CREATE THIS DELICIOUS LOW-FAT DISH — JUST WAIT TILL YOU OPEN THE OVEN DOOR.

SERVES FOUR

INGREDIENTS
    500g/1¼lb waxy potatoes
    12 shallots
    2 yellow (bell) peppers
    15ml/1 tbsp olive oil
    2 fresh rosemary sprigs
    salt and ground black pepper
    crushed peppercorns, to garnish

1 Preheat the oven to 200ºC/400ºF/ Gas 6. Par-boil the potatoes in their skins in a pan of salted boiling water for 5 minutes. Drain and when they are cool, peel them and halve lengthways.

VARIATION
Use red (bell) peppers in place of yellow (bell) peppers.

2 Peel the shallots, allowing them to fall into their natural segments. Cut each pepper lengthways into eight strips, discarding the seeds and pith.

3 Oil a shallow ovenproof dish with a little olive oil. Arrange the potatoes and peppers in alternating rows and stud with the shallots.

4 Cut the rosemary sprigs into 5cm/2in lengths and tuck among the vegetables. Season the vegetables generously with salt and pepper, add the olive oil, then roast, uncovered, for 30–40 minutes, until all the vegetables are tender. Turn the vegetables occasionally to cook and brown evenly. Serve hot or at room temperature, with crushed peppercorns.

Energy 176Kcal/742kJ; Protein 4.2g; Carbohydrate 33.6g, of which sugars 12.6g; Fat 3.7g, of which saturates 0.6g; Cholesterol 0mg; Calcium 40mg; Fibre 4.1g; Sodium 20mg.

FENNEL, POTATO AND GARLIC MASH ⋆

THIS SOUR-SWEET MASH OF POTATO, FENNEL AND GARLIC CREATES A DELICIOUS LIGHT
ACCOMPANIMENT TO VEGETARIAN SAUSAGES, BURGERS OR CUTLETS.

SERVES SIX

INGREDIENTS

1 head of garlic, separated
   into cloves
800g/1¾lb potatoes, cut into chunks
2 large fennel bulbs
25g/1oz/2 tbsp butter or 30ml/
  2 tbsp extra virgin olive oil
120–150ml/4–5fl oz/½–⅔ cup
  semi-skimmed (low-fat) milk or
  single cream
freshly grated nutmeg
salt and ground black pepper

1 If using a food mill to mash the
potato, leave the garlic unpeeled,
otherwise peel it. Cook the garlic with
the potatoes in a pan of salted boiling
water for 20 minutes.

2 Meanwhile, trim and roughly chop
the fennel, reserving any feathery tops.
Chop the tops and set aside. Heat 15g/
½oz/1 tbsp of the butter or 15ml/1 tbsp
of the oil in a heavy non-stick pan. Add
the fennel, cover and cook gently for
20–30 minutes, until soft but not browned.

3 Drain and mash the potatoes and
garlic. Purée the fennel in a food mill or
food processor and beat it into the
potato with the remaining butter or oil.

COOK'S TIP
A food mill is good for mashing potatoes
as it ensures a smooth texture. Never
mash potatoes in a blender or food
processor as this releases the starch, giving
a result that resembles wallpaper paste.

4 Warm the milk in a pan and beat
sufficient into the potato and fennel to
make a creamy, light mixture. Season to
taste with salt, pepper and nutmeg.

5 Reheat gently, then beat in any
chopped fennel tops. Transfer to a
warmed dish and serve immediately.

VARIATIONS
• For a stronger garlic flavour, use
30–45ml/2–3 tbsp roasted garlic
purée (paste).
• To give a stronger fennel flavour, cook
2.5–5ml/½–1 tsp ground fennel seeds
with the fennel.
• For an even healthier mash, substitute
hot vegetable stock for some or all of
the milk.

Energy 144Kcal/608kJ; Protein 4g; Carbohydrate 24.4g, of which sugars 4.6g; Fat 4.1g, of which saturates 2.3g; Cholesterol 10mg; Calcium 60mg; Fibre 4g; Sodium 61mg.

MIXED VEGETABLES MONK-STYLE ★

*CHINESE MONKS EAT NEITHER MEAT NOR FISH, SO "MONK-STYLE" DISHES ARE IDEAL FOR
VEGETARIANS. THIS TASTY VEGETABLE MIXTURE CREATES A TANGY, LOW-FAT SIDE DISH.*

SERVES FOUR

INGREDIENTS

   50g/2oz dried beancurd or tofu sticks
   115g/4oz fresh lotus root, or
     50g/2oz dried
   10g/¼oz dried cloud ears (wood ears)
   8 dried Chinese mushrooms
   10ml/2 tsp vegetable oil
   75g/3oz/¾ cup drained, canned
     straw mushrooms
   115g/4oz/1 cup baby corn cobs,
     cut in half
   30ml/2 tbsp light soy sauce
   15ml/1 tbsp dry sherry
   10ml/2 tsp caster (superfine) sugar
   150ml/¼ pint/⅔ cup vegetable stock
   75g/3oz mangetouts (snow peas),
     trimmed and cut in half
   5ml/1 tsp cornflour (cornstarch)
   15ml/1 tbsp cold water
   salt

1 Put the beancurd or tofu sticks in a
bowl. Cover with hot water and leave to
soak for 1 hour. If using fresh lotus root,
peel and slice it; if using dried lotus
root, place it in a bowl of hot water and
leave to soak for 1 hour.

2 Prepare the dried wood ears and
Chinese mushrooms by soaking them in
separate bowls of hot water for 15
minutes. Drain the wood ears, trim off
and discard the hard base from each
and cut the rest into bitesize pieces.
Drain the soaked mushrooms, trim off
and discard the stems and chop the
caps roughly.

3 Drain the beancurd or tofu sticks.
Cut them into 5cm/2in long pieces,
discarding any hard pieces. If using
dried lotus root, drain it well.

4 Heat the oil in a non-stick wok or
frying pan. Add the wood ears, Chinese
mushrooms and lotus root and stir-fry
for about 30 seconds.

5 Add the pieces of beancurd or tofu
sticks, straw mushrooms, baby corn cobs,
soy sauce, sherry, sugar and stock.
Bring to the boil, then reduce the heat,
cover the wok or pan, lower the heat
and simmer for about 20 minutes.

6 Stir in the mangetouts, with salt to
taste, then cook, uncovered, for a
further 2 minutes. In a small bowl, mix
the cornflour and water to a smooth
paste. Add the cornflour mixture to the
wok or pan. Cook until the sauce
thickens, stirring. Serve immediately.

COOK'S TIP
The flavour of this tasty vegetable mix
improves on keeping, so any leftovers
would taste even better the next day.

VARIATIONS
• Use sugar-snap peas in place of
mangetouts (snow peas).
• Use canned or frozen (defrosted) corn
kernels in place of baby corn cobs.

Energy 48Kcal/203kJ; Protein 3.3g; Carbohydrate 6.2g, of which sugars 4.6g; Fat 0.9g, of which saturates 0.1g; Cholesterol 0mg; Calcium 90mg; Fibre 1.4g; Sodium 882mg.

STIR-FRIED BROCCOLI AND SESAME SEEDS ★

PURPLE SPROUTING BROCCOLI HAS BEEN USED FOR THIS TASTY, LIGHT RECIPE, BUT AN ORDINARY VARIETY OF BROCCOLI, SUCH AS CALABRESE, WORKS JUST AS WELL. SOY SAUCE IS ESSENTIAL.

SERVES TWO

INGREDIENTS
 225g/8oz purple sprouting broccoli
 5ml/1 tsp olive oil
 10ml/2 tsp soy sauce
 10ml/2 tsp toasted sesame seeds
 salt and ground black pepper

COOK'S TIP
Sesame seeds are widely used in cooking, and they add a delicious, nutty flavour to many dishes. Sesame seeds are available in three different colours – beige (unhulled), black (found in Asian or oriental shops) and pearly white. Sesame seeds are also ground into two types of oil – a light, almost tasteless oil for frying, and a dark toasted oil used in small quantities as a flavouring.

1 Using a sharp knife, cut off and discard any thick stems from the broccoli and cut the broccoli into long, thin florets.

2 Heat the oil in a non-stick wok or large, non-stick frying pan and add the broccoli. Stir-fry for 3–4 minutes, or until tender, adding a splash of water if the pan becomes too dry.

3 Add the soy sauce to the broccoli, then season to taste with salt and pepper. Add the sesame seeds and toss to combine, then serve immediately.

VARIATIONS
Use poppy, sunflower or pumpkin seeds in place of sesame seeds.
Use sesame oil in place of olive oil.

Energy 68Kcal/282kJ; Protein 5.6g; Carbohydrate 2.5g, of which sugars 2.1g; Fat 4g, of which saturates 0.7g; Cholesterol 0mg; Calcium 81mg; Fibre 3.1g; Sodium 366mg.

SAFFRON RICE WITH ONION AND CARDAMOM ★

THIS DELIGHTFULLY FRAGRANT, LIGHT PILAFF IS WONDERFUL SERVED WITH BOTH INDIAN AND MIDDLE-EASTERN VEGETARIAN DISHES.

SERVES FOUR

INGREDIENTS

350g/12oz/generous 1½ cups
   basmati rice
a good pinch of saffron threads
   (about 15 threads)
15g/½oz/1 tbsp butter
1 onion, finely chopped
6 green cardamom pods,
   lightly crushed
5ml/1 tsp salt
2–3 fresh bay leaves
600ml/1 pint/2½ cups well-flavoured
   vegetable stock or water

1 Put the rice into a sieve (strainer) and rinse it well under cold running water. Tip the rice into a bowl, add cold water to cover and set aside to soak for 30–40 minutes. Drain in the sieve.

2 Toast the saffron threads in a dry pan over a low heat for 1–2 minutes, then place in a small bowl and add 30ml/2 tbsp warm water. Leave to soak for 10–15 minutes.

3 Melt the butter in a heavy, non-stick pan, add the onion and cardamom pods and cook very gently for 8–10 minutes, until soft and buttery yellow.

4 Add the drained rice and stir to coat the grains. Add the salt and bay leaves, followed by the stock and saffron with its liquid. Bring to the boil, stir, then reduce the heat to very low and cover tightly. Cook for 10–12 minutes, until the rice has absorbed all the liquid.

5 Lay a clean, folded dish towel over the pan under the lid and press on the lid to wedge it firmly in place. Leave to stand for 10–15 minutes.

6 Fluff up the grains of rice with a fork. Turn it into a warmed serving dish and serve immediately.

COOK'S TIP
After boiling, when all the liquid has been absorbed, basmati rice is set aside to finish cooking in its own heat and become tender. Wedging a folded dish towel under the pan lid ensures the heat is not lost and the steam is absorbed.

Energy 348Kcal/1452kJ; Protein 6.7g; Carbohydrate 71g, of which sugars 0.9g; Fat 3.6g, of which saturates 2g; Cholesterol 8mg; Calcium 21mg; Fibre 0.2g; Sodium 515mg.

PERSIAN BAKED RICE ★

IN THIS PERSIAN-STYLE DISH, RICE IS COOKED SLOWLY OVER A LOW HEAT SO THAT A CRUST FORMS ON THE BOTTOM. THE MILD FLAVOURS OF SAFFRON AND ALMONDS GO PERFECTLY TOGETHER. THIS LIGHT DISH IS AN IDEAL ACCOMPANIMENT FOR VEGETARIAN CUTLETS OR SAUSAGES.

SERVES SIX

INGREDIENTS
    450g/1lb/2¼ cups basmati rice
    a good pinch of saffron threads
    15g/1oz/1 tbsp butter
    25g/1oz/¼ cup flaked
      (sliced) almonds
    salt and ground black pepper

COOK'S TIP
Saffron comes from a flower of the crocus family and is sold either as whole threads or strands, or in powdered form. Saffron threads should be soaked or steeped in a little warm or hot liquid, stock, milk or water, to infuse and disperse their flavour and colour, before adding the saffron and its liquid to dishes. Powdered saffron can be added directly to dishes. Saffron is expensive to buy but it adds a lovely orange hue and a subtle, aromatic flavour to dishes such as this one.

1   Cook the rice in a pan of salted boiling water for 5 minutes, then drain thoroughly. Meanwhile, put the saffron threads in a small bowl with 30ml/ 2 tbsp warm water and leave to infuse for at least 5 minutes.

2   Heat the butter in a large, non-stick pan and add the almonds. Cook over a medium heat for 2–3 minutes, or until golden, stirring occasionally. Add the rice and stir well, then stir in the saffron and its liquid, plus 1 litre/1¾ pints/ 4 cups water. Season with salt and pepper and cover with a tight-fitting lid.

3   Cook over a very low heat for 30 minutes, or until the rice is tender and a crust has formed on the bottom of the pan. Fork up the rice to mix in the crust before serving.

Energy 313Kcal/1309kJ; Protein 6.5g; Carbohydrate 60.2g, of which sugars 0.2g; Fat 4.8g, of which saturates 1.5g; Cholesterol 5mg; Calcium 25mg; Fibre 0.3g; Sodium 16mg.

THAI-SPICED RICE SALAD ★

THIS IS A LOVELY, SOFT, FLUFFY RICE DISH, PERFUMED WITH LIMES AND FRESH LEMON GRASS. AS WELL AS BEING A GOOD, LOW-FAT ACCOMPANIMENT FOR A FAMILY VEGETARIAN SUPPER, IT WOULD BE AN EXCELLENT CHOICE, IN DOUBLE OR EVEN TRIPLE THE QUANTITY, FOR A VEGETARIAN BUFFET TABLE.

SERVES FOUR

INGREDIENTS

2 limes
1 lemon grass stalk
225g/8oz/generous 1 cup long grain
  brown rice
15ml/1 tbsp olive oil
1 onion, chopped
2.5cm/1in piece fresh root ginger,
  finely chopped
7.5ml/1½ tsp coriander seeds
7.5ml/1½ tsp cumin seeds
750ml/1¼ pints/3 cups
  vegetable stock
60ml/4 tbsp chopped fresh
  coriander (cilantro)
1 spring onion (scallion) thinly
  sliced, and toasted coconut strips,
  to garnish
lime wedges, to serve

3 Heat the oil in a non-stick pan. Add the onion, ginger, spices, lemon grass and lime rind and cook over a gentle heat for about 3 minutes or until the onion is soft, stirring occasionally.

4 Add the drained rice and cook for 1 minute, stirring constantly, then pour in the stock and bring to the boil. Reduce the heat to very low and cover the pan with a tight-fitting lid. Cook gently for 30 minutes, then check the rice. If it is still crunchy, re-cover and leave for 3–5 minutes more. Remove the pan from the heat when done.

5 Stir in the fresh coriander, fluff up the grains, cover the pan again and leave for about 10 minutes. Transfer to a large serving dish or individual bowls, garnish with strips of spring onion and toasted coconut, and serve with plenty of lime wedges.

1 Thinly pare the limes using a zester or a fine grater, taking care to avoid cutting the bitter pith. Set aside the rind. Finely chop the lower portion of the lemon grass stalk and set aside.

2 Rinse the rice in plenty of cold water until the water runs clear. Tip it into a sieve (strainer) and drain thoroughly.

COOK'S TIP
You could substitute the finely grated rind of kaffir limes for an authentic Thai flavour, but you will need to use juicier Tahitian or Mexican limes for cutting into wedges to serve.

Energy 232Kcal/981kJ; Protein 4g; Carbohydrate 47g, of which sugars 1.7g; Fat 4.4g, of which saturates 0.8g; Cholesterol 0mg; Calcium 10mg; Fibre 1.3g; Sodium 2mg.

RED ONION, GARLIC AND LEMON RELISH ★

THIS POWERFUL LOW-FAT RELISH IS FLAVOURED WITH NORTH-AFRICAN SPICES AND PRESERVED LEMONS, AVAILABLE FROM DELICATESSENS OR FROM MIDDLE-EASTERN FOOD STORES.

SERVES SIX

INGREDIENTS
    30ml/2 tbsp olive oil
    3 large red onions, sliced
    2 heads of garlic, separated into
        cloves and peeled
    10ml/2 tsp coriander seeds, crushed
    10ml/2 tsp light muscovado (brown)
        sugar, plus a little extra
    pinch of saffron threads
    5cm/2in piece cinnamon stick
    2–3 small whole dried red
        chillies (optional)
    2 fresh bay leaves
    30–45ml/2–3 tbsp sherry vinegar
    juice of ½ small orange
    30ml/2 tbsp chopped
        preserved lemon
    salt and ground black pepper

1 Heat the oil in a heavy pan. Add the onions and stir, then cover and reduce the heat to the lowest setting. Cook for 10–15 minutes, until the onions are soft, stirring occasionally.

2 Add the garlic cloves and coriander seeds (crushed but not finely ground). Cover and cook for 5–8 minutes, until soft.

3 Add a pinch of salt, lots of pepper and the sugar, and cook, uncovered, for 5 minutes. Soak the saffron threads in about 45ml/3 tbsp warm water for 5 minutes, then add to the onions, with the soaking water. Add the cinnamon stick, dried chillies, if using, and bay leaves. Stir in 30ml/2 tbsp of the sherry vinegar and the orange juice.

4 Cook over a low heat, uncovered, until the onions are very soft and most of the liquid has evaporated. Stir in the preserved lemon and cook gently for a further 5 minutes. Taste and adjust the seasoning, adding more salt, sugar and/or vinegar to taste.

5 Serve warm or cold, but not hot or chilled. The relish tastes best if it is allowed to stand for 24 hours.

VARIATION
To make a quick Lebanese onion relish, to serve 6, chop 500g/1¼lb ripe tomatoes and combine with 1 bunch of sliced spring onions (scallions). Crush 2 cloves of garlic with a large pinch of salt and gradually work in 15ml/1 tbsp lemon juice and 30ml/2 tbsp extra virgin olive oil. Toss the tomatoes and onions with the dressing and stir in a small bunch of chopped purslane or 30ml/2 tbsp of chopped marjoram or lemon thyme, then adjust the seasoning with salt, pepper, a pinch or two of sugar and maybe more lemon juice. Serve with a vegetarian grain salad made with bulgur wheat or couscous.

Energy 79Kcal/326kJ; Protein 1.3g; Carbohydrate 10.4g, of which sugars 8.1g; Fat 3.9g, of which saturates 0.5g; Cholesterol 0mg; Calcium 27mg; Fibre 1.4g; Sodium 4mg.

APPLE AND TOMATO CHUTNEY ★

THIS MELLOW, GOLDEN, SPICY CHUTNEY MAKES THE MOST OF FRESH AUTUMN PRODUCE. ANY TYPE OF WELL-FLAVOURED TOMATOES CAN BE USED SUCCESSFULLY IN THIS LOW-FAT VEGETARIAN RECIPE.

MAKES ABOUT 36 50G/2OZ SERVINGS

INGREDIENTS

    1.3kg/3lb cooking apples
    1.3kg/3lb tomatoes
    2 large onions
    2 garlic cloves
    250g/9oz/1½ cups pitted dried dates
    2 red (bell) peppers
    3 dried red chillies
    15ml/1 tbsp black peppercorns
    4 cardamom pods
    15ml/1 tbsp coriander seeds
    10ml/2 tsp cumin seeds
    10ml/2 tsp ground turmeric
    5ml/1 tsp sea salt
    600ml/1 pint/2½ cups distilled
      malt vinegar
    1kg/2¼lb/5¼ cups unrefined
      granulated sugar

3 Add the vinegar and sugar and bring to boil. Leave to simmer for 30 minutes; stir occasionally. Add the red pepper and cook for 30 minutes, stirring as the chutney becomes thick and pulpy.

4 Spoon the chutney into warm, dry, sterilized jars. Seal each jar with a waxed circle and cover with a tightly fitting cellophane top. Leave to cool, then label and store in a cool, dry place.

1 Peel, core and chop the apples. Peel and chop the tomatoes, onions and garlic. Quarter the dates. Core and seed the peppers, then cut into chunky pieces. Put all the prepared ingredients, except the red peppers, into a preserving pan.

2 Slit the chillies and set aside. Put the peppercorns and remaining spices into a mortar and roughly crush with a pestle. Add the chillies, spices and salt to the pan.

VARIATIONS

Use red onions or 8 shallots in place of standard onions. Use dried apricots or pears in place of dates.

Energy 151Kcal/644kJ; Protein 0.9g; Carbohydrate 39g, of which sugars 38.7g; Fat 0.2g, of which saturates 0g; Cholesterol 0mg; Calcium 25mg; Fibre 1.4g; Sodium 7mg.

LIGHT MEALS

*Vegetarian light meals make ideal low-fat lunch
or supper options — which is good news as there
are plenty of recipes to choose from. The
selection is as varied as it is plentiful: try tasty
and tempting recipes such as Potato Gnocchi,
Vegetable Tofu Burgers, Italian Stuffed Peppers,
Fresh Herb Risotto or Toasted Noodles with
Vegetables, all of which combine full-on flavours
with a light touch on the calories and fat.*

POTATO GNOCCHI ★

GNOCCHI ARE LITTLE ITALIAN DUMPLINGS MADE EITHER WITH MASHED POTATO AND FLOUR, AS HERE, OR WITH SEMOLINA. THEY SHOULD BE LIGHT IN TEXTURE, AND MUST NOT BE OVERWORKED WHILE BEING MADE. GNOCCHI ARE IDEAL SERVED FOR A TASTY LIGHT MEAL OR LOW-FAT SUPPER.

5 Hold an ordinary table fork with long tines sideways, leaning on the board. One by one, press and roll the gnocchi lightly along the tines of the fork towards the points, making ridges on one side and a depression from your thumb on the other.

6 Bring a large pan of water to a fast boil. Add salt and drop in about half the gnocchi.

SERVES SIX

INGREDIENTS
  1kg/2¼lb waxy potatoes, scrubbed
  250–300g/9–11oz/2¼–2½ cups
    plain (all-purpose) flour
  1 egg
  pinch of freshly grated nutmeg
  25g/1oz/2 tbsp butter
  salt
  a little grated fresh Parmesan cheese,
    to serve (optional)

VARIATION
• Green gnocchi are made in exactly the same way as potato gnocchi, with the addition of fresh or frozen spinach. Use 675g/1½lb fresh spinach, or 400g/14oz frozen leaf spinach. Mix with the potato and the flour in Step 2.
• Almost any pasta sauce is suitable for serving with gnocchi; they are particularly good with a fresh tomato sauce, or simply drizzled with a little olive oil. Gnocchi can also be served in clear low-fat soup.

1 Place the unpeeled potatoes in a large pan of salted water. Bring to the boil and cook until the potatoes are tender but not falling apart. Drain. Peel as soon as possible, while the potatoes are still hot.

2 On a work surface, spread out a layer of flour. Mash the hot potatoes with a food mill, dropping them on to the flour. Sprinkle with about half of the remaining flour. Mix the flour very lightly into the potatoes.

3 Break the egg into the mixture, add the nutmeg and knead lightly, drawing in more flour as necessary. When the dough is light to the touch and no longer moist or sticky, it is ready to be rolled. Do not overwork or the gnocchi will be heavy.

4 Divide the dough into four portions. On a lightly floured board, form each portion into a roll about 2cm/¾in in diameter, taking care not to overhandle the dough. Cut the rolls crossways into pieces about 2cm/¾in long.

7 When they rise to the surface, after 3–4 minutes, the gnocchi are done. Scoop them out, allow to drain and place in a warmed serving bowl. Dot with butter. Keep warm while the remaining gnocchi are boiling.

8 As soon as they are cooked, toss the drained gnocchi with the butter, sprinkle with a little grated Parmesan, if using, and serve.

Energy 296Kcal/1254kJ; Protein 7.8g; Carbohydrate 59.2g, of which sugars 2.8g; Fat 4.7g, of which saturates 2.3g; Cholesterol 39mg; Calcium 74mg; Fibre 3g; Sodium 52mg.

BAKED POTATOES AND THREE FILLINGS ★

POTATOES BAKED IN THEIR SKINS UNTIL THEY ARE CRISP ON THE OUTSIDE AND FLUFFY IN THE MIDDLE MAKE AN EXCELLENT AND NOURISHING LIGHT MEAL ON THEIR OWN. FOR AN EVEN BETTER TREAT, ADD ONE OF THESE DELICIOUS AND EASY LOW-FAT TOPPINGS. EACH TOPPING IS ENOUGH FOR FOUR BAKED POTATOES.

SERVES FOUR

INGREDIENTS
4 medium baking potatoes
10ml/2 tsp olive oil
sea salt
filling of your choice (see below)

1 Preheat the oven to 200°C/400°F/ Gas 6. Score the potatoes with a cross and lightly rub all over with the olive oil.

2 Place on a baking sheet and cook in the oven for 45 minutes to 1 hour, until a knife inserted into the centres indicates they are cooked. Or, cook the potatoes in the microwave according to your manufacturer's instructions.

3 Cut the potatoes open along the score lines and push up the flesh. Season and fill with your chosen filling.

RED BEAN CHILLIES
425g/15oz can red kidney beans, rinsed and drained
200g/7oz/scant 1 cup low-fat cottage cheese
30ml/2 tbsp mild chilli sauce
5ml/1 tsp ground cumin

1 Heat the beans in a pan on the hob (stovetop) or in a microwave until hot. Stir in the cottage cheese, chilli sauce and cumin.

2 Fill the baked potatoes with the bean mixture and top with a little chilli sauce.

STIR-FRY VEG
10ml/2 tsp sunflower oil
2 leeks, thinly sliced
2 carrots, cut into sticks
1 courgette (zucchini), thinly sliced
115g/4oz baby corn, halved
115g/4oz/1½ cup button (white) mushrooms, sliced
45ml/3 tbsp soy sauce
30ml/2 tbsp dry sherry or vermouth
10ml/2 tsp sesame oil
sesame seeds, to garnish

1 Heat the oil in a non-stick wok or large frying pan until really hot. Add the veg and stir-fry for about 2 minutes, then add the mushrooms and stir-fry for a further minute.

2 Mix the soy sauce, sherry and sesame oil and pour on.

3 Heat through until just bubbling, then scatter over the sesame seeds. Serve.

HERBY CHEESE AND CORN
425g/15oz can creamed corn
50g/2oz half-fat hard cheese, grated
5ml/1 tsp mixed dried herbs
fresh parsley sprigs, to garnish

1 Gently heat the corn in a pan with the cheese and mixed herbs until well blended and hot.

2 Use to fill the potatoes and garnish with fresh parsley sprigs.

COOK'S TIP
Choose potatoes which are evenly sized and have undamaged skins, and scrub them thoroughly. If they are done before you are ready to serve them, take them out of the oven and wrap them up in a warmed cloth until they are needed.

Red Bean Chillies: Energy 270Kcal/1147kJ; Protein 14.9g; Carbohydrate 48.2g, of which sugars 8.8g; Fat 3.3g, of which saturates 1g; Cholesterol 3mg; Calcium 125mg; Fibre 6.3g; Sodium 563mg.
Stir-fry Veg: Energy 225Kcal/950kJ; Protein 7.4g; Carbohydrate 39g, of which sugars 8.3g; Fat 4.5g, of which saturates 0.8g; Cholesterol 0mg; Calcium 55mg; Fibre 5.5g; Sodium 1161mg.
Cheese and Corn: Energy 304Kcal/1290kJ; Protein 10.6g; Carbohydrate 60.5g, of which sugars 12.8g; Fat 3.9g, of which saturates 1.7g; Cholesterol 5mg; Calcium 121mg; Fibre 3.5g; Sodium 393mg.

HERB POLENTA WITH GRILLED TOMATOES ★

*GOLDEN POLENTA FLAVOURED WITH FRESH SUMMER HERBS AND SERVED WITH SWEET GRILLED
TOMATOES CREATES THIS TASTY LOW-FAT ITALIAN DISH, IDEAL FOR LUNCH OR SUPPER.*

SERVES SIX

INGREDIENTS
750ml/1¼ pints/3 cups vegetable
   stock or water
5ml/1 tsp salt
175g/6oz/1½ cups polenta
15g/½oz/1 tbsp butter
75ml/5 tbsp chopped mixed fresh
   parsley, chives and basil, plus extra
   to garnish
10ml/2 tsp olive oil
4 large plum or beefsteak
   tomatoes, halved
salt and ground black pepper

1 Prepare the polenta in advance:
place the stock or water in a pan with
the salt, and bring to the boil.

2 Reduce the heat and gradually add
the polenta, stirring constantly to ensure
that it doesn't form any lumps.

3 Stir constantly over a medium heat
for 5 minutes, until the polenta begins
to thicken and comes away from the
sides of the pan.

4 Remove the pan from the heat and
stir in the butter, chopped herbs
and pepper.

5 Transfer the polenta mixture to a
wide, lightly greased dish or baking tin
(pan) and spread it out evenly. Leave
until it is completely cool and has set.

6 Turn the polenta out on to a chopping
board and cut it into squares or stamp out
rounds with a large biscuit cutter. Lightly
brush the squares or rounds with oil.

7 Lightly brush the tomatoes with oil
and sprinkle with salt and pepper.

8 Cook the tomatoes and polenta over
a medium hot barbecue or under a
preheated grill (broiler) for 5 minutes,
turning once. Serve hot, garnished
with herbs.

VARIATION
Any mixture of fresh herbs can be used,
or try using just basil or chives alone, for
a really distinctive flavour.

Energy 146Kcal/611kJ; Protein 3.2g; Carbohydrate 23.4g, of which sugars 2.1g; Fat 4.2g, of which saturates 1.5g; Cholesterol 5mg; Calcium 6mg; Fibre 1.3g; Sodium 349mg.

RATATOUILLE PANCAKES ★

BY USING COOKING SPRAY, YOU CAN CONTROL THE AMOUNT OF FAT YOU ARE USING AND KEEP IT TO A MINIMUM. SERVE WITH A MIXED SALAD FOR A TASTY LIGHT VEGETARIAN MEAL.

SERVES FOUR

INGREDIENTS
   75g/3oz/²⁄₃ cup plain (all-purpose)
      flour
   a pinch of salt
   25g/1oz/¼ cup medium oatmeal
   1 egg
   300ml/½ pint/1¼ cups skimmed milk
   non-stick cooking spray
   mixed salad, to serve
For the filling
   1 large aubergine (eggplant), cut into
      2.5cm/1in cubes
   1 garlic clove, crushed
   2 medium courgettes (zucchini), sliced
   1 green (bell) pepper, seeded
      and sliced
   1 red (bell) pepper, seeded and sliced
   75ml/5 tbsp vegetable stock
   200g/7oz can chopped tomatoes
   5ml/1 tsp cornflour (cornstarch)
   salt and ground black pepper

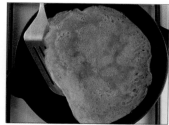

1 Sift the flour and a pinch of salt into a bowl. Stir in the oatmeal. Make a well in the centre, add the egg and half the milk and mix to a smooth batter. Gradually beat in the remaining milk. Cover the bowl and leave to stand for 30 minutes. Give the batter a quick stir just before using it to make the pancakes.

COOK'S TIP
Adding oatmeal to the batter mixture adds flavour, colour and texture to the cooked pancakes. If you like, wholemeal (whole-wheat) flour may be used in place of white flour to add extra fibre and flavour too.

2 Spray an 18cm/7in heavy, non-stick frying pan with cooking spray. Heat the pan, then pour in just enough batter to cover the base of the pan thinly. Cook for 2–3 minutes, until the underside is golden brown. Flip over and cook for a further 1–2 minutes.

3 Slide the pancake out on to a plate lined with baking parchment. Stack the other pancakes on top as they are made, interleaving each with baking parchment. Keep warm.

4 For the filling, put the aubergine in a colander and sprinkle well with salt. Leave to stand on a plate for 30 minutes. Rinse thoroughly and drain well.

5 Put the garlic, courgettes, peppers, stock and tomatoes into a large pan. Bring to the boil, then reduce the heat and simmer, uncovered for 10 minutes, stirring occasionally. Add the aubergine and cook for a further 15 minutes. In a small bowl, blend the cornflour with 10ml/2 tsp water and stir into the pan. Simmer for 2 minutes, stirring. Season to taste with salt and pepper.

6 Spoon some of the ratatouille mixture into the middle of each pancake. Fold each one in half, then in half again to make a cone shape. Serve hot with a mixed salad.

Energy 202Kcal/852kJ; Protein 9.5g; Carbohydrate 35.6g, of which sugars 12.8g; Fat 3.4g, of which saturates 0.8g; Cholesterol 50mg; Calcium 160mg; Fibre 4.9g; Sodium 65mg.

HUSK-GRILLED CORN <u>ON THE</u> COB ★

KEEPING THE HUSK ON THE CORN PROTECTS THE KERNELS AND ENCLOSES THE JUICES, SO THE
FLAVOURS ARE CONTAINED. IF YOU CAN'T GET FRESH HUSKS USE A DOUBLE LAYER OF FOIL.

SERVES EIGHT

INGREDIENTS

   1–2 dried chipotle chillies
   40g/1½oz/3 tbsp butter, softened
   2.5ml/½ tsp lemon juice
   15–30ml/1–2 tbsp chopped fresh
      flat leaf parsley
   8 corn on the cob, with husks intact
   salt and ground black pepper

1 Heat a heavy frying pan. Add the dried chillies and roast them by stirring them continuously for 1 minute without letting them scorch.

Put the chillies in a bowl with almost boiling water to cover. Use a saucer to keep them submerged, and leave them to rehydrate for up to 1 hour. Drain, remove the seeds and chop the chillies finely.

2 Place the butter in a bowl and add the chillies, lemon juice and parsley. Season to taste with salt and pepper and mix well.

3 Peel back the husks from each cob without tearing them. Remove the silk. Smear a little of the chilli butter over each cob. Pull the husks back over the cobs, ensuring that the butter is well hidden. Put any remaining butter in a small pot, smooth the top and chill to use later. Place the cobs in a bowl of cold water and leave in a cool place for 1–3 hours; longer if that suits your work plan better.

4 Prepare the barbecue, if using, or heat the grill (broiler) to its highest setting. Remove the corn cobs from the water and wrap in pairs in foil. Once the flames have died down, position a lightly oiled grill rack over the coals to heat. When the coals are medium-hot, or have a moderate coating of ash, cook the corn for 15–20 minutes. Remove the foil and cook them for a further 5 minutes, turning them often to char the husks a little. Serve hot, with any remaining butter.

Energy 114Kcal/477kJ; Protein 1.8g; Carbohydrate 16.7g, of which sugars 6g; Fat 4.9g, of which saturates 2.7g; Cholesterol 11mg; Calcium 3mg; Fibre 0.9g; Sodium 199mg.

VEGETABLE TOFU BURGERS ★

THESE SOFT GOLDEN PATTIES ARE STUFFED FULL OF DELICIOUS VEGETABLES. THEY ARE QUICK AND EASY TO MAKE AND ARE LOW IN FAT TOO. SERVE IN SESAME SEED BAPS WITH SALAD AND KETCHUP.

MAKES EIGHT BURGERS

INGREDIENTS
  4 potatoes, diced
  250g/9oz frozen mixed vegetables,
    such as corn, green beans, (bell)
    peppers
  30ml/2 tbsp vegetable oil
  2 leeks, coarsely chopped
  1 garlic clove, crushed
  250g/9oz firm tofu, drained and
    crumbled
  30ml/2 tbsp soy sauce
  15ml/1 tbsp tomato purée (paste)
  115g/4oz/2 cups fresh breadcrumbs
  a small bunch of fresh coriander
    (cilantro) or parsley (optional)
  sea salt and ground black pepper

COOK'S TIP
To preserve their vitamins, cook the potatoes whole for 20 minutes, then peel.

1 Cook the potatoes in a pan of salted boiling water for 10–12 minutes, until tender, then drain. Meanwhile, cook the frozen vegetables in a separate pan of salted boiling water for 5 minutes, or until tender, then drain well.

2 Heat 10ml/2 tsp of the oil in a large, non-stick frying pan. Add the leeks and garlic and cook over a low heat for about 5 minutes, until softened and golden, stirring occasionally.

3 Mash the potatoes, then add the vegetables and all the other ingredients except the oil but including the cooked leeks and garlic. Season to taste with salt and pepper, mix together well, then divide the mixture into eight equal size mounds.

4 Squash and shape each mound into a burger. Heat another 10ml/2 tsp oil in the frying pan. Cook four burgers at a time over a gentle heat for 4–5 minutes on each side, until golden brown and warmed through. Repeat with the other four burgers, using the remaining oil. Keep the first batch warm in a low oven. Serve hot.

Energy 167Kcal/704kJ; Protein 6.7g; Carbohydrate 25.7g, of which sugars 3.3g; Fat 4.9g, of which saturates 0.6g; Cholesterol 0mg; Calcium 201mg; Fibre 2.4g; Sodium 391mg.

VEGETABLE KEBABS WITH MUSTARD AND HONEY ★

*A COLOURFUL MIXTURE OF VEGETABLES AND TOFU, SKEWERED, GLAZED AND GRILLED UNTIL TENDER,
CREATES THIS SIMPLE BUT INVENTIVE LOW-FAT LUNCH OR SUPPER DISH.*

SERVES FOUR

INGREDIENTS
  1 yellow (bell) pepper
  2 small courgettes (zucchini)
  225g/8oz firm tofu, drained
  8 cherry tomatoes
  8 button (white) mushrooms
  20ml/4 tsp wholegrain mustard
  20ml/4 tsp clear honey
  10ml/2 tsp olive oil
  salt and ground black pepper
  lime segments and flat leaf parsley
    sprigs, to garnish
  cooked hot rice, to serve (optional)

1 Cut the pepper in half and remove the seeds. Cut each half into eight.

2 Trim the courgettes and peel them decoratively, if you like. Cut each courgette into eight chunks.

3 Rinse the tofu under cold running water and drain well. Cut the tofu into neat, square pieces of a similar size to the vegetables.

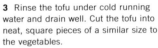

4 Thread the pepper pieces, courgette chunks, tofu, cherry tomatoes and mushrooms alternately on to four metal or wooden skewers.

5 Whisk the mustard, honey and olive oil together in a small bowl. Add salt and pepper to taste.

6 Brush the kebabs with the mustard and honey glaze. Cook under a grill (broiler) or over a hot barbecue for 8 minutes, turning once or twice during cooking. Serve with a mixture of cooked long grain and wild rice, if you like, and garnish with lime segments and parsley.

Energy 102Kcal/426kJ; Protein 6.7g; Carbohydrate 9.2g, of which sugars 8.7g; Fat 4.5g, of which saturates 0.7g; Cholesterol 0mg; Calcium 312mg; Fibre 1.7g; Sodium 8mg.

SUMMER VEGETABLES WITH YOGURT PESTO ★

CHARGRILLED VEGETABLES CREATE A DELICIOUS LIGHT MEAL ON THEIR OWN, OR ARE EQUALLY GOOD SERVED AS A MEDITERRANEAN-STYLE ACCOMPANIMENT TO VEGETARIAN MAIN MEALS.

SERVES FOUR

INGREDIENTS

2 small aubergines (eggplants)
2 large courgettes (zucchini)
1 red (bell) pepper
1 yellow (bell) pepper
1 fennel bulb
1 red onion
10ml/2 tsp olive oil
salt and ground black pepper
For the yogurt pesto
150ml/¼ pint/⅔ cup fat-free Greek
  (US strained plain) yogurt
15ml/1 tbsp pesto

1 Cut the aubergines into 1cm/½in slices. Sprinkle with salt and leave to drain for about 30 minutes. Rinse well in cold running water and pat dry.

2 Cut the courgettes in half lengthways. Cut the peppers in half, removing the seeds but leaving the stalks intact. Set aside.

3 Slice the fennel bulb and the red onion into thick wedges. Set aside.

COOK'S TIP
Baby vegetables make excellent candidates for grilling (broiling) whole, so look out for baby aubergines (eggplants) and (bell) peppers, in particular. There's no need to salt the aubergines if they're small.

4 Stir the yogurt and pesto lightly together in a serving bowl, to make a marbled sauce. Set aside.

5 Arrange the vegetables over a hot barbecue, or under a hot grill (broiler), lightly brush with the olive oil and sprinkle with plenty of salt and pepper.

6 Cook the vegetables until golden brown and tender, turning occasionally. The aubergines and peppers will take about 6–8 minutes to cook, and the courgettes, onion and fennel will take about 4–5 minutes. Serve the vegetables immediately, with the yogurt pesto.

Energy 107Kcal/448kJ; Protein 5.7g; Carbohydrate 13g, of which sugars 12.1g; Fat 4g, of which saturates 1g; Cholesterol 2mg; Calcium 133mg; Fibre 4.5g; Sodium 56mg.

CHEESE-TOPPED ROAST BABY VEGETABLES ★

THIS IS A SIMPLE WAY OF SERVING TASTY AND TENDER BABY VEGETABLES. ROASTING THEM REALLY BRINGS OUT THEIR SWEET FLAVOUR, AND THE ADDITION OF CHEESE MAKES THIS A TASTY, LIGHT MEAL.

SERVES SIX

INGREDIENTS

1kg/2¼lb mixed baby vegetables, such as aubergines (eggplants), onions or shallots, courgettes (zucchini), corn cobs and mushrooms
1 red (bell) pepper, seeded and cut into large pieces
1–2 garlic cloves, finely chopped
15ml/1 tbsp olive oil
30ml/2 tbsp chopped mixed fresh herbs
225g/8oz cherry tomatoes
115g/4oz/1 cup coarsely grated half-fat mozzarella cheese
salt and ground black pepper
black olives, to serve (optional)

1 Preheat the oven to 220°C/425°F/Gas 7. Cut the mixed baby vegetables in half lengthways.

2 Place them and the pepper pieces in an ovenproof dish with the garlic. Add salt and pepper. Drizzle with oil and toss the vegetables to lightly coat them in the oil.

3 Bake in the oven for 20 minutes, or until the vegetables are tinged brown at the edges.

4 Remove from the oven and stir in the chopped herbs. Sprinkle the cherry tomatoes over the surface and top with the grated mozzarella cheese. Return to the oven and bake for a further 5–10 minutes, or until the cheese has melted. Serve immediately with black olives, if you like.

COOK'S TIP
Treat all fresh herbs gently during preparation, as they contain volatile oils that can easily be lost. Most herbs are best added towards the end of cooking (as with this recipe), to preserve their flavour and colour.

VARIATIONS
• Use 2–3 sprigs of fresh rosemary instead of fresh mixed herbs.
• Use grated half-fat hard cheese such as Cheddar in place of mozzarella.

Energy 107Kcal/445kJ; Protein 5.2g; Carbohydrate 11.1g, of which sugars 9g; Fat 4.9g, of which saturates 2g; Cholesterol 7mg; Calcium 89mg; Fibre 2.8g; Sodium 54mg.

RATATOUILLE ★

A TOMATO AND MIXED VEGETABLE STEW FROM PROVENÇE, FRANCE, THIS LOW-FAT VERSION OF RATATOUILLE IS STIRRED AND SERVED WARM OR COOL, WITH CRUSTY BREAD TO MOP UP THE JUICES.

SERVES SIX

INGREDIENTS
  900g/2lb ripe tomatoes
  30ml/2 tbsp olive oil
  2 onions, thinly sliced
  2 red and 1 yellow (bell) pepper,
    seeded and cut into chunks
  1 large aubergine (eggplant), cut
    into chunks
  2 courgettes (zucchini), sliced
  4 garlic cloves, crushed
  2 bay leaves
  15ml/1 tbsp chopped fresh thyme
  salt and ground black pepper

1 Plunge the tomatoes into a bowl of boiling water for 30 seconds, then refresh in cold water. Peel away the skins and chop the flesh roughly.

2 Heat a little of the oil in a large, heavy non-stick pan and gently cook the onions for 5 minutes. Stir them constantly so that they do not brown, as this will adversely affect their flavour and make them bitter. Cook them until they are just transparent.

3 Add the peppers to the softened onions and cook for a further 2 minutes. Using a slotted spoon, transfer the onions and peppers to a plate and set them aside.

4 Add a little more oil to the pan, add the aubergine and cook gently for 5 minutes. Add the remaining oil and courgettes, and cook for 3 minutes. Lift out the courgettes and aubergine and set them aside.

5 Add the garlic and tomatoes to the pan with the bay leaves and thyme, and a little salt and pepper. Cook gently until the tomatoes have softened and are turning pulpy.

6 Return all the vegetables to the pan and cook gently for about 15 minutes, until fairly pulpy but retaining a little texture, stirring frequently. Season to taste. Serve warm or refrigerate overnight.

Energy 115Kcal/480kJ; Protein 3.9g; Carbohydrate 14.6g, of which sugars 13.1g; Fat 4.9g, of which saturates 0.9g; Cholesterol 0mg; Calcium 49mg; Fibre 4.7g; Sodium 19mg.

STUFFED AUBERGINES ★

THIS DISH FROM THE LIGURIAN REGION OF ITALY IS SPIKED WITH PAPRIKA AND ALLSPICE, A LEGACY FROM THE DAYS WHEN SPICES FROM THE EAST CAME INTO NORTHERN ITALY VIA THE PORT OF GENOA.

SERVES SIX

INGREDIENTS

2 aubergines (eggplants), about
  225g/8oz each, stalks removed
275g/10oz potatoes, diced
15ml/1 tbsp olive oil
1 small onion, finely chopped
1 garlic clove, finely chopped
a good pinch of ground allspice
  and paprika
30ml/2 tbsp skimmed milk
25g/1oz grated fresh Parmesan
  cheese
15ml/1 tbsp fresh white breadcrumbs
salt and ground black pepper
fresh mint sprigs, to garnish
salad leaves, to serve

1 Bring a large pan of lightly salted water to the boil. Add the whole aubergines and cook for 5 minutes, turning frequently. Remove with a slotted spoon and set aside. Add the diced potatoes to the pan and boil for about 15 minutes or until cooked.

2 Meanwhile, cut the aubergines in half lengthways and gently scoop out the flesh with a small sharp knife and a spoon, leaving 5mm/¼in of the shell intact. Select an ovenproof baking dish that will hold the aubergine shells snugly in a single layer. Brush it lightly with oil. Put the shells in the baking dish and chop the aubergine flesh roughly. Set aside.

3 Heat the remaining oil in a non-stick frying pan, add the onion and cook gently until softened, stirring frequently. Add the chopped aubergine flesh and the garlic. Cook for 6–8 minutes, stirring frequently. Tip the mixture into a bowl and set aside. Preheat the oven to 190°C/375°F/Gas 5.

4 Drain and mash the potatoes. Add to the aubergine mixture with the ground spices and milk, mixing well. Set aside 15ml/1 tbsp of the Parmesan cheese and add the rest to the aubergine mixture, stirring in salt and pepper to taste.

5 Spoon the mixture into the aubergine shells. Mix the breadcrumbs with the reserved Parmesan cheese and sprinkle the mixture evenly over the aubergines. Bake in the oven for 30–40 minutes or until the topping is crisp. Garnish with mint sprigs and serve with salad leaves.

COOK'S TIPS
• To make fine fresh breadcrumbs quickly, drop pieces or small slices of fresh bread through the feeder tube onto the moving blade of a food processor.
• If you only need a small amount of breadcrumbs, such as with this recipe, use a coffee grinder to grind small pieces of fresh bread.
• Freshly made breadcrumbs will keep in a polythene freezer bag in the freezer for up to 6 months.

Energy 94Kcal/396kJ; Protein 3.8g; Carbohydrate 12.2g, of which sugars 3.1g; Fat 3.8g, of which saturates 1.3g; Cholesterol 4mg; Calcium 73mg; Fibre 2.3g; Sodium 74mg.

ITALIAN STUFFED PEPPERS ★

THESE FLAVOURFUL ITALIAN STUFFED PEPPERS ARE EASY TO MAKE FOR A LIGHT AND HEALTHY LUNCH OR SUPPER, AND ARE IDEAL SERVED WITH A MIXED LEAF SALAD.

SERVES FOUR

INGREDIENTS

10ml/2 tsp olive oil
1 red onion, sliced
1 courgette (zucchini), diced
115g/4oz/1½ cups mushrooms, sliced
1 garlic clove, crushed
400g/14oz can chopped tomatoes
15ml/1 tbsp tomato purée (paste)
25g/1oz pine nuts (optional)
30ml/2 tbsp torn fresh basil leaves
4 large (bell) peppers
25g/1oz/⅓ cup finely grated fresh
  Parmesan or Fontina cheese
  (optional)
salt and ground black pepper
fresh basil leaves, to garnish

1 Preheat the oven to 180°C/350°F/ Gas 4. Heat the oil in a non-stick pan, add the onion, courgette, mushrooms and garlic and cook gently for 3 minutes, stirring occasionally.

COOK'S TIP
Tear fresh basil leaves with your fingers, instead of chopping them with a knife, to avoid losing the flavour and colour too quickly from this delicate leaved herb.

2 Stir in the tomatoes and tomato purée, then bring to the boil and simmer, uncovered, for 10–15 minutes until thickened slightly, stirring occasionally. Remove the pan from the heat and stir in the basil, seasoning and pine nuts, if using. Set aside.

3 Cut the peppers in half lengthways and deseed them. Blanch the pepper halves in a pan of boiling water for about 3 minutes. Drain.

4 Place the peppers cut side up in a shallow ovenproof dish and fill with the vegetable mixture.

5 Cover the dish with foil and bake in the oven for 20 minutes. Uncover, sprinkle each pepper half with a little grated cheese, if using, and bake, uncovered, for a further 5–10 minutes. Garnish with fresh basil leaves and serve immediately.

Energy 108Kcal/450kJ; Protein 4.2g; Carbohydrate 17g, of which sugars 16.1g; Fat 2.9g, of which saturates 0.6g; Cholesterol 0mg; Calcium 40mg; Fibre 4.9g; Sodium 28mg.

BAKED MEDITERRANEAN VEGETABLES ★

CRUNCHY GOLDEN BATTER SURROUNDS THESE VEGETABLES, MAKING THEM COMFORTING AND FILLING. SERVE WITH SALAD AS A LIGHT LUNCH, OR WITH GRILLED VEGETARIAN SAUSAGES FOR A MORE HEARTY MEAL.

SERVES SIX

INGREDIENTS

1 small aubergine (eggplant),
    trimmed, halved and thickly sliced
1 egg
115g/4oz/1 cup plain
    (all-purpose) flour
300ml/½ pint/1¼ cups
    semi-skimmed (low-fat) milk
30ml/2 tbsp fresh thyme leaves,
    or 10ml/2 tsp dried thyme
1 red onion
2 large courgettes (zucchini)
1 red (bell) pepper
1 yellow (bell) pepper
30ml/2 tbsp sunflower oil
30ml/2 tbsp grated fresh Parmesan
    cheese (optional)
salt and ground black pepper
fresh herb sprigs, to serve

1 Place the aubergine in a colander or sieve (strainer), sprinkle generously with salt and leave for 10 minutes. Drain, rinse well and pat dry on kitchen paper.

2 Meanwhile, beat the egg in a bowl, then gradually mix in the flour and a little milk to make a smooth thick paste. Gradually blend in the rest of the milk, add the thyme leaves and seasoning to taste and stir until smooth. Leave the batter in a cool place until required. Preheat the oven to 220°C/425°F/Gas 7.

3 Quarter the onion, slice the courgettes and seed and quarter the peppers. Put the oil in a roasting pan and heat in the oven for a few minutes, until hot. Add the prepared vegetables, toss in the oil to coat thoroughly and return to the oven for 20 minutes.

4 Give the batter a whisk, then pour it over the vegetables. Return the pan to the oven for 30 minutes. When puffed up and golden, reduce the heat to 190°C/375°F/Gas 5 and bake for 10–15 minutes until crisp around the edges. Sprinkle with Parmesan, if using, and herbs. Serve.

COOK'S TIP
As with Yorkshire pudding, it is essential to get the oil in the dish really hot before adding the batter, which should sizzle slightly as it goes in. If the fat is not hot enough, the batter will not rise well. Use a dish that is not too deep.

Energy 151Kcal/635kJ; Protein 6.3g; Carbohydrate 23g, of which sugars 7.9g; Fat 4.4g, of which saturates 1.2g; Cholesterol 35mg; Calcium 113mg; Fibre 2.5g; Sodium 37mg.

MEDITERRANEAN VEGETABLES WITH CHICKPEAS ★

THE FLAVOURS OF THE MEDITERRANEAN ARE CAPTURED IN THIS EXOTIC LOW-FAT VEGETARIAN DISH, IDEAL FOR A LUNCHTIME SNACK OR LIGHT SUPPER, SERVED WITH FLATBREADS SUCH AS PITTA.

SERVES SIX

INGREDIENTS
1 onion, sliced
2 leeks, sliced
2 garlic cloves, crushed
1 red (bell) pepper, seeded
   and sliced
1 green (bell) pepper, seeded
   and sliced
1 yellow (bell) pepper, seeded
   and sliced
350g/12oz courgettes
   (zucchini), sliced
225g/8oz/3 cups mushrooms, sliced
400g/14oz can chopped tomatoes
30ml/2 tbsp ruby port or red wine
30ml/2 tbsp tomato purée (paste)
15ml/1 tbsp tomato ketchup
   (optional)
400g/14oz can chickpeas, rinsed
   and drained
115g/4oz/1 cup pitted black olives
45ml/3 tbsp chopped mixed
   fresh herbs
salt and ground black pepper
chopped mixed fresh herbs,
   to garnish

1 Put the onion, leeks, garlic, red, yellow and green peppers, courgettes and mushrooms into a large saucepan.

2 Add the tomatoes, port or red wine, tomato purée, tomato ketchup, if using, and chickpeas to the pan and mix all the ingredients together well.

3 Rinse and drain the chick-peas and add to the pan. Stir to mix.

4 Cover, bring to the boil, then reduce the heat and simmer the mixture gently for 20–30 minutes, until the vegetables are cooked and tender but not overcooked, stirring occasionally.

5 Remove the lid of the pan and increase the heat slightly for the last 10 minutes of the cooking time, to thicken the sauce, if you like.

6 Stir in the olives, herbs and seasoning. Serve either hot or cold, garnished with chopped mixed herbs.

Energy 161Kcal/678kJ; Protein 7.9g; Carbohydrate 21.7g, of which sugars 13.4g; Fat 4.7g, of which saturates 0.8g; Cholesterol 0mg; Calcium 78mg; Fibre 7g; Sodium 639mg.

LEMONY OKRA AND TOMATO TAGINE ★

*IN THIS SPICY VEGETABLE DISH, THE HEAT OF THE CHILLI IS OFFSET BY THE REFRESHING FLAVOUR OF
LEMON JUICE. BASED ON A MOROCCAN RECIPE, THIS IS IDEAL SERVED WITH A MIXED LEAF SIDE SALAD.*

4 Heat the sunflower oil in a large,
non-stick pan. Thinly slice the second
onion and cook it gently in the oil for
about 5–6 minutes, or until soft and
golden brown. Transfer the cooked onion
slices to a plate with a slotted spoon.

5 Reduce the heat and pour the onion
and coriander mixture into the pan.
Cook for 1–2 minutes, stirring
frequently. Add the okra pieces,
chopped tomatoes, lemon juice and
about 120ml/4fl oz/½ cup water. Stir
well to mix, cover tightly, and simmer
gently over a low heat for about
15 minutes, or until the okra is tender.

6 Transfer to a large warmed serving
dish, sprinkle with the fried onion rings,
garnish with fresh coriander and serve
immediately.

VARIATIONS
Use vine-ripened or plum tomatoes for
this recipe. Use 2 small red onions or
4–6 shallots in place of standard onions.

SERVES FOUR

INGREDIENTS
  350g/12oz okra
  5–6 tomatoes
  2 small onions
  2 garlic cloves, crushed
  1 fresh green chilli, seeded
  5ml/1 tsp paprika
  a small handful of fresh coriander
    (cilantro), plus extra to garnish
  15ml/1 tbsp sunflower oil
  juice of 1 lemon

1 Trim the okra and then cut them into
1cm/½in lengths. Set aside.

2 Cut the tomatoes in half and scoop
out the seeds with a teaspoon. Chop the
flesh coarsely and set aside.

3 Coarsely chop one of the onions,
then place it in a blender or food
processor with the garlic, green chilli,
paprika, coriander and 60ml/4 tbsp
water. Process to a smooth paste.

Energy 79Kcal/329kJ; Protein 3.7g; Carbohydrate 7.3g, of which sugars 6.4g; Fat 4.1g, of which saturates 0.7g; Cholesterol 0mg; Calcium 176mg; Fibre 5.3g; Sodium 21mg.

SPICED TURNIPS WITH SPINACH AND TOMATOES ★

SWEET BABY TURNIPS, TENDER SPINACH AND RIPE TOMATOES MAKE TEMPTING PARTNERS IN THIS SIMPLE BUT VERY TASTY LIGHT, EASTERN MEDITERRANEAN VEGETABLE STEW.

SERVES SIX

INGREDIENTS

450g/1lb plum tomatoes
25ml/5 tsp olive oil
2 onions, sliced
450g/1lb baby turnips, peeled
5ml/1 tsp paprika
2.5ml/½ tsp granulated sugar
60ml/4 tbsp chopped fresh
  coriander (cilantro)
450g/1lb fresh young spinach
salt and ground black pepper

VARIATION
Try this with celery hearts instead of baby turnips. It is also good with fennel or drained canned artichoke hearts.

1 Plunge the tomatoes into a bowl of boiling water for 30 seconds or so, then refresh in a bowl of cold water. Drain, peel away the tomato skins and chop the flesh roughly.

2 Heat the olive oil in a large, non-stick frying pan or sauté pan, add the onions and cook gently for about 5 minutes until golden. Ensure that they do not blacken.

3 Add the baby turnips, tomatoes and paprika to the pan with 60ml/4 tbsp water and cook until the tomatoes are pulpy. Cover the pan with a lid and continue cooking until the baby turnips have softened.

4 Stir in the sugar and coriander, then add the spinach and a little salt and pepper. Cook the mixture for a further 2–3 minutes or until the spinach has wilted. The dish can be served warm or cold.

Energy 77Kcal/320kJ; Protein 3.4g; Carbohydrate 8.3g, of which sugars 7.8g; Fat 3.6g, of which saturates 0.5g; Cholesterol 0mg; Calcium 172mg; Fibre 4.3g; Sodium 123mg.

LINGUINE <u>WITH</u> SUN-DRIED TOMATOES ★

CHOOSE PLAIN SUN-DRIED TOMATOES FOR THIS SAUCE, INSTEAD OF THOSE PRESERVED IN OIL, AS THEY WILL INCREASE THE FAT CONTENT. SERVE WITH A MIXED BABY LEAF SALAD FOR A TASTY LIGHT SUPPER.

SERVES FOUR

INGREDIENTS

1 garlic clove, crushed
1 celery stick, thinly sliced
115g/4oz/2 cups sun-dried tomatoes,
   finely chopped
90ml/6 tbsp red wine
8 fresh ripe plum tomatoes
350g/12oz dried linguine
salt and ground black pepper
fresh basil leaves, to garnish

1 Put the garlic, celery, sun-dried tomatoes and wine into a pan, and cook gently for 15 minutes.

2 Meanwhile, plunge the plum tomatoes into a separate pan of boiling water for 30 seconds, then transfer the tomatoes to a pan of cold water. Drain, then slip off their skins. Halve them, remove and discard the seeds and cores, and roughly chop the flesh.

3 Add the tomato flesh to the pan and simmer for a further 5 minutes. Season to taste with salt and pepper.

4 Meanwhile, cook the linguine in a large pan of lightly salted boiling water for 8–10 minutes, or until *al dente*. Drain well.

5 Return the pasta to the pan, add half the tomato sauce and toss to mix well. Serve immediately on warmed plates, topped with the remaining sauce, and garnished with basil leaves.

COOK'S TIP
Add shavings of fresh Parmesan for extra flavour, if you like, but remember this will add extra calories and fat.

Energy 346Kcal/1474kJ; Protein 12.1g; Carbohydrate 71.5g, of which sugars 9.6g; Fat 2.2g, of which saturates 0.4g; Cholesterol 0mg; Calcium 41mg; Fibre 4.8g; Sodium 27mg.

RIGATONI WITH TOMATOES AND WILD MUSHROOMS ★

THIS IS A GOOD STORE-CUPBOARD STAND-BY AS IT DOESN'T RELY ON ANYTHING FRESH, APART FROM THE SHALLOTS AND HERBS. IT IS PERFECT FOR A LOW-FAT END-OF-WEEK MEAL.

SERVES SIX

INGREDIENTS

2 x 15g/½oz packets dried
　wild mushrooms
175ml/6fl oz/¾ cup warm water
10ml/2 tsp olive oil
2 shallots, finely chopped
2 garlic cloves, crushed
a few sprigs of fresh marjoram,
　chopped, plus extra to garnish
1 handful fresh flat leaf
　parsley, chopped
15g/½oz/1 tbsp cold butter
400g/14oz can chopped tomatoes
400g/14oz/3½ cups dried rigatoni
25g/1oz/⅓ cup grated fresh
　Parmesan cheese
salt and ground black pepper

1 Put the dried mushrooms in a bowl, pour the warm water over to cover and leave to soak for 15–20 minutes. Tip into a fine sieve (strainer) set over a bowl and squeeze the mushrooms with your fingers to release as much liquid as possible. Reserve the mushrooms and the strained liquid.

2 Heat the oil in a non-stick frying pan and cook the shallots, garlic and chopped herbs over a low heat for about 5 minutes, stirring frequently. Add the butter and soaked mushrooms, and stir until the butter has melted. Season well with salt and pepper.

3 Stir in the tomatoes and the reserved liquid from the soaked mushrooms. Bring to the boil, then reduce the heat, cover and simmer for about 20 minutes, stirring occasionally. Meanwhile, cook the pasta according to the instructions on the packet.

4 Taste the sauce and adjust the seasoning. Drain the pasta, reserving some of the cooking water, and tip the pasta into a warmed large bowl. Add the sauce and the grated Parmesan and toss to mix. Add a little cooking water if you prefer a runnier sauce. Serve immediately, garnished with marjoram sprigs.

VARIATION
If you have a bottle of wine open, red or white, add a splash when you add the canned tomatoes.

COOK'S TIP
Serve with a little extra Parmesan cheese, which can be handed around separately, if you like, but remember this will add to the calorie and fat content of the dish.

Energy 281Kcal/1193kJ; Protein 10.4g; Carbohydrate 52.3g, of which sugars 4.9g; Fat 4.9g, of which saturates 1.9g; Cholesterol 7mg; Calcium 75mg; Fibre 2.8g; Sodium 62mg.

FRESH HERB RISOTTO ★

HERE IS A LIGHT AND TASTY RISOTTO TO CELEBRATE THE ABUNDANCE OF SUMMER HERBS. AN AROMATIC BLEND OF OREGANO, CHIVES, PARSLEY AND BASIL IS COMBINED WITH ARBORIO RICE.

SERVES SIX

INGREDIENTS
  90g/3½oz/½ cup wild rice
  15g/½oz/1 tbsp butter
  10ml/2 tsp olive oil
  1 small onion, finely chopped
  450g/1lb/2¼ cups arborio rice
  300ml/½ pint/1¼ cups dry white
    wine
  1.2 litres/2 pints/5 cups simmering
    vegetable stock
  45ml/3 tbsp chopped fresh oregano
  45ml/3 tbsp chopped fresh chives
  60ml/4 tbsp chopped fresh flat
    leaf parsley
  60ml/4 tbsp chopped fresh basil
  40g/1½oz/½ cup grated fresh
    Parmesan cheese
  salt and ground black pepper

1 Cook the wild rice in a pan of salted boiling water according to the instructions on the packet, then drain and set aside.

2 Heat the butter and oil in a large, heavy, non-stick pan. When the butter has melted, add the onion and cook for 3 minutes. Add the arborio rice and cook for 2 minutes, stirring to coat.

COOK'S TIPS
Risotto rice is essential to achieve the correct creamy texture in this dish. Other types of rice simply will not do. Fresh herbs are also a must, but you can use tarragon, chervil, marjoram or thyme instead of the ones listed here, if you prefer.

3 Pour in the white wine and bring to the boil. Reduce the heat and cook for 10 minutes, or until all the wine has been absorbed.

4 Add the hot vegetable stock, a little at a time, waiting for each quantity to be absorbed before adding more, and stirring constantly. After 20–25 minutes the rice should be tender and creamy. Season well with salt and pepper.

5 Add the chopped herbs and wild rice, then heat for 2 minutes, stirring frequently. Stir in two-thirds of the Parmesan, if using, and cook until melted. Serve sprinkled with the remaining Parmesan, if using.

Energy 378Kcal/1578kJ; Protein 9.6g; Carbohydrate 72.8g, of which sugars 0.7g; Fat 4.8g, of which saturates 2.1g; Cholesterol 9mg; Calcium 115mg; Fibre 0.5g; Sodium 83mg.

CLASSIC MIXED MUSHROOM RISOTTO ⋆

A CLASSIC LOW-FAT RISOTTO OF MIXED MUSHROOMS, HERBS AND FRESH PARMESAN CHEESE, THIS IS BEST SIMPLY SERVED WITH A MIXED LEAF SALAD TOSSED IN A LIGHT FAT-FREE DRESSING.

SERVES FOUR

INGREDIENTS
10ml/2 tsp olive oil
4 shallots, finely chopped
2 garlic cloves, crushed
10g/¼oz dried porcini mushrooms,
    soaked in 150ml/¼ pint/⅔ cup hot
    water for 20 minutes
450g/1lb/6 cups mixed mushrooms,
    such as closed cup, chestnut and
    field (portobello) mushrooms, sliced
250g/9oz/1¼ cups long grain rice
900ml/1½ pints/3¾ cups well-
    flavoured vegetable stock
30–45ml/2–3 tbsp chopped fresh
    flat leaf parsley
40g/1½oz/½ cup grated fresh
    Parmesan cheese (optional)
salt and ground black pepper

1 Heat the oil in a large, non-stick pan. Add the shallots and garlic and cook gently for 5 minutes, stirring constantly.

2 Drain the porcini, reserving their liquid, and chop roughly. Add all the mushrooms to the pan with the porcini soaking liquid, the rice and 300ml/½ pint/1¼ cups of the stock.

3 Bring to the boil, then reduce the heat and simmer uncovered until all the liquid has been absorbed, stirring frequently. Add a ladleful of hot stock and stir until it has been absorbed.

4 Continue cooking and adding the hot stock, a ladleful at a time, until the rice is cooked and creamy but *al dente*, stirring frequently. This should take about 35 minutes and it may not be necessary to add all the stock.

5 Season to taste with salt and pepper, then stir in the chopped parsley and grated Parmesan, if using. Serve at once. Alternatively, sprinkle the Parmesan, if using, over the risotto just before serving.

Energy 256Kcal/1071kJ; Protein 7g; Carbohydrate 50.5g, of which sugars 0.3g; Fat 2.6g, of which saturates 0.4g; Cholesterol 0mg; Calcium 20mg; Fibre 1.4g; Sodium 132mg.

LENTILS WITH MUSHROOMS AND ANIS ★

IN THIS SPANISH RECIPE, LENTEJAS CON CHAMPIÑONES, *LENTILS ARE FLAVOURED WITH ANOTHER PRODUCT OF CASTILLE, ANIS SPIRIT, PLUS A LARGE QUANTITY OF PARSLEY. SERVE THIS DELICATE LOW-FAT DISH ON ITS OWN, OR WITH FRESH CRUSTY BREAD.*

SERVES FOUR

INGREDIENTS
    15ml/1 tbsp olive oil
    1 large onion, sliced
    2 garlic cloves, finely chopped
    250g/9oz/generous 3 cups brown cap
      (cremini) mushrooms, sliced
    150g/5oz/generous ½ cup brown or
      green lentils, soaked overnight
      and drained
    4 tomatoes, each cut into eighths
    1 bay leaf
    25g/1oz/½ cup chopped fresh parsley
    30ml/2 tbsp anis spirit or anisette
    salt, paprika and black pepper

COOK'S TIP
If you forget to soak the lentils, add at
least 30 minutes to the cooking time.

1 Heat the oil in a flameproof casserole. Add the onion and cook gently, with the garlic, until softened but not browned.

2 Add the mushrooms and stir to combine with the onion and garlic. Continue cooking for a couple of minutes, stirring gently.

3 Add the lentils, tomatoes and bay leaf with 175ml/6fl oz/¾ cup water. Simmer gently, covered, for 30–40 minutes until the lentils are soft, and the liquid has almost disappeared.

4 Stir in the parsley and anis. Season with salt, paprika and black pepper.

Energy 216Kcal/910kJ; Protein 12.4g; Carbohydrate 29.3g, of which sugars 9.6g; Fat 4.5g, of which saturates 0.7g; Cholesterol 0mg; Calcium 72mg; Fibre 6.9g; Sodium 26mg.

LENTIL DHAL WITH ROASTED GARLIC ★

THIS LENTIL DHAL MAKES A COMFORTING LIGHT MEAL WHEN SERVED WITH BROWN RICE OR LOW-FAT INDIAN BREADS AND ANY DRY-SPICED VEGETARIAN DISH, PARTICULARLY A CAULIFLOWER OR POTATO DISH. THE ROASTED GARLIC MAKES FOR A SMOKEY, SPICY GARNISH.

SERVES SIX

INGREDIENTS
    15g/½oz/1 tbsp butter or ghee
    1 onion, chopped
    2 fresh green chillies, seeded
      and chopped
    15ml/1 tbsp chopped fresh root ginger
    225g/8oz/1 cup yellow or red lentils
    900ml/1½ pints/3¾ cups water
    45ml/3 tbsp roasted garlic purée
      (paste)
    5ml/1 tsp ground cumin
    5ml/1 tsp ground coriander
    200g/7oz tomatoes, skinned and diced
    a little lemon juice
    salt and ground black pepper
    30–45ml/2–3 tbsp fresh coriander
      (cilantro) sprigs, to garnish
For the spicy garnish
    10ml/2 tsp sunflower oil
    4–5 shallots, sliced
    2 garlic cloves, thinly sliced
    15g/½oz/1 tbsp butter or ghee
    5ml/1 tsp cumin seeds
    5ml/1 tsp mustard seeds
    3–4 small dried red chillies
    8–10 fresh curry leaves

1 First begin the spicy garnish. Heat the oil in a large, heavy, non-stick pan. Add the shallots and cook them over a medium heat for 5–10 minutes until they are crisp and browned, stirring occasionally. Add the garlic and cook for a moment or two until the garlic colours slightly, stirring frequently. Remove the pan from the heat and use a slotted spoon to remove the shallots and garlic from the pan. Set aside.

COOK'S TIP
Mustard seeds (both yellow and black ones) are widely used in Indian dishes such as this one, to add a delicious flavour and texture. The yellow seeds are milder than the black ones.

2 Melt the butter or ghee for the dhal in the pan, add the onion, chillies and ginger, and cook for 10 minutes until golden.

3 Stir in the yellow or red lentils and water, then bring to the boil, reduce the heat and part-cover the pan. Simmer for 50–60 minutes until it is the same consistency as a very thick soup, stirring occasionally.

4 Stir in the roasted garlic purée, cumin and ground coriander, then season to taste with salt and pepper. Cook the dhal, uncovered, for a further 10–15 minutes, stirring frequently.

5 Stir in the tomatoes, then adjust the seasoning, adding a little lemon juice to taste, if necessary.

6 To finish the spicy garnish: melt the butter or ghee in a non-stick frying pan. Add the cumin and mustard seeds and cook until the mustard seeds begin to pop. Stir in the dried red chillies and fresh curry leaves, then immediately swirl the mixture into the cooked dhal. Garnish with coriander sprigs and the spicy fried shallots and garlic. Serve.

Energy 147Kcal/623kJ; Protein 9.3g; Carbohydrate 23g, of which sugars 2.5g; Fat 2.7g, of which saturates 1.4g; Cholesterol 5mg; Calcium 24mg; Fibre 2.3g; Sodium 32mg.

WILD RICE WITH GRILLED VEGETABLES ★

THE MIXTURE OF WILD RICE AND LONG GRAIN RICE WORKS VERY WELL IN THIS DISH, COMBINED WITH THE GRILLED PEPPERS, MUSHROOMS, COURGETTES AND AUBERGINE, TO MAKE A COMFORTING LIGHT MEAL.

SERVES FOUR

INGREDIENTS

225g/8oz/generous 1 cup mixed wild
  and long grain rice
1 large aubergine (eggplant),
  thickly sliced
1 red, 1 yellow and 1 green (bell)
  pepper, seeded and cut into quarters
2 red onions, sliced
225g/8oz/3 cups brown cap (cremini)
  or shiitake mushrooms
2 small courgettes (zucchini), cut in
  half lengthways
10ml/2 tsp olive oil
30ml/2 tbsp chopped fresh thyme,
  plus extra to garnish
For the dressing
120ml/4fl oz/½ cup low-fat French
  dressing (*see recipe on page 14*)
2 garlic cloves, crushed
salt and ground black pepper

1 Put all the rice in a pan of salted cold water. Bring to the boil, then reduce the heat, cover and cook gently for 30–40 minutes (or according to the instructions on the packet) until tender.

2 Make the dressing. Whisk the French dressing, garlic and seasoning together in a bowl or shake in a screw-top jar until thoroughly blended. Set aside while you grill (broil) the vegetables.

3 Preheat the grill (broiler) to high. Arrange all the vegetables on a grill (broiler) rack. Lightly brush the vegetables with olive oil and grill for about 5 minutes.

4 Turn the vegetables over, lightly brush them with a little more olive oil and grill for a further 5–8 minutes, or until tender and charred in places.

5 Drain the rice, transfer it to a bowl and toss in half the dressing. Spoon the rice on to individual plates and arrange the grilled vegetables on top. Pour over the remaining dressing, scatter over the chopped thyme and serve.

VARIATION
Use standard onions in place of red onions.

Energy 296Kcal/1237kJ; Protein 7.8g; Carbohydrate 59.3g, of which sugars 13.5g; Fat 3g, of which saturates 0.5g; Cholesterol 0mg; Calcium 39mg; Fibre 4.7g; Sodium 460mg.

FRIED RICE WITH MUSHROOMS ★

A TASTY LOW-FAT VERSION OF THIS POPULAR RICE DISH THAT IS IDEAL SERVED AS A QUICK AND EASY DISH. A LITTLE SESAME OIL ADDS A HINT OF NUTTY FLAVOUR.

SERVES FOUR

INGREDIENTS
    225g/8oz/generous 1 cup long
       grain rice
    10ml/2 tsp vegetable oil
    1 egg, lightly beaten
    2 garlic cloves, crushed
    175g/6oz/scant 2½ cups button
      (white) mushrooms, sliced
    15ml/1 tbsp light soy sauce
    1.5ml/¼ tsp salt
    2.5ml/½ tsp sesame oil
    cucumber matchsticks, to garnish

1 Rinse the rice until the water runs clear, then drain thoroughly. Place it in a pan. Measure the depth of the rice against your index finger, then bring the finger up to just above the surface of the rice and add cold water to the same depth as the rice.

2 Bring the water to the boil. Stir, boil for a few minutes, then cover the pan. Reduce the heat to a simmer and cook the rice gently for 5–8 minutes, until all the water has been absorbed. Remove the pan from the heat and, without lifting the lid, leave for a further 10 minutes before stirring or forking up the rice.

COOK'S TIP
When you cook rice this way, you may find there is a crust at the bottom of the pan. Don't worry; simply soak the crust in water for a couple of minutes to break it up, then drain it and fry it with the rest of the rice.

3 Heat 5ml/1 tsp of the vegetable oil in a non-stick frying pan or wok. Add the egg and cook until scrambled, stirring with chopsticks or wooden spoon. Remove the egg to a plate and set aside.

4 Heat the remaining vegetable oil in the pan or wok. Stir-fry the garlic for a few seconds, then add the mushrooms and stir-fry for 2 minutes, adding a little water, if needed, to prevent burning.

5 Stir in the cooked rice and cook for about 4 minutes, or until the rice is hot, stirring occasionally.

6 Add the scrambled egg, soy sauce, salt and sesame oil. Cook for 1 minute to heat through. Serve immediately, garnished with cucumber matchsticks.

Energy 245Kcal/1022kJ; Protein 6.6g; Carbohydrate 45.4g, of which sugars 0.4g; Fat 3.8g, of which saturates 0.7g; Cholesterol 48mg; Calcium 21mg; Fibre 0.5g; Sodium 287mg.

CHINESE LEAVES AND BLACK RICE STIR-FRY ★

THE SLIGHTLY NUTTY, CHEWY BLACK GLUTINOUS RICE CONTRASTS BEAUTIFULLY WITH THE CHINESE LEAVES, TO CREATE THIS FLAVOURFUL LIGHT VEGETARIAN DISH.

SERVES FOUR

INGREDIENTS

225g/8oz/generous 1 cup black glutinous rice or brown rice
900ml/1½ pints/3¾ cups vegetable stock
10ml/2 tsp vegetable oil
225g/8oz Chinese leaves (Chinese cabbage), cut into 1cm/½in strips
4 spring onions (scallions), thinly sliced
salt and ground white pepper
2.5ml/½ tsp sesame oil

1 Rinse the rice until the water runs clear, then drain and transfer to a pan. Add the stock and bring to the boil. Reduce the heat, cover the pan and cook gently for 30 minutes. Remove the pan from the heat and leave to stand for 15 minutes without lifting the lid.

2 Heat the vegetable oil in a non-stick frying pan or wok. Stir-fry the Chinese leaves for 2 minutes, adding a little water to prevent them burning.

3 Drain the rice, stir it into the pan and cook for 4 minutes, using two spatulas or wooden spoons to toss it with the Chinese leaves over the heat.

4 Add the spring onions, with the salt and pepper and sesame oil. Cook for a further 1 minute. Serve immediately.

Energy 236Kcal/988kJ; Protein 5.7g; Carbohydrate 45.3g, of which sugars 3g; Fat 2.9g, of which saturates 0.3g; Cholesterol 0mg; Calcium 41mg; Fibre 1.3g; Sodium 6mg.

TOASTED NOODLES WITH VEGETABLES ★

SLIGHTLY CRISP NOODLE CAKES TOPPED WITH VEGETABLES CREATE THIS SUPERB LOW-FAT LUNCH OR SUPPER DISH. EACH NOODLE CAKE SERVES TWO PEOPLE.

SERVES FOUR

INGREDIENTS

    175g/6oz/1½ cups dried egg vermicelli
    10ml/2 tsp vegetable oil
    2 garlic cloves, finely chopped
    115g/4oz/1 cup baby corn cobs
    115g/4oz/1½ cups fresh shiitake
      mushrooms, halved
    3 celery sticks, sliced
    1 carrot, sliced diagonally
    115g/4oz/1 cup mangetouts (snow peas)
    75g/3oz/¾ cup canned, sliced
      bamboo shoots, drained
    15ml/1 tbsp cornflour (cornstarch)
    15ml/1 tbsp cold water
    15ml/1 tbsp dark soy sauce
    5ml/1 tsp caster (superfine) sugar
    300ml/½ pint/1¼ cups
      vegetable stock
salt and ground white pepper
spring onion (scallion) curls,
    to garnish

1 Bring a pan of water to the boil. Add the egg vermicelli and cook according to instructions on the packet until just tender. Drain, refresh under cold water, drain again, then dry thoroughly on kitchen paper. Set aside.

2 Heat 2.5ml/½ tsp oil in a non-stick frying pan or wok. When it starts to smoke, spread half the noodles over the base. Cook for 2–3 minutes until lightly toasted. Carefully turn the noodles over (they stick together like a cake), cook the other side, then slide on to a heated serving plate. Repeat with the remaining noodles to make two cakes. Keep hot.

3 Heat the remaining oil in the clean pan, then cook the garlic for a few seconds. Halve the corn cobs lengthways, add to the pan with the mushrooms, then stir-fry for 3 minutes, adding a little water, if needed, to prevent the mixture burning. Add the celery, carrot, mangetouts and bamboo shoots. Stir-fry for 2 minutes or until the vegetables are tender-crisp.

4 In a small bowl, mix the cornflour to a paste with the water. Add the mixture to the pan with the soy sauce, sugar and stock. Cook until the sauce thickens, stirring. Season to taste with salt and pepper. Divide the vegetable mixture between the noodle cakes, garnish with the spring onion curls and serve immediately.

Energy 230Kcal/964kJ; Protein 7.9g; Carbohydrate 44.6g, of which sugars 5.4g; Fat 2.4g, of which saturates 0.3g; Cholesterol 0mg; Calcium 52mg; Fibre 2.8g; Sodium 623mg.

MAIN DISHES

Healthy certainly, but vegetarian main meals can be quite high in calories and fat, and they can soon eat into your daily calorie and fat limits. But be reassured: the main dishes included here are low in fat (all virtually containing 10g of fat or less per serving) while being full of flavour. The following versatile collection includes classic dishes such as Vegetable Moussaka or Spanish Omelette, and other favourites including Pasta with Tomato and Chilli Sauce, Grilled Vegetable Pizza, Red Pepper Risotto or Spicy Chickpea and Aubergine Stew.

LEEK, SQUASH AND TOMATO GRATIN ★★

COLOURFUL AND SUCCULENT, YOU CAN USE VIRTUALLY ANY KIND OF SQUASH FOR THIS DELICIOUS, LOW-FAT AUTUMN GRATIN, FROM PATTY PANS AND ACORN SQUASH TO PUMPKINS.

SERVES SIX

INGREDIENTS

450g/1lb peeled and seeded squash, cut into 1cm/½in slices
20ml/4 tsp olive oil
450g/1lb leeks, cut into thick, diagonal slices
675g/1½lb tomatoes, skinned and thickly sliced
2.5ml/½ tsp ground toasted cumin seeds
175ml/6fl oz/¾ cups single (light) cream
120ml/4fl oz/½ cup vegetable stock
1 fresh red chilli, seeded and sliced
1 garlic clove, finely chopped
15ml/1 tbsp chopped fresh mint
30ml/2 tbsp chopped fresh parsley
60ml/4 tbsp fresh white breadcrumbs
salt and ground black pepper

1 Steam the squash over a pan of salted boiling water for 10 minutes.

2 Heat half the oil in a non-stick frying pan and cook the leeks gently for 5–6 minutes until lightly coloured. Try to keep the slices intact. Preheat the oven to 190°C/375°F/Gas 5.

3 Layer all the squash, leeks and tomatoes in a 2 litre/3½ pint/8 cup gratin dish, arranging them in rows. Season with salt, pepper and cumin.

4 Pour the cream and stock into a small pan and add the chilli and garlic. Bring to the boil over a low heat, stirring, then stir in the mint. Pour the mixture evenly over the layered vegetables, using a rubber spatula to scrape all the sauce out of the pan.

5 Bake in the oven for 50–55 minutes, or until the gratin is bubbling and tinged brown. Sprinkle the parsley and breadcrumbs on top and drizzle over the remaining oil. Bake for a further 15–20 minutes until the breadcrumbs are browned and crisp. Serve immediately.

VARIATION
For a curried version, use ground coriander as well as cumin, and coconut milk instead of cream. Use fresh coriander (cilantro) instead of mint and parsley.

Energy 157Kcal/660kJ; Protein 4.8g; Carbohydrate 15.9g, of which sugars 7.5g; Fat 8.7g, of which saturates 4.1g; Cholesterol 16mg; Calcium 100mg; Fibre 4.1g; Sodium 98mg.

RICH VEGETABLE HOT-POT ★★

HERE'S A ONE-DISH MEAL THAT'S SUITABLE FOR FEEDING LARGE NUMBERS OF PEOPLE. IT'S LIGHTLY SPICED, LOW IN FAT AND HAS PLENTY OF GARLIC TOO — WHO COULD REFUSE?

SERVES FOUR

INGREDIENTS

30ml/2 tbsp extra virgin olive oil or
  sunflower oil
1 large onion, chopped
2 small–medium aubergines
  (eggplants), cut into small cubes
4 courgettes (zucchini), cut into
  small chunks
2 red, yellow or green (bell) peppers,
  seeded and chopped
115g/4oz/1 cup fresh or frozen peas
115g/4oz green beans
200g/7oz can flageolet (small
  cannellini) beans, rinsed and drained
450g/1lb new or salad potatoes,
  peeled and diced
2.5ml/½ tsp ground cinnamon
2.5ml/½ tsp ground cumin
5ml/1 tsp paprika
4–5 fresh tomatoes, skinned
400g/14oz can chopped tomatoes
30ml/2 tbsp chopped fresh parsley
3–4 garlic cloves, crushed
350ml/12fl oz/1½ cups vegetable stock
salt and ground black pepper
black olives, to garnish
fresh parsley, to garnish

1 Preheat the oven to 190°C/375°F/ Gas 5. Heat 15ml/1 tbsp of the oil in a heavy, non-stick pan, and cook the onion until golden. Add the aubergines, cook for 3 minutes, then add the courgettes, peppers, peas, beans and potatoes, and stir in the spices and seasoning. Cook for 3 minutes, stirring constantly.

2 Cut the fresh tomatoes in half and scoop out the seeds. Chop the tomatoes finely and place them in a bowl. Stir in the canned tomatoes with the chopped parsley, garlic and the remaining olive oil. Spoon the aubergine mixture into a shallow ovenproof dish and level the surface.

3 Pour the stock over the aubergine mixture, then spoon the prepared tomato mixture over the top.

4 Cover the dish with foil and bake in the oven for 30–45 minutes until the vegetables are tender. Serve hot, garnished with black olives and parsley.

Energy 310Kcal/1303kJ; Protein 12.9g; Carbohydrate 49.3g, of which sugars 20.4g; Fat 8.2g, of which saturates 1.3g; Cholesterol 0mg; Calcium 124mg; Fibre 12.1g; Sodium 225mg.

VEGETABLE MOUSSAKA ★★

THIS IS A REALLY FLAVOURSOME AND LOW-FAT VEGETARIAN ALTERNATIVE TO CLASSIC MEAT MOUSSAKA.
SERVE IT WITH WARM BREAD AND A GLASS OR TWO OF RUSTIC RED WINE.

SERVES SIX

INGREDIENTS
450g/1lb aubergines (eggplants),
    sliced
115g/4oz/½ cup whole green lentils
600ml/1 pint/2½ cups vegetable stock
1 bay leaf
225g/8oz tomatoes
25ml/5 tsp olive oil
1 onion, sliced
1 garlic clove, crushed
225g/8oz/3 cups mushrooms, sliced
400g/14oz can chickpeas, rinsed
    and drained
400g/14oz can chopped tomatoes
30ml/2 tbsp tomato purée (paste)
10ml/2 tsp dried basil
300ml/½ pint/1¼ cups low-fat
    natural (plain) yogurt
3 eggs
50g/2oz/½ cup reduced-fat mature
    (sharp) Cheddar cheese, grated
salt and ground black pepper
fresh flat leaf parsley sprigs,
    to garnish

1 Sprinkle the aubergine slices with
salt and place in a colander. Cover and
leave for 30 minutes to allow any bitter
juices to be extracted.

2 Meanwhile, place the lentils, stock
and bay leaf in a pan. Cover, bring to
the boil and simmer for about
20 minutes until the lentils are just
tender. Drain well and keep warm.

3 If you like, skin the fresh tomatoes
then cut them into pieces.

4 Heat 10ml/2 tsp of the oil in a large,
non-stick pan, add the onion and garlic,
and cook for 5 minutes, stirring. Stir in
the lentils, mushrooms, chickpeas, fresh
and canned tomatoes, tomato purée,
basil and 45ml/3 tbsp water. Bring to
the boil, cover and simmer gently for
10 minutes.

5 Preheat the oven to 180°C/350°F/
Gas 4. Rinse the aubergine slices, drain
and pat dry. Heat the remaining oil in a
non-stick frying pan and cook the
aubergines in batches for 3–4 minutes,
turning once.

VARIATIONS
Use 5–10ml/1–2 tsp mixed dried herbs
in place of dried basil. Use other
reduced-fat hard cheese such as Red
Leicester in place of Cheddar. Use fresh
Parmesan cheese in place of Cheddar,
but remember this will increase the
calorie and fat contents of the dish.

6 Season the lentil mixture. Layer the
aubergines and lentils in an ovenproof
dish, starting with aubergines and
finishing with the lentil mixture.

7 Beat together the yogurt, eggs and
salt and pepper, and pour the mixture
evenly into the dish. Sprinkle the cheese
on top. Bake in the oven for 45 minutes.
Serve, garnished with parsley sprigs.

Energy 768Kcal/3255kJ; Protein 60.2g; Carbohydrate 109.6g, of which sugars 10.3g; Fat 13.1g, of which saturates 2.9g; Cholesterol 99mg; Calcium 357mg; Fibre 21.8g; Sodium 320mg.

VEGETABLE STEW WITH ROASTED TOMATO AND GARLIC SAUCE ★★

THIS LIGHTLY SPICED LOW-FAT VEGETARIAN STEW MAKES A PERFECT MATCH FOR COUSCOUS, ENRICHED WITH A LITTLE BUTTER OR OLIVE OIL. ADD SOME CHOPPED FRESH CORIANDER AND A HANDFUL EACH OF RAISINS AND TOASTED PINE NUTS TO THE COUSCOUS TO MAKE IT EXTRA SPECIAL.

SERVES SIX

INGREDIENTS

- 30ml/2 tbsp olive oil
- 250g/9oz small pickling (pearl) onions or shallots
- 1 large onion, chopped
- 2 garlic cloves, finely chopped
- 5ml/1 tsp cumin seeds
- 5ml/1 tsp ground coriander seeds
- 5ml/1 tsp paprika
- 5cm/2in piece of cinnamon stick
- 2 fresh bay leaves
- 300–450ml/½–¾ pint/ 1¼–scant 2 cups vegetable stock
- good pinch of saffron threads
- 450g/1lb carrots, thickly sliced
- 2 green (bell) peppers, seeded and thickly sliced
- 115g/4oz ready-to-eat dried apricots, halved if large
- 5–7.5ml/1–1½ tsp ground toasted cumin seeds
- 450g/1lb squash, peeled, seeded and cut into chunks
- a pinch of granulated sugar, to taste
- 15g/½oz/1 tbsp butter (optional)
- salt and ground black pepper
- 45ml/3 tbsp fresh coriander (cilantro) leaves, to garnish

For the roasted tomato and garlic sauce

- 1kg/2¼lb tomatoes, halved
- 5ml/1 tsp granulated sugar
- 15ml/1 tbsp olive oil
- 1–2 fresh red chillies, seeded and chopped
- 2–3 garlic cloves, chopped
- 5ml/1 tsp fresh thyme leaves
- salt and pepper

VARIATION

Other vegetables could be used. A mixture of aubergine (eggplant) and potato is good. Cook the cubed aubergine with the shallots until brown and cook the potatoes as you would the squash. Allow 2 medium aubergines and about 500g/1¼lb small potatoes. Omit the carrots and apricots.

1 Preheat the oven to 180°C/350°F/ Gas 4. First make the tomato and garlic sauce. Place the tomatoes, cut sides uppermost, in a roasting pan. Season well with salt and pepper and sprinkle the sugar over the top, then drizzle with the olive oil. Roast in the oven for 30 minutes.

2 Scatter the chillies, garlic and thyme over the tomatoes, stir to mix, then roast for a further 30–45 minutes, until the tomatoes are collapsed but still a little juicy. Cool, then process in a blender or food processor to make a thick sauce. Strain to remove the seeds.

3 Heat 15ml/1 tbsp of the oil in a large, wide non-stick pan or deep frying pan and cook the pickling onions or shallots until browned all over. Remove from the pan and set aside. Add the chopped onion to the pan and cook over a low heat for 5–7 minutes, until softened. Stir in the garlic and cumin seeds and cook for a further 3–4 minutes.

4 Add the ground coriander seeds, paprika, cinnamon stick and bay leaves. Cook for a further 2 minutes, stirring constantly, then mix in the stock, saffron, carrots and green peppers. Season well, cover and simmer gently for 10 minutes.

5 Stir in the apricots, 5ml/1 tsp of the ground toasted cumin, the browned onions or shallots and the squash. Stir in the tomato sauce.

6 Cover the pan and cook for a further 5 minutes. Uncover the pan and continue to cook for 10–15 minutes, until the vegetables are all fully cooked, stirring occasionally.

7 Adjust the seasoning, adding a little more cumin and a pinch of sugar to taste. Remove and discard the cinnamon stick. Stir in the butter, if using, and serve scattered with the fresh coriander leaves.

Energy 204Kcal/857kJ; Protein 4.8g; Carbohydrate 32.7g, of which sugars 29.3g; Fat 6.9g, of which saturates 1.2g; Cholesterol 0mg; Calcium 98mg; Fibre 7.9g; Sodium 42mg.

SPANISH OMELETTE ★★

SPANISH TORTILLA, OR OMELETTE, CONSISTS SIMPLY OF POTATOES, ONIONS AND EGGS. THIS VARIATION FROM NORTHERN SPAIN HAS OTHER VEGETABLES INCLUDING WHITE BEANS, AND MAKES A HEARTY LOW-FAT VEGETARIAN MAIN COURSE OR, BECAUSE IT IS GOOD SERVED COLD, AN EXCELLENT PICNIC FOOD.

<u>SERVES EIGHT</u>

INGREDIENTS
   15ml/1 tbsp olive oil
   1 Spanish (Bermuda) onion, chopped
   1 small red (bell) pepper, seeded
      and diced
   2 celery sticks, chopped
   225g/8oz potatoes, diced and cooked
   400g/14oz can cannellini beans,
      rinsed and drained
   8 eggs
   salt and ground black pepper
   sprigs of fresh oregano, to garnish
   green salad and olives, to serve

1 Heat the oil in a 30cm/12in non-stick frying pan or paella pan. Add the onion, red pepper and celery and cook for 3–5 minutes until the vegetables are soft, but not coloured.

2 Add the potatoes and beans and cook for several minutes to heat through.

3 In a small bowl, beat the eggs with a fork, then season well and pour over the ingredients in the pan.

4 Stir the egg mixture with a wooden spatula until it begins to thicken, then allow it to cook over a low heat for about 8 minutes. The omelette should be firm, but still moist in the middle. Cool slightly then invert on to a serving plate.

5 Cut the omelette into wedges. Serve warm or cool with a green salad and olives. Garnish with fresh oregano sprigs.

COOK'S TIP
In Spain, this omelette is often served as a tapas dish or appetizer. It is delicious served cold, cut into bitesize pieces and accompanied by a low-fat chilli sauce for dipping. Other sliced seasonal vegetables, baby artichoke hearts and chickpeas can also be used in this recipe.

Energy 223Kcal/937kJ; Protein 15.2g; Carbohydrate 25.1g, of which sugars 5.4g; Fat 7.7g, of which saturates 1.9g; Cholesterol 190mg; Calcium 82mg; Fibre 6.8g; Sodium 86mg.

POTATO AND ONION CAKES WITH BEETROOT ★★

THESE IRRESISTIBLE LOW-FAT PANCAKES ARE BASED ON LATKE (JEWISH CRISPY, SAVOURY POTATO CAKES TRADITIONALLY EATEN AT HANUKKAH). THEY ARE ESPECIALLY DELICIOUS SERVED WITH A SWEET-SHARP BEETROOT RELISH AND SOUR CREAM, AND ARE A TREAT ANYTIME.

SERVES FOUR

INGREDIENTS
500g/1¼lb potatoes (such as King
    Edward, Estima or Desirée)
1 small Bramley cooking apple,
    peeled, cored and coarsely grated
1 small onion, finely chopped
50g/2oz/½ cup plain
    (all-purpose) flour
2 large (US extra large) eggs, beaten
30ml/2 tbsp chopped fresh chives
30ml/2 tbsp vegetable oil
salt and ground black pepper
fresh dill sprigs and fresh chives
    or chive flowers, to garnish
250ml/8fl oz/1 cup sour cream or
    reduced-fat crème fraîche, to serve
    (optional)
For the beetroot relish
250g/9oz beetroot (beets), cooked
    and peeled
1 large dessert apple, cored and
    finely chopped
15ml/1 tbsp finely chopped red onion
15–30ml/1–2 tbsp tarragon vinegar
15ml/1 tbsp chopped fresh dill
15ml/1 tbsp light olive oil
a pinch of caster (superfine)
    sugar (optional)

1 To make the relish, finely dice the beetroot, then mix it with the apple and onion in a bowl. Add 15ml/1 tbsp of the vinegar, the dill and oil. Season, adding a little more vinegar and a pinch of caster sugar to taste. Set aside.

2 Coarsely grate the potatoes, then rinse, drain and dry them on a clean dish towel.

3 Mix the potatoes, cooking apple and onion in a bowl. Stir in the flour, eggs and chives. Season and mix again.

4 Heat the oil in a non-stick frying pan and cook spoonfuls of the potato mixture. Flatten them to make pancakes 7.5–10cm/3–4in across and cook for 3–4 minutes on each side, until browned. Drain on kitchen paper and keep warm until the mixture is used up.

VARIATION
Use sweet potatoes in place of standard potatoes.

5 Serve a stack of pancakes – there should be about 16–20 in total – with spoonfuls of sour cream or crème fraîche if you like, and the beetroot relish. Garnish with dill sprigs and chives or chive flowers and grind black pepper on top just before serving.

VARIATION
To make a leek and potato cake, melt 15g/½oz/1 tbsp butter in a non-stick pan, add 400g/14oz thinly sliced leeks and cook until tender. Season well. Coarsely grate 500g/1¼lb peeled potatoes, then season. Melt another 25g/1oz/2 tbsp butter in a non-stick frying pan and add a layer of half the potatoes. Cover with the leeks, then add the remaining potatoes, pressing down with a spatula to form a cake. Cook over a low heat for 20–25 minutes until the potatoes are browned, then turn over and cook for 15–20 minutes, until the potatoes are browned.

Energy 265Kcal/1116kJ; Protein 7.8g; Carbohydrate 38.8g, of which sugars 10g; Fat 9.9g, of which saturates 1.7g; Cholesterol 95mg; Calcium 57mg; Fibre 3.6g; Sodium 92mg.

LENTIL FRITTATA ★★

OMELETTES TEND TO HAVE THE EGG MIXTURE COOKED AND FOLDED AROUND A FILLING, WHILE A FRITTATA JUST MIXES IT ALL UP. THIS RECIPE COMBINES GREEN LENTILS, RED ONIONS, BROCCOLI AND TOMATOES.

SERVES EIGHT

INGREDIENTS
    75g/3oz/scant ½ cup green lentils
    225g/8oz small broccoli florets
    2 red onions, halved and thickly sliced
    15ml/1 tbsp olive oil
    8 eggs
    45ml/3 tbsp water
    45ml/3 tbsp chopped mixed fresh
        herbs, such as oregano, parsley,
        tarragon and chives, plus extra
        sprigs to garnish
    175g/6oz cherry tomatoes, halved
    salt and ground black pepper

1 Place the lentils in a pan, cover with cold water and bring to the boil, then reduce the heat and simmer for 25 minutes until tender. Add the broccoli, return to the boil and cook for 1 minute.

VARIATIONS
Use green beans, halved, in place of broccoli florets. Use standard white onions in place of red onions.

2 Meanwhile place the onion slices and olive oil in a shallow earthenware dish or cazuela about 23–25cm/9–10in in diameter, and place in a cold (unheated) oven. Set the oven to 200°C/400°F/Gas 6 and cook for 25 minutes.

3 In a bowl, whisk together the eggs, water, a pinch of salt and plenty of pepper. Stir in the chopped herbs and set aside.

4 Drain the lentils and broccoli and stir into the onions. Add the cherry tomatoes and stir gently to combine.

5 Pour the egg mixture evenly over the vegetables. Reduce the oven temperature to 190°C/375°F/Gas 5. Return the dish to the oven and cook for 10 minutes, then push the mixture into the centre of the dish using a spatula, allowing the raw egg mixture in the centre to flow to the edges.

6 Return the dish to the oven and cook the frittata for a further 15 minutes, or until it is just set. Garnish with sprigs of fresh herbs and serve warm, cut into wedges.

Energy 145Kcal/605kJ; Protein 10.5g; Carbohydrate 9.7g, of which sugars 4g; Fat 7.5g, of which saturates 1.8g; Cholesterol 190mg; Calcium 65mg; Fibre 2.5g; Sodium 77mg.

BAKED CHEESE POLENTA WITH TOMATO SAUCE ★★

POLENTA, OR CORNMEAL, IS A STAPLE FOOD IN ITALY THAT IS LOW IN FAT. IT IS COOKED NOT UNLIKE A PORRIDGE, AND EATEN SOFT, OR SET AND CUT INTO SHAPES THEN BAKED OR GRILLED.

SERVES FOUR

INGREDIENTS

5ml/1 tsp salt
250g/9oz/2¼ cups quick-cook polenta
5ml/1 tsp paprika
2.5ml/½ tsp freshly grated nutmeg
10ml/2 tsp olive oil
1 large onion, finely chopped
2 garlic cloves, crushed
2 x 400g/14oz cans chopped tomatoes
15ml/1 tbsp tomato purée (paste)
5ml/1 tsp granulated sugar
salt and ground black pepper
75g/3oz/¾ cup Gruyère cheese, finely grated

1 Lightly grease an ovenproof dish and set aside. Line a 28 x 18cm/11 x 7in baking tin (pan) with clear film (plastic wrap). In a pan, bring 1 litre/1¾ pints/4 cups water to the boil with the salt.

2 Pour in the polenta in a steady stream and cook, stirring continuously, for 5 minutes. Beat in the paprika and nutmeg, then pour the mixture into the prepared tin and smooth the surface. Leave to cool.

3 Heat the oil in a non-stick pan and cook the onion and garlic until they go soft. Add the tomatoes, tomato purée and sugar. Season to taste with salt and pepper. Bring to the boil, then reduce the heat and allow the mixture to simmer for about 20 minutes.

4 Meanwhile, preheat the oven to 200°C/400°F/Gas 6. Turn out the polenta on to a chopping board, and cut into 5cm/2in squares. Place half the squares in the prepared ovenproof dish. Spoon over half the tomato sauce, and sprinkle with half the cheese. Repeat the layers. Bake in the oven for about 25 minutes, or until golden. Serve hot.

Energy 369Kcal/1548kJ; Protein 14.6g; Carbohydrate 61.4g, of which sugars 13.4g; Fat 7.2g, of which saturates 2.2g; Cholesterol 8mg; Calcium 200mg; Fibre 4.9g; Sodium 647mg.

SPAGHETTI WITH FRESH TOMATO SAUCE ★★

THE HEAT FROM THE PASTA WILL RELEASE THE AROMATIC FLAVOURS OF SOFT PLUM OR SWEET CHERRY TOMATOES — TOP QUALITY TOMATOES REALLY ADD TO THE TASTE OF THIS SAUCE.

SERVES FOUR

INGREDIENTS

675g/1½lb ripe Italian
   plum tomatoes or sweet
   cherry tomatoes
30ml/2 tbsp extra virgin olive oil or
   sunflower oil
1 onion, finely chopped
350g/12oz fresh or dried spaghetti
a small handful of fresh basil leaves
salt and ground black pepper
coarsely shaved fresh Parmesan
   cheese, to serve

COOK'S TIPS

• The Italian plum tomatoes called San Marzano are the best variety to use. When fully ripe, they have thin skins that peel off easily.
• In Italy, cooks often make this sauce in bulk in the summer months and freeze it for later use. Let it cool, then freeze in usable quantities in rigid containers. Thaw, before reheating thoroughly.

1 With a sharp knife, cut a cross in the base end of each tomato. Plunge the tomatoes, a few at a time, into a bowl of boiling water. Leave for 30 seconds or so, then lift them out with a slotted spoon and drop them into a bowl of cold water. Drain well. The skin will have begun to peel back from the crosses. Remove it entirely.

2 Place the tomatoes on a chopping board and cut into quarters, then eighths, then chop as finely as possible.

3 Heat the oil in a large, non-stick pan, add the onion and cook over a low heat for about 5 minutes until softened and lightly coloured, stirring frequently.

4 Add the tomatoes, season with salt and pepper to taste, bring to a simmer, then reduce the heat to low and cover the pan with a lid. Cook for 30–40 minutes until the mixture is thick, stirring occasionally.

5 Meanwhile, cook the pasta according to the instructions on the packet. Shred the basil leaves finely, or tear them into small pieces.

6 Remove the sauce from the heat, stir in the basil and adjust the seasoning to taste. Drain the pasta in a colander. Transfer the spaghetti to a warmed bowl, pour the sauce over and toss the mixture well. Serve immediately, with shaved Parmesan handed around in a separate bowl.

Energy 383Kcal/1623kJ; Protein 11.9g; Carbohydrate 71.3g, of which sugars 9g; Fat 7.6g, of which saturates 1.1g; Cholesterol 0mg; Calcium 38mg; Fibre 4.4g; Sodium 18mg.

CONCHIGLIE WITH ROASTED VEGETABLES ★★

NOTHING COULD BE SIMPLER — OR MORE DELICIOUS — THAN TOSSING FRESHLY COOKED PASTA WITH ROASTED VEGETABLES. THE COMBINATION IS SUPERB AND THIS DISH IS LOW IN FAT TOO!

SERVES SIX

INGREDIENTS

1 red (bell) pepper, seeded and cut into 1cm/½in squares
1 yellow or orange (bell) pepper, seeded and cut into 1cm/½in squares
1 small aubergine (eggplant), roughly diced
2 courgettes (zucchini), roughly diced
30ml/2 tbsp extra virgin olive oil
15ml/1 tbsp chopped fresh flat leaf parsley
5ml/1 tsp dried oregano or marjoram
250g/9oz baby Italian plum tomatoes, halved lengthways
2 garlic cloves, roughly chopped
350–400g/12–14oz/3–3½ cups dried conchiglie
salt and ground black pepper
4–6 fresh marjoram or oregano flowers, to garnish

1 Preheat the oven to 190°C/375°F/Gas 5. Rinse the prepared peppers, aubergine and courgettes in a colander under cold running water, drain well, then put the vegetables in a large, non-stick roasting pan.

2 Drizzle the olive oil over the vegetables and sprinkle with the chopped fresh and dried herbs. Add salt and pepper to taste and toss to mix well. Roast in the oven for about 30 minutes, stirring two or three time during cooking.

3 Stir the halved tomatoes and chopped garlic into the vegetable mixture, then roast for a further 20 minutes, stirring once or twice. Meanwhile, cook the pasta according to the instructions on the packet.

4 Drain the pasta and transfer it to a warmed serving bowl. Add the roasted vegetables and any cooking juices and toss to mix well. Serve the hot pasta and vegetables in warmed bowls, sprinkling each portion with fresh herb flowers, to garnish.

Energy 277Kcal/1171kJ; Protein 9.5g; Carbohydrate 50.3g, of which sugars 8.7g; Fat 5.5g, of which saturates 0.8g; Cholesterol 0mg; Calcium 52mg; Fibre 4.6g; Sodium 11mg.

PASTA, SUN-DRIED TOMATOES AND RADICCHIO ★★

USE PAGLIA E FIENO PASTA TO GET THE BEST FROM THIS MODERN PASTA DISH. CAREFUL DRIZZLING OF THE TOMATO SAUCE AND PLACING OF THE PASTA ARE KEY TO THIS RECIPE.

2 Cook the pasta according to the packet instructions, keeping the colours separate by using two pans.

3 While the pasta is cooking, heat 15ml/1 tbsp of the oil in a non-stick pan or frying pan. Add the sun-dried tomato paste and the sun-dried tomatoes, then stir in 2 ladlefuls of the water used for cooking the pasta. Simmer until the sauce is slightly reduced, stirring constantly.

4 Mix in the radicchio, then taste and season with salt and pepper, if necessary. Keep on a low heat. Drain the *paglia e fieno*, keeping the colours separate, and return the pasta to the pans. Add about 7.5ml/1½ tsp oil to each pan and toss over a medium to high heat until the pasta is glistening with the oil.

5 Arrange a portion of green and white pasta in each of 6 warmed bowls, then spoon the sun-dried tomato and radicchio mixture in the centre. Sprinkle the spring onions and pine nuts over the top and serve immediately. Before eating, each diner should toss the sauce ingredients with the pasta.

SERVES SIX

INGREDIENTS
45ml/3 tbsp pine nuts
350g/12oz *paglia e fieno* (or two different colours of tagliatelle)
30ml/2 tbsp extra virgin olive oil or sunflower oil
30ml/2 tbsp sun-dried tomato paste
2 pieces drained sun-dried tomatoes in olive oil, cut into very thin slivers
40g/1½oz radicchio leaves, finely shredded
4–6 spring onions (scallions), thinly sliced into rings
salt and ground black pepper

1 Put the pine nuts in a non-stick frying pan and toss over a low to medium heat for 1–2 minutes, or until they are lightly toasted and golden. Remove from the heat and set aside.

COOK'S TIP
If you find the presentation too fussy, you can toss the tomato and radicchio mixture with the pasta in a large bowl before serving, then sprinkle the spring onions and toasted pine nuts on top.

Energy 293Kcal/1237kJ; Protein 8.7g; Carbohydrate 45.1g, of which sugars 3.7g; Fat 10g, of which saturates 1g; Cholesterol 0mg; Calcium 24mg; Fibre 2.3g; Sodium 23mg.

FUSILLI WITH BASIL AND PEPPERS ★ ★

CHARGRILLED PEPPERS HAVE A WONDERFUL, SMOKY FLAVOUR THAT MARRIES WELL WITH GARLIC, OLIVES, BASIL AND TOMATOES IN THIS DELECTABLE LOW-FAT PASTA DISH.

SERVES FOUR

INGREDIENTS

3 large (bell) peppers (red, yellow and orange)
350g/12oz/3 cups fresh or dried fusilli
30ml/2 tbsp extra virgin olive oil
1–2 garlic cloves, to taste, finely chopped
4 ripe plum tomatoes, skinned, seeded and diced
50g/2oz/½ cup pitted black olives, halved or quartered lengthways
a handful of fresh basil leaves
salt and ground black pepper

VARIATION
Use vine-ripened tomatoes in place of plum tomatoes.

1 put the whole peppers under a hot grill (broiler) and grill (broil) for about 10 minutes, until charred on all sides, turning frequently.

2 Put the hot peppers in a plastic bag, seal the bag and set aside until the peppers are cold.

3 Remove the peppers from the bag and hold them, one at a time, under cold running water. Peel off the charred skins with your fingers, split the peppers open and pull out the cores. Rub off all the seeds under the running water, then pat the peppers dry on kitchen paper.

4 Cook the pasta in a pan of salted boiling water until *al dente*.

5 Meanwhile, thinly slice the peppers and place them in a large bowl with the olive oil, garlic, tomatoes, olives and basil. Add salt and pepper to taste.

6 Drain the cooked pasta and transfer it to the bowl with the other ingredients. Toss well to mix and serve immediately.

Energy 420Kcal/1778kJ; Protein 12.6g; Carbohydrate 76.4g, of which sugars 14g; Fat 9.3g, of which saturates 1.4g; Cholesterol 0mg; Calcium 46mg; Fibre 6g; Sodium 297mg.

PENNE WITH GREEN VEGETABLE SAUCE ★★

LIGHTLY COOKED FRESH GREEN VEGETABLES ARE TOSSED WITH HOT PASTA TO CREATE THIS DELICATELY-FAVOURED LOW-FAT DISH, IDEAL FOR A DECEPTIVELY FILLING SUPPER.

2 Heat the oil in a non-stick frying pan. Add the carrots and leek. Sprinkle the sugar over and cook for about 5 minutes, all the time stirring.

3 Stir in the courgette, green beans, peas and plenty of salt and pepper. Cover and cook over a low to medium heat for 5–8 minutes, or until the vegetables are tender, stirring occasionally.

4 Meanwhile, cook the pasta in a large pan of salted boiling water, according to the packet instructions, until it is tender or *al dente*. Drain the pasta well and keep it hot until it is ready to serve.

5 Stir the chopped parsley and plum tomatoes into the vegetable mixture and adjust the seasoning to taste. Toss the vegetable mixture with the cooked pasta and serve immediately.

VARIATIONS

Use 1 standard or red onion in place of leek. Use frozen baby broad (fava) beans in place of peas.

SERVES FOUR

INGREDIENTS
   2 carrots
   1 courgette (zucchini)
   75g/3oz green beans
   1 small leek
   2 ripe Italian plum tomatoes
   1 handful fresh flat leaf parsley
   15ml/1 tbsp extra virgin olive oil
   2.5ml/½ tsp granulated sugar
   115g/4oz/1 cup frozen peas
   350g/12oz/3 cups dried penne
   salt and ground black pepper

1 Dice the carrots and the courgette finely. Trim the green beans, then cut them into 2cm/¾in lengths. Slice the leek thinly. Skin and dice the tomatoes. Finely chop the parsley and set aside.

Energy 400Kcal/1692kJ; Protein 15.3g; Carbohydrate 76.9g, of which sugars 11.7g; Fat 5.6g, of which saturates 0.9g; Cholesterol 0mg; Calcium 76mg; Fibre 7.2g; Sodium 21mg.

PASTA WITH TOMATO AND CHILLI SAUCE ★★

THIS DELICIOUS LOW-FAT PASTA DISH COMES FROM LAZIO, IN ITALY, WHERE IT IS DESCRIBED AS
"ALL'ARRABBIATA" WHICH MEANS ANGRY — REFERRING TO THE HEAT THAT COMES FROM THE CHILLI.

SERVES FOUR

INGREDIENTS

500g/1¼lb sugocasa (see Cook's Tip)
2 garlic cloves, crushed
150ml/¼ pint/½ cup dry white wine
15ml/1 tbsp sun-dried tomato paste
1 fresh red chilli
300g/11oz/2¾ cups penne or tortiglioni
60ml/4 tbsp finely chopped fresh flat
   leaf parsley
salt and ground black pepper
grated fresh Pecorino cheese,
   to serve

COOK'S TIP
Sugocasa resembles passata (bottled strained tomatoes), but it is rougher.

3 Remove the chilli from the tomato sauce and add 30ml/2 tbsp of the parsley. Taste for seasoning. If you prefer a hotter taste, chop some or all of the chilli and return it to the sauce.

4 Drain the pasta and transfer it to a warmed large bowl. Pour the tomato sauce over the pasta and toss to mix. Serve at once, sprinkled with grated Pecorino and the remaining parsley.

1 Mix the sugocasa, garlic, wine, sun-dried tomato paste and whole chilli in a pan and bring to the boil. Cover and simmer gently, stirring occasionally.

2 Meanwhile, drop the pasta into a large pan of salted rapidly boiling water. Reduce the heat and simmer for 10–12 minutes or until *al dente*.

Energy 310Kcal/1316kJ; Protein 10.5g; Carbohydrate 60.6g, of which sugars 7.4g; Fat 1.9g, of which saturates 0.3g; Cholesterol 0mg; Calcium 57mg; Fibre 4.2g; Sodium 28mg.

TAGLIATELLE ᴼᴺ BROCCOLI ᴬᴺᴰ SPINACH ★★

THIS IS A HEARTY, FRESHLY-PREPARED VEGETARIAN SUPPER DISH. IT IS NUTRITIOUS AND FILLING, AND NEEDS NO ACCOMPANIMENT. IF YOU LIKE, YOU CAN USE TAGLIATELLE FLECKED WITH HERBS.

SERVES FOUR

INGREDIENTS
2 heads of broccoli
450g/1lb fresh spinach,
   stalks removed
freshly grated nutmeg, to taste
450g/1lb fresh or dried
   egg tagliatelle
30ml/2 tbsp extra virgin olive oil
juice of ½ lemon, or to taste
salt and ground black pepper
grated fresh Parmesan cheese,
   to serve

COOK'S TIP
Always grate nutmeg freshly as the ground spice loses its flavour quickly.

1 Put the broccoli in the basket of a steamer, cover and steam over a pan of boiling water for 10 minutes. Add the spinach to the broccoli, cover and steam for 4–5 minutes or until both are tender. Towards the end of the cooking time, sprinkle the vegetables with freshly grated nutmeg and salt and pepper to taste. Transfer the vegetables to a colander.

2 Add salt to the water in the steamer and fill the steamer pan with boiling water, then add the pasta and cook according to the instructions on the packet. Meanwhile, chop the broccoli and spinach in the colander.

3 Drain the pasta. Heat the oil in the pasta pan, add the pasta and chopped vegetables and toss over a medium heat until evenly mixed. Sprinkle in the lemon juice and plenty of black pepper, then taste and add more lemon juice, salt and nutmeg, if you like. Serve immediately, sprinkled with grated fresh Parmesan cheese and black pepper.

VARIATIONS
• If you like, add a sprinkling of crushed dried chillies with the black pepper in Step 3.
• To add both texture and protein, garnish the finished dish with one or two handfuls of toasted pine nuts. They are often served with broccoli and spinach in Italy. Remember though, they will add extra calories and fat to the recipe.

Energy 504Kcal/2130kJ; Protein 22.2g; Carbohydrate 87.4g, of which sugars 7.3g; Fat 9.6g, of which saturates 1.4g; Cholesterol 0mg; Calcium 290mg; Fibre 8.9g; Sodium 171mg.

TAGLIATELLE WITH FRESH HERBS ★★

FRESH ROSEMARY, PARSLEY, MINT, SAGE, BASIL, BAY AND GARLIC ARE ALL HERE, MERGING TOGETHER TO CREATE AN AROMATIC PASTA DISH THAT IS PACKED WITH TASTE.

SERVES SIX

INGREDIENTS

3 fresh rosemary sprigs
1 small handful fresh flat leaf parsley
5–6 fresh mint leaves
5–6 fresh sage leaves
8–10 large fresh basil leaves
30ml/2 tbsp extra virgin olive oil
25g/1oz/2 tbsp butter
1 shallot, finely chopped
2 garlic cloves, finely chopped
a pinch of chilli powder, to taste
400g/14oz fresh egg tagliatelle
1 bay leaf
120ml/4fl oz/½ cup dry white wine
90–120ml/6–8 tbsp vegetable stock
salt and ground black pepper
fresh basil leaves, to garnish

1 Strip the rosemary and parsley leaves from their stalks and chop them together with the other fresh herbs.

2 Heat the oil and half the butter in a large non-stick pan. Add the shallot, garlic and chilli powder. Cook over a very low heat for 2–3 minutes, stirring frequently.

3 Meanwhile, cook the fresh pasta in a large pan of salted boiling water according to the packet instructions.

4 Add the chopped herbs and the bay leaf to the shallot mixture and cook for 2–3 minutes, stirring, then add the wine and increase the heat. Boil rapidly for 1–2 minutes, or until reduced. Reduce the heat, add the stock and simmer gently for 1–2 minutes. Season.

5 Drain the pasta and add it to the herb mixture. Toss well to mix and remove and discard the bay leaf.

6 Put the remaining butter in a warmed large bowl, transfer the dressed pasta to it and toss well to mix. Serve immediately, garnished with basil.

Energy 289Kcal/1223kJ; Protein 8.5g; Carbohydrate 50.7g, of which sugars 3.2g; Fat 5.8g, of which saturates 2.5g; Cholesterol 9mg; Calcium 47mg; Fibre 2.7g; Sodium 33mg.

PASTA WITH ONION AND SHREDDED CABBAGE ★ ★

SLOWLY-COOKED ONIONS, CABBAGE, PARMESAN AND PINE NUTS COMBINE WITH BALSAMIC VINEGAR TO PRODUCE A LOVELY SPICY TANG TO THIS PASTA CLASSIC.

SERVES SIX

INGREDIENTS

15g/½oz/1 tbsp butter
15ml/1 tbsp extra virgin olive oil
500g/1¼lb Spanish (Bermuda) onions, halved and thinly sliced
5–10ml/1–2 tsp balsamic vinegar
400–500g/14oz–1¼lb cavolo nero, spring greens (collards), kale or Brussels sprout tops, shredded
400–500g/14–1¼lb/3½–5 cups dried pasta shapes (such as penne or fusilli)
50g/2oz/⅔ cup grated fresh Parmesan cheese
25g/1oz/¼ cup pine nuts, toasted, to serve
salt and ground black pepper

VARIATION
To make a delicious pilaff, cook 250g/9oz/1¼ cups brown basmati rice and use in place of the pasta.

1 Heat the butter and olive oil together in a large, non-stick pan. Stir in the onions, cover and cook very gently for about 20 minutes, until very soft, stirring occasionally.

2 Uncover the pan and continue to cook gently until the onions have turned golden. Add the balsamic vinegar and season well, then cook for a further 1–2 minutes. Remove from the heat and set aside.

3 Blanch the cavolo nero, spring greens, kale or Brussels sprout tops in a pan of lightly salted boiling water for about 3 minutes. Drain well and add to the onions, then cook over a low heat for 3–4 minutes.

4 Cook the pasta in a separate pan of lightly salted boiling water for 8–12 minutes, or according to the packet instructions, until *al dente*. Drain the pasta, then add it to the pan of onions and greens and toss thoroughly to mix.

5 Season well with salt and pepper and stir in half the grated Parmesan cheese. Transfer the pasta to warmed plates. Scatter the pine nuts and more Parmesan on top and serve immediately.

Energy 349Kcal/1472kJ; Protein 13.2g; Carbohydrate 59.3g, of which sugars 10.2g; Fat 8.1g, of which saturates 3.4g; Cholesterol 14mg; Calcium 171mg; Fibre 4.5g; Sodium 115mg.

PASTA WITH AUBERGINES ★★

THIS SICILIAN RECIPE IS TRADITIONALLY MADE FROM FRIED AUBERGINES. THIS VERSION IS LIGHTER AS THE AUBERGINES ARE ROASTED. IT IS A GREAT MAKE-AHEAD FAMILY DISH.

SERVES FOUR

INGREDIENTS

    2 medium aubergines (eggplants),
      about 225g/8oz each, diced small
    45ml/3 tbsp olive oil
    275g/10oz dried macaroni or fusilli
    50g/2oz/$\frac{2}{3}$ cup grated Pecorino
      cheese
    salt and ground black pepper
    shredded fresh basil leaves,
      to garnish
    crusty bread, to serve
For the tomato sauce
    30ml/2 tbsp olive oil
    1 onion, finely chopped
    400g/14oz can chopped tomatoes
      or 400g/14oz passata (bottled
      strained tomatoes)

1 Soak the diced aubergine in a bowl of cold salted water for 30 minutes. Meanwhile, preheat the oven to 220°C/425°F/Gas 7. Make the sauce. Heat the oil in a large pan, add the onion and cook gently for about 3 minutes until softened. Add the tomatoes, and season. Bring to the boil, lower the heat, cover and simmer for about 20 minutes. Stir the sauce and add a few spoonfuls of water from time to time, to prevent it from becoming too thick. Remove from the heat.

2 Drain the aubergines and pat dry. Spread out in a roasting pan, add the oil and toss to coat. Bake the aubergines for 20–25 minutes, turning every 4–5 minutes.

3 Cook the pasta in a large pan of rapidly boiling salted water for 10–12 minutes or until *al dente*. Reheat the tomato sauce.

4 Drain the pasta and add it to the tomato sauce, with half the roasted aubergines and half the Pecorino. Toss to mix, then taste for seasoning.

5 Spoon the pasta and sauce mixture into a warmed large serving dish and top with the remaining roasted aubergines. Scatter the shredded fresh basil leaves over the top, followed by the remaining Pecorino. Serve with generous chunks of crusty bread.

COOK'S TIP

In Sicily, a cheese called ricotta salata is used for this recipe. This is a matured salted ricotta that is grated. It is unlikely that you will find ricotta salata outside Sicily; Pecorino is the best substitute.

Energy 506kcal/2126kJ; Protein 15g; Carbohydrate 61g, of which sugars 9g; Fat 24g, of which saturates 5g; Cholesterol 12mg; Calcium 178mg; Fibre 7g; Sodium 144mg.

FRESH RAVIOLI WITH PUMPKIN ★★

This is a very simple, low-fat version of a Christmas Eve speciality from Lombardy. In traditional recipes the pumpkin filling is flavoured with mostarda di frutta (a kind of sweet fruit pickle), crushed amaretti and sugar. Here the pumpkin is seasoned with fresh Parmesan and nutmeg. It is quite sweet enough for most tastes.

SERVES EIGHT

INGREDIENTS
1 quantity Pasta with Eggs
40g/1½oz/3 tbsp butter
grated fresh Parmesan cheese,
   to serve
For the filling
450g/1lb piece of pumpkin
10ml/2 tsp olive oil
25g/1oz/⅓ cup grated fresh
   Parmesan cheese
freshly grated nutmeg, to taste
salt and ground black pepper

1 Make the filling. Preheat the oven to 220°C/425°F/Gas 7. Cut the piece of pumpkin into chunks and remove the seeds and fibres. Put the chunks, skin side down, in a roasting pan and drizzle the oil over the pumpkin flesh. Roast in the oven for 30 minutes, turning the pieces over once or twice.

2 Leave the roasted pumpkin until it is cool enough to handle, then scrape the flesh out into a bowl and discard the pumpkin skin.

3 Mash the roasted pumpkin flesh with a fork, then add the grated Parmesan and freshly grated nutmeg and salt and pepper to taste. Stir well to mix, then set aside until cold.

4 Using a pasta machine, roll out one-quarter of the pasta into a 90cm–1m/36in–1yd strip. Cut the strip with a sharp knife into two 45–50cm/18–20in lengths (you can do this during rolling if the strip gets too long to manage).

5 Using a teaspoon, put 10–12 little mounds of the filling along one side of one of the pasta strips, spacing them evenly.

6 Brush a little water around each mound, then fold the plain side of the pasta strip over the mounds of filling. Starting from the folded edge, press down gently with your fingertips around each mound, pushing the air out at the unfolded edge. Sprinkle lightly with flour.

7 With a fluted pasta wheel, cut along each long side, then in between each mound to make small square shapes. Put the ravioli on floured dish towels, sprinkle lightly with flour and leave to dry, while repeating the process with the remaining pasta to get 80–96 ravioli altogether.

8 Drop the ravioli into a large pan of salted boiling water, bring back to the boil and boil for 4–5 minutes. Meanwhile, melt the butter in a small pan until it is sizzling.

9 Drain the ravioli and divide them equally among eight warmed dinner plates or large bowls. Drizzle the sizzling butter over the ravioli and serve immediately, sprinkled with grated Parmesan. Hand round a little more grated Parmesan separately, if you like.

VARIATION
You can buy *mostarda di frutta* at Italian delicatessens, especially at Christmas time. If you would like to try some in the filling, add about 45ml/3 tbsp, together with a few crushed amaretti.

Energy 236Kcal/998kJ; Protein 7.7g; Carbohydrate 38.3g, of which sugars 2.6g; Fat 6.9g, of which saturates 3.5g; Cholesterol 14mg; Calcium 67mg; Fibre 2g; Sodium 66mg.

GRILLED VEGETABLE PIZZA ★★

YOU REALLY CAN'T GO TOO FAR WRONG WITH THIS CLASSIC MIXTURE OF GRILLED VEGETABLES ON HOME-MADE PIZZA DOUGH. IT IS LOW IN FAT, AND LOOKS AND TASTES GREAT TOO.

3 Place the pizza dough on a sheet of baking parchment on top of a baking sheet, and roll or gently press it out to form a 25cm/10in round, making the edges slightly thicker than the centre.

4 Lightly brush the pizza dough with any remaining oil, then spread the chopped plum tomatoes evenly over the dough.

SERVES EIGHT

INGREDIENTS

1 courgette (zucchini), sliced
2 baby aubergines (eggplants) or
  1 small aubergine, sliced
15ml/1 tbsp olive oil
1 yellow (bell) pepper, seeded
  and sliced
115g/4oz/1 cup cornmeal
50g/2oz/½ cup potato flour
50g/2oz/½ cup soya flour
5ml/1 tsp baking powder
2.5ml/½ tsp sea salt
50g/2oz/¼ cup butter or
  non-hydrogenated margarine
about 105ml/7 tbsp semi-skimmed
  (low-fat) milk
4 plum tomatoes, skinned
  and chopped
30ml/2 tbsp chopped fresh basil
115g/4oz half-fat mozzarella
  cheese, sliced
salt and ground black pepper
fresh basil sprigs, to garnish

1 Preheat the grill (broiler) to high. Brush the courgette and aubergine slices with a little oil and place on a grill (broiler) rack with the pepper slices. Cook under the grill until lightly browned, turning once.

2 Meanwhile, preheat the oven to 200°C/400°F/Gas 6. Place the cornmeal, potato flour, soya flour, baking powder and sea salt in a mixing bowl and stir to mix. Lightly rub in the butter or margarine until the mixture resembles coarse breadcrumbs, then stir in enough of the milk to make a soft but not sticky dough.

COOK'S TIP
This recipe uses a combination of different types of flours to give an interesting flavour and texture to the base. If you prefer, use 225g/8oz/ 2 cups of plain (all-purpose) flour or a combination of half plain and half wholemeal (whole-wheat) flours.

5 Sprinkle with the chopped basil and season with salt and pepper. Arrange the grilled vegetables over the tomatoes and top with the cheese.

6 Bake in the oven for 25–30 minutes until crisp and golden brown. Garnish the pizza with fresh basil sprigs and serve immediately, cut into slices.

VARIATION
Top the pizza with 115g/4oz sliced chevre cheese (goat's cheese) instead of the mozzarella for a creamy alternative. Remember, this will increase the calorie and fat contents of the recipe.

Energy 217Kcal/907kJ; Protein 12g; Carbohydrate 20.7g, of which sugars 8.1g; Fat 9.7g, of which saturates 4.4g; Cholesterol 16mg; Calcium 114mg; Fibre 4.7g; Sodium 74mg.

TOMATO AND OLIVE MINI PIZZAS ★★

FOR A QUICK AND LIGHT VEGETARIAN SUPPER, TRY THESE DELICIOUS LITTLE PIZZAS MADE WITH FRESH AND SUN-DRIED TOMATOES. SERVE SIMPLY WITH A MIXED LEAF SIDE SALAD.

MAKES FOUR

INGREDIENTS

150g/5oz packet of pizza base mix
8 halves sun-dried tomatoes in olive oil, drained
50g/2oz/½ cup pitted black olives
1 ripe beefsteak tomato, sliced
50g/2oz/¼ cup chevre cheese (goat's cheese)
30ml/2 tbsp fresh basil leaves

3 Place the sun-dried tomatoes and olives in a blender or food processor and process until smooth. Spread the mixture evenly over the pizza bases.

4 Top with the tomato slices, then crumble over the goat's cheese. Bake in the oven for 10–15 minutes. Sprinkle with the fresh basil and serve immediately.

1 Preheat the oven to 200°C/400°F/ Gas 6. Lightly oil 2 baking sheets and set aside. Make up the pizza base following the instructions on the packet.

2 Divide the dough into four equal portions and roll out each portion of dough to form a 13cm/5in round. Place on the oiled baking sheets.

COOK'S TIP
You could use loose sun-dried tomatoes (preserved without oil) instead. Leave in a bowl of warm water for 10–15 minutes to soften, then drain and process with the olives.

Energy 195Kcal/823kJ; Protein 6.8g; Carbohydrate 29.9g, of which sugars 3.2g; Fat 6.2g, of which saturates 2.7g; Cholesterol 12mg; Calcium 80mg; Fibre 2.1g; Sodium 385mg.

PROVENÇAL RICE ★★

Sweet cherry tomatoes, purple aubergines and tender green courgettes are a delicious combination in this flavourful low-fat dish originating from the south of France.

<u>SERVES FOUR</u>

INGREDIENTS

2 onions
30ml/2 tbsp extra virgin olive oil or sunflower oil
225g/8oz/generous 1 cup long grain brown rice
10ml/2 tsp mustard seeds
600ml/1 pint/2½ cups vegetable stock
1 large or 2 small red (bell) peppers, seeded and cut into chunks
1 small aubergine (eggplant), diced
2–3 courgettes (zucchini), sliced
about 12 cherry tomatoes
5–6 fresh basil leaves, torn into pieces
2 garlic cloves, finely chopped
60ml/4 tbsp white wine
60ml/4 tbsp passata (bottled strained tomatoes) or tomato juice
2 hard-boiled eggs, peeled and cut into wedges
8 stuffed green olives, sliced
15ml/1 tbsp capers
3 sun-dried tomatoes in oil, drained and sliced (optional)
salt and ground black pepper

1 Preheat the oven to 200°C/400°F/Gas 6. Roughly chop 1 onion. Heat 10ml/2 tsp of the oil in a non-stick pan and cook the chopped onion over a low heat for 5–6 minutes until softened.

2 Add the rice and mustard seeds. Cook for 2 minutes, stirring, then add the stock and a little salt. Bring to the boil, then reduce the heat, cover and simmer for 35 minutes or until the rice is tender and fairly dry.

3 Meanwhile, cut the remaining onion into wedges. Put these in a roasting pan with the peppers, aubergine, courgettes and cherry tomatoes. Sprinkle over the basil and garlic. Drizzle over the remaining oil and sprinkle with salt and pepper. Roast in the oven for 15–20 minutes or until the vegetables begin to char, stirring halfway through cooking. Remove from the oven, then reduce the oven temperature to 180°C/350°F/Gas 4.

4 Spoon the rice into an earthenware casserole. Put the roasted vegetables on top, together with any juices from the roasting pan, then pour over the combined wine and passata or tomato juice.

5 Arrange the egg wedges on top of the vegetables, with the sliced olives, capers and sun-dried tomatoes, if using. Cover and cook for 15–20 minutes until heated through. Serve immediately, in warmed bowls.

Energy 359Kcal/1511kJ; Protein 9.5g; Carbohydrate 59.2g, of which sugars 12.1g; Fat 10g, of which saturates 1.8g; Cholesterol 48mg; Calcium 74mg; Fibre 5.7g; Sodium 114mg.

SPICED TOMATO RICE ★★

THIS RECIPE IS PROOF THAT YOU DON'T NEED ELABORATE INGREDIENTS OR COMPLICATED COOKING METHODS TO CREATE A DELICIOUS LOW-FAT VEGETARIAN DISH.

SERVES FOUR

INGREDIENTS

15ml/1 tbsp sunflower oil
2.5ml/½ tsp onion seeds
1 onion, sliced
4 tomatoes, sliced
1 orange or yellow (bell) pepper,
   seeded and sliced
5ml/1 tsp grated fresh root ginger
1 garlic clove
5ml/1 tsp chilli powder
1 potato, diced
7.5ml/1½ tsp salt
400g/14oz/2 cups basmati
   rice, soaked
750ml/1¼ pints/3 cups water
30–45ml/2–3 tbsp chopped
   fresh coriander (cilantro)

1 Heat the oil in a non-stick pan and cook the onion seeds for 30 seconds. Add the onion and cook for about 5 minutes.

2 Stir in the tomatoes, pepper, ginger, garlic, chilli powder, potato and salt. Stir-fry over a medium heat for about 5 minutes.

3 Drain the rice and add it to the pan, then stir for about 1 minute until the grains are well coated. Pour in the water and bring the rice to the boil, then reduce the heat, give the mixture a stir, cover the pan and cook the rice for 12–15 minutes.

4 Remove the pan from the heat, without lifting the lid, and leave the rice to stand for 5 minutes. Stir in the chopped coriander. Serve in warmed bowls, forking the rice over gently as you do so. If you like, sprinkle a little extra coriander on top of each portion.

Energy 463Kcal/1940kJ; Protein 10g; Carbohydrate 96.2g, of which sugars 7.6g; Fat 4.1g, of which saturates 0.5g; Cholesterol 0mg; Calcium 57mg; Fibre 3g; Sodium 21mg.

SPINACH WITH BEANS, RAISINS AND PINE NUTS ★★

THIS LIGHT VEGETARIAN DISH IS TRADITIONALLY MADE WITH CHICKPEAS, BUT CAN ALSO BE MADE WITH HARICOT BEANS AS HERE. USE EITHER DRIED OR CANNED BEANS.

SERVES FOUR

INGREDIENTS

115g/4oz/²⁄₃ cup haricot (navy) beans, soaked overnight, or 400g/14oz can haricot beans, rinsed and drained
30ml/2 tbsp olive oil
1 thick slice white bread
1 onion, chopped
3–4 tomatoes, skinned, seeded and chopped
2.5ml/½ tsp ground cumin
450g/1lb fresh spinach leaves
5ml/1 tsp paprika
1 garlic clove, halved
25g/1oz/generous ¼ cup raisins
15g/½oz pine nuts, toasted
salt and ground black pepper

1 Cook the dried beans in a pan of boiling water for about 1 hour, or until tender. Drain and set aside.

2 Heat 10ml/2 tsp of the oil in a non-stick frying pan and cook the bread until golden all over. Transfer to a plate and set aside.

3 Cook the onion in a further 10ml/2 tsp of the oil over a gentle heat, until soft but not brown, then add the tomatoes and cumin and continue cooking over a gentle heat.

4 Meanwhile, wash the spinach thoroughly, removing any tough stalks. Heat the remaining oil in a large, non-stick pan, stir in the paprika, then add the spinach and 45ml/3 tbsp water. Cover and cook for a few minutes, or until the spinach has wilted.

5 Add the onion and tomato mixture to the spinach and stir in the haricot beans, then season to taste with salt and pepper.

6 Place the garlic and fried bread in a blender or food processor and process until smooth. Stir the bread mixture into the spinach and bean mixture, together with the raisins. Add 175ml/6fl oz/¾ cup water and bring to the boil, then reduce the heat, cover and simmer very gently for 20–30 minutes, adding more water, if necessary.

7 Place the spinach mixture on a warmed serving plate and sprinkle with toasted pine nuts. Serve hot with Moroccan bread or other fresh bread.

Energy 231Kcal/969kJ; Protein 11.4g; Carbohydrate 25.8g, of which sugars 10.2g; Fat 9.8g, of which saturates 1.2g; Cholesterol 0mg; Calcium 240mg; Fibre 8.1g; Sodium 209mg.

MEXICAN RICE ★★

VERSIONS OF THIS DISH — A RELATIVE OF SPANISH RICE — ARE POPULAR ALL OVER SOUTH AMERICA. IT IS A TASTY LOW-FAT MEDLEY OF RICE, TOMATOES AND AROMATIC FLAVOURINGS, IDEAL FOR VEGETARIANS.

SERVES SIX

INGREDIENTS
200g/7oz/1 cup long grain rice
400g/14oz can chopped tomatoes
½ onion, roughly chopped
2 garlic cloves, roughly chopped
15ml/1 tbsp olive oil
225ml/7½fl oz/scant 1 cup
   vegetable stock
2.5ml/½ tsp salt
3 fresh red or green chillies
150g/5oz/generous 1 cup frozen peas
ground black pepper

1 Put the rice in a large heatproof bowl and pour over boiling water to cover. Stir once, then leave to stand for 10 minutes. Transfer to a strainer over the sink, rinse under cold water, then drain again. Set aside to dry slightly.

2 Meanwhile, pour the canned tomatoes into a blender or food processor, add the onion and garlic and process until smooth.

3 Heat the oil in a large, heavy, non-stick pan, add the rice and cook over a medium heat until the rice becomes a delicate golden brown colour. Stir occasionally with a wooden spatula to ensure that the rice does not stick to the base of the pan.

4 Add the tomato mixture and stir over a medium heat until all the liquid has been absorbed. Stir in the stock, salt, whole chillies and peas. Continue to cook the mixture until all the liquid has been absorbed and the rice is just tender, stirring occasionally.

5 Remove the pan from the heat, cover it with a tight-fitting lid and leave it to stand in a warm place for 5–10 minutes. Remove the chillies, fluff up the rice lightly with a fork, and serve in warmed bowls, sprinkled with black pepper. The chillies may be used as a garnish, if you like.

COOK'S TIP
Do not stir the rice too often after adding the stock or the grains will break down and the mixture will become starchy.

Energy 186Kcal/778kJ; Protein 5.3g; Carbohydrate 35.4g, of which sugars 5.5g; Fat 2.7g, of which saturates 0.4g; Cholesterol 0mg; Calcium 29mg; Fibre 2.6g; Sodium 8mg.

LEEK, MUSHROOM AND LEMON RISOTTO ★★

THE DELICIOUS COMBINATION OF LEEKS AND LEMON IS PERFECT IN THIS LIGHT VEGETARIAN RISOTTO.
BROWN CAP MUSHROOMS PROVIDE ADDITIONAL TEXTURE AND EXTRA FLAVOUR.

SERVES FOUR

INGREDIENTS

    225g/8oz trimmed leeks
    225g/8oz/3 cups brown cap
      (cremini) mushrooms
    15ml/1 tbsp olive oil
    3 garlic cloves, crushed
    25g/1oz/2 tbsp butter
    1 large onion, coarsely chopped
    350g/12oz/1¾ cups risotto rice, such
      as arborio or carnaroli
    1.2 litres/2 pints/5 cups simmering
      vegetable stock
    finely grated rind of 1 lemon
    45ml/3 tbsp lemon juice
    25g/1oz/⅓ cup grated fresh
      Parmesan cheese
    60ml/4 tbsp mixed chopped fresh
      chives and flat leaf parsley
    salt and ground black pepper

1 Slice the leeks in half lengthways, wash them well and then slice them evenly. Wipe the mushrooms with kitchen paper and chop them coarsely.

COOK'S TIP
Risotto rice is a rounder grain than long grain and is capable of absorbing a lot of liquid, which gives it a creamy texture.

2 Heat the oil in a large, non-stick pan and cook the garlic for 1 minute. Add the leeks, mushrooms and plenty of seasoning and cook over a medium heat for about 10 minutes, or until the leeks have softened and browned. Spoon into a bowl and set aside.

3 Add 15g/½oz/1 tbsp of the butter to the pan. When it has melted, add the onion and cook over a medium heat for 5 minutes, or until it has softened and is golden.

4 Stir in the rice and cook for about 1 minute, or until the grains begin to look translucent and are coated in the fat. Add a ladleful of stock and cook gently, until the liquid has been absorbed, stirring occasionally.

5 Continue to add stock, a ladleful at a time, until all of it has been absorbed, stirring constantly. This will take about 30 minutes. The risotto will become thick and creamy, and the rice should be tender, but not sticky.

6 Just before serving, add the leeks and mushrooms with the remaining butter. Stir in the grated lemon rind and juice. Add the Parmesan cheese and the herbs. Adjust the seasoning, if necessary and serve immediately.

Energy 442Kcal/1844kJ; Protein 11.8g; Carbohydrate 77.6g, of which sugars 5.6g; Fat 9g, of which saturates 3.8g; Cholesterol 14mg; Calcium 128mg; Fibre 2.9g; Sodium 97mg.

RED PEPPER RISOTTO ★★

THIS PEPPER-BASED RISOTTO CREATES A SATISFYING LOW-FAT SUPPER OR MAIN-COURSE DISH, IDEAL SERVED WITH A MIXED BABY LEAF SALAD AND FRESH ITALIAN BREAD.

SERVES FOUR

INGREDIENTS

3 large red (bell) peppers
15ml/1 tbsp olive oil
3 large garlic cloves, thinly sliced
400g/14oz can chopped tomatoes
225g/8oz can chopped tomatoes
2 bay leaves
about 1.2–1.5 litres/2–2½ pints/
   5–6¼ cups vegetable stock
450g/1lb/2¼ cups arborio rice or
   long grain brown rice
6 fresh basil leaves, shredded
salt and ground black pepper

1 Preheat the grill (broiler) to high. Put the peppers in a grill (broiling) pan and grill (broil) until the skins are blackened and blistered all over. Transfer the peppers to a bowl, cover with a clean, damp dish towel and leave for 10 minutes. Peel off and discard the skins, then slice the peppers, discarding the cores and seeds. Set aside.

2 Heat the oil in a wide, shallow, non-stick pan. Add the garlic and tomatoes and cook gently for 5 minutes, stirring occasionally, then add the prepared pepper slices and the bay leaves. Stir well, then cook gently for 15 minutes, stirring occasionally.

3 Pour the vegetable stock into a separate heavy pan and heat it to simmering point. Stir the rice into the vegetable mixture and cook for about 2 minutes, then add two or three ladlefuls of the hot stock. Cook until all the stock has been absorbed into the rice, stirring occasionally.

VARIATION
Use yellow or green (bell) peppers or mixed (bell) peppers in place of all red.

4 Continue to add stock, making sure each addition has been absorbed before adding the next. When the rice is cooked and tender, season to taste.

5 Remove the pan from the heat, cover and leave to stand for 10 minutes. Remove and discard the bay leaves, then stir in the shredded basil. Serve.

Energy 501Kcal/2098kJ; Protein 10.9g; Carbohydrate 103.8g, of which sugars 13.6g; Fat 4.4g, of which saturates 0.7g; Cholesterol 0mg; Calcium 44mg; Fibre 3.9g; Sodium 20mg.

RISOTTO WITH BASIL AND RICOTTA ★★

THIS IS A WELL-FLAVOURED, LIGHT VEGETARIAN RISOTTO, WHICH BENEFITS FROM THE DISTINCTIVE PUNGENCY OF BASIL, MELLOWED WITH SMOOTH RICOTTA.

SERVES FOUR

INGREDIENTS

10ml/2 tsp olive oil
1 onion, finely chopped
275g/10oz/scant 1½ cups risotto rice
1 litre/1¾ pints/4 cups simmering
  vegetable stock
175g/6oz/¾ cup ricotta cheese
50g/2oz/generous 1 cup finely
  chopped fresh basil leaves, plus
  extra leaves to garnish
40g/1½oz/½ cup grated fresh
  Parmesan cheese
salt and ground black pepper

1 Heat the oil in a large, non-stick pan and cook the onion pieces over a gentle heat stirring frequently until they are soft.

2 Stir in the rice. Cook for a few minutes until the rice is coated with oil and is slightly translucent, stirring.

3 Pour in about a quarter of the stock. Cook until all the stock has been absorbed, stirring, then add another ladleful of stock. Continue in this manner, adding more stock when the previous ladleful has been absorbed, for about 20 minutes, or until the rice is just tender.

4 Spoon the ricotta cheese into a bowl and break it up a little with a fork. Stir into the risotto along with the basil and Parmesan. Adjust the seasoning to taste, then cover and allow to stand for 2–3 minutes before serving, garnished with basil leaves.

Energy 373Kcal/1557kJ; Protein 16.1g; Carbohydrate 57.9g, of which sugars 2.7g; Fat 8.8g, of which saturates 4.6g; Cholesterol 21mg; Calcium 213mg; Fibre 0.8g; Sodium 305mg.

ROSEMARY RISOTTO <u>WITH</u> BORLOTTI BEANS ★★

THIS IS A TASTY, LOW-FAT RISOTTO WITH A SUBTLE AND COMPLEX TASTE, FROM THE HEADY FLAVOURS OF ROSEMARY TO THE SAVOURY BEANS AND THE FRUITY-SWEET TASTES OF THE CHEESES.

<u>SERVES FOUR</u>

INGREDIENTS

 400g/14oz can borlotti beans
 10ml/2 tsp olive oil
 1 onion, chopped
 2 garlic cloves, crushed
 275g/10oz/scant 1½ cups risotto rice
 175ml/6fl oz/¾ cup dry white wine
 900ml–1 litre/1½–1¾ pints/
  3¾–4 cups simmering
  vegetable stock
 30ml/2 tbsp mascarpone
 40g/1½oz/½ cup grated fresh
  Parmesan cheese, plus extra
  to serve (optional)
 5ml/1 tsp chopped fresh rosemary
 salt and ground black pepper

1 Drain the canned borlotti beans, rinse them well under plenty of cold water and drain again.

2 Purée about two-thirds of the beans fairly coarsely in a blender or food processor. Set the remainder aside.

3 Heat the oil in a large, non-stick pan and gently cook the onion and garlic for 6–8 minutes, or until very soft. Add the rice and cook over a medium heat for a few minutes until the grains are thoroughly coated in oil and are slightly translucent, stirring constantly.

VARIATION
Fresh thyme or marjoram could be used for this risotto instead of rosemary, if you prefer. Experiment with different herbs to make your own speciality dish.

4 Pour in the wine. Cook over a medium heat for 2–3 minutes until the wine has been absorbed, stirring constantly. Gradually add the stock, a ladleful at a time, waiting for each quantity to be absorbed before adding more, and stirring constantly.

5 When the rice is about three-quarters cooked, stir in the bean purée. Continue to cook the risotto, adding any stock that remains, until it has reached a creamy consistency and the rice is tender but still has a bit of "bite".

6 Add the reserved beans, with the mascarpone, Parmesan and rosemary, then season to taste with salt and pepper. Stir thoroughly, then cover and leave to stand for about 5 minutes, so that the risotto absorbs the flavours fully and the rice finishes cooking. Serve with extra Parmesan, if you like.

Energy 419Kcal/1752kJ; Protein 15.1g; Carbohydrate 68.8g, of which sugars 3.9g; Fat 6.2g, of which saturates 2.7g; Cholesterol 12mg; Calcium 198mg; Fibre 4.5g; Sodium 412mg.

THREE-ALLIUM RISOTTO
WITH FRIZZLED ONIONS AND PARMESAN ★ ★

IN THIS RECIPE, GARLIC AND CHIVES ARE ADDED TO SOFTENED, GOLDEN BROWN ONIONS TO CREATE THIS LIGHT AND FLAVOURFUL RISOTTO. A FINAL SPRINKLING OF CRISP FRIED ONIONS BRINGS A DELICIOUS CHANGE OF TEXTURE TO THE COOKED DISH.

SERVES SIX

INGREDIENTS

25g/1oz/2 tbsp butter
30ml/2 tbsp olive oil
1 onion, finely chopped
4 garlic cloves, finely chopped
350g/12oz/1¾ cups risotto rice
150ml/¼ pint/⅔ cup dry white wine
a pinch of saffron threads
about 1.2 litres/2 pints/5 cups hot
  vegetable stock
1 large yellow onion, thinly sliced
15g/½oz fresh chives, chopped,
  plus extra to garnish
25g/1oz/⅓ cup grated fresh
  Parmesan cheese
salt and ground black pepper

1 Melt half the butter with 15ml/1 tbsp of the oil in a large, deep, non-stick frying pan or heavy pan. Add the onion with a pinch of salt and cook over a very low heat, for 10–15 minutes, until softened and just turning golden, stirring frequently.

2 Add the garlic and rice and cook, for 3–4 minutes, until the rice is coated and looks translucent, stirring constantly. Season to taste with a little salt and pepper.

3 Pour in the wine and stir in the saffron with a ladleful of hot stock. Cook slowly until the liquid is absorbed, stirring frequently.

4 Continue cooking for 18–20 minutes, adding 1–2 ladlefuls of stock at a time, until the rice is swollen and tender outside, but still *al dente* on the inside. Keep the heat low and stir frequently. The finished risotto should be moist, but not like soup.

5 Meanwhile, separate the slices of yellow onion into rings while the risotto is cooking. Heat the remaining oil in a non-stick frying pan. Cook the onion rings slowly at first until soft, then increase the heat and fry briskly until they are brown and crisp. Drain on kitchen paper.

6 Beat the chives, the remaining butter and half the Parmesan into the risotto until it looks creamy. Taste and adjust the seasoning, if necessary.

7 Serve the risotto in warm serving bowls, topped with the crisp onions and chives.

Energy 316Kcal/1316kJ; Protein 6.3g; Carbohydrate 48.3g, of which sugars 1.3g; Fat 8.8g, of which saturates 3.6g; Cholesterol 13mg; Calcium 69mg; Fibre 0.3g; Sodium 72mg.

BARLEY RISOTTO WITH ROASTED SQUASH AND LEEKS ★★

THIS IS MORE LIKE A SEASONED RICE PILAFF MADE WITH SLIGHTLY CHEWY, NUTTY-FLAVOURED PEARL BARLEY THAN A CLASSIC RISOTTO. LEEKS, ROASTED BUTTERNUT SQUASH OR ANOTHER WINTER SQUASH GO REALLY WELL TOGETHER WITH THIS EARTHY GRAIN.

SERVES SIX

INGREDIENTS

200g/7oz/1 cup pearl barley
1 butternut squash, peeled, seeded and cut into chunks
10ml/2 tsp chopped fresh thyme
30ml/2 tbsp olive oil
15g/½oz/1 tbsp butter
4 leeks, cut into fairly thick diagonal slices
2 garlic cloves, finely chopped
175g/6oz/2¼ cups chestnut mushrooms, sliced
2 carrots, coarsely grated
about 120ml/4fl oz/½ cup vegetable stock
30ml/2 tbsp chopped fresh flat leaf parsley
25g/1oz/⅓ cup fresh Parmesan cheese, grated or shaved
45ml/3 tbsp pumpkin seeds, toasted, or chopped walnuts
salt and ground black pepper

1 Rinse the pearl barley, then cook it in a pan of simmering water, keeping the pan part-covered, for 35–45 minutes, or until tender. Drain. Preheat the oven to 200°C/400°F/Gas 6.

2 Place the squash in a roasting pan with half the thyme. Season with pepper and toss with half the oil. Roast in the oven for 30–35 minutes, until the squash is tender and beginning to brown, stirring once.

3 Heat half the butter with the remaining olive oil in a large non-stick frying pan. Add the leeks and garlic and cook gently for 5 minutes. Add the mushrooms and remaining thyme, then cook until the liquid from the mushrooms evaporates and they begin to fry.

COOK'S TIP
To chop fresh parsley quickly and easily, remove the stems and wash and dry the sprigs. Place the parsley sprigs in a jug or cup and snip the parsley into small pieces inside the jug or cup, using a pair of kitchen scissors.

VARIATIONS
• Make the risotto with brown rice instead of the pearl barley – cook following the packet instructions and continue from Step 2.
• Any type of mushrooms can be used in this recipe – try sliced field (portobello) smushrooms for a hearty flavour.

4 Stir in the carrots and cook for about 2 minutes, then add the pearl barley and most of the vegetable stock. Season well and partially cover the pan. Cook for a further 5 minutes. Pour in the remaining stock if the mixture seems dry.

5 Stir in the parsley, the remaining butter and half the cheese, then stir in the squash. Adjust the seasoning to taste and serve immediately, sprinkled with the toasted pumpkin seeds or walnuts and the remaining cheese.

Energy 237Kcal/1000kJ; Protein 7.3g; Carbohydrate 34.8g, of which sugars 5.5g; Fat 8.6g, of which saturates 3g; Cholesterol 10mg; Calcium 121mg; Fibre 4.1g; Sodium 69mg.

SPICED VEGETABLE COUSCOUS ★★

THIS TASTY LOW-FAT VEGETARIAN MAIN COURSE IS EASY TO MAKE AND CAN BE PREPARED WITH ANY NUMBER OF SEASONAL VEGETABLES SUCH AS SPINACH, PEAS, BROAD BEANS OR CORN.

SERVES SIX

INGREDIENTS
25ml/5 tsp olive oil
1 large onion, finely chopped
2 garlic cloves, crushed
15ml/1 tbsp tomato purée (paste)
2.5ml/½ tsp ground turmeric
2.5ml/½ tsp cayenne pepper
5ml/1 tsp ground coriander
5ml/1 tsp ground cumin
225g/8oz cauliflower florets
225g/8oz baby carrots, trimmed
1 red (bell) pepper, seeded and diced
225g/8oz courgettes (zucchini), sliced
400g/14oz can chickpeas, rinsed and drained
4 beefsteak tomatoes, skinned and sliced
45ml/3 tbsp chopped fresh coriander (cilantro)
salt and ground black pepper
fresh coriander sprigs, to garnish
For the couscous
2.5ml/½ tsp sea salt
450g/1lb/2⅔ cups couscous
25g/1oz/2 tbsp butter or
30ml/2 tbsp sunflower oil

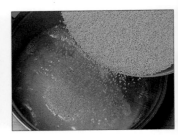

1 Heat 15ml/1 tbsp olive oil in a large non-stick pan, add the onion and garlic and cook until soft and translucent. Stir in the tomato purée, turmeric, cayenne, ground coriander and cumin. Cook for 2 minutes, stirring.

2 Add the cauliflower, baby carrots and red pepper, with enough water to come halfway up the vegetables. Bring to the boil, then reduce the heat, cover and simmer for 10 minutes.

3 Add the courgettes, chickpeas and tomatoes to the pan and cook for 10 minutes. Stir in the fresh coriander and seasoning. Keep hot.

4 To cook the couscous, bring about 475ml/16fl oz/2 cups water to the boil in a large pan. Add the remaining olive oil and the salt. Remove the pan from the heat and add the couscous, stirring. Allow to swell for 2 minutes.

5 Add the butter or sunflower oil, and heat through gently, stirring to separate the grains.

6 Turn the couscous out on to a warm serving dish, and spoon the cooked vegetables on top, pouring over any liquid. Garnish with coriander sprigs and serve immediately.

Energy 382Kcal/1597kJ; Protein 13.3g; Carbohydrate 63g, of which sugars 12.4g; Fat 10g, of which saturates 1.3g; Cholesterol 0mg; Calcium 108mg; Fibre 7.1g; Sodium 187mg.

HOT VEGETABLE COUSCOUS WITH HARISSA ★★

A NORTH AFRICAN FAVOURITE, THIS DELICIOUSLY SPICY DISH, MADE RICH WITH TOMATOES AND PRUNES, MAKES AN EXCELLENT AND UNUSUAL LOW-FAT MEAL FOR VEGETARIANS.

SERVES FOUR

INGREDIENTS

15ml/1 tbsp extra virgin olive oil or
  sunflower oil
1 onion, chopped
2 garlic cloves, crushed
5ml/1 tsp ground cumin
5ml/1 tsp paprika
400g/14oz can chopped tomatoes
300ml/½ pint/1¼ cups
  vegetable stock
1 cinnamon stick
a generous pinch of saffron threads
4 baby aubergines (eggplants),
  quartered
8 baby courgettes (zucchini), trimmed
8 baby carrots
225g/8oz/1⅓ cups couscous, soaked
400g/14oz can chickpeas, rinsed
  and drained
175g/6oz/¾ cup pitted prunes
45ml/3 tbsp chopped fresh parsley
45ml/3 tbsp chopped fresh
  coriander (cilantro)
10–15ml/2–3 tsp harissa
salt

COOK'S TIPS
Harissa is a very hot chilli sauce from North Africa. It looks rather like puréed tomatoes but needs to be treated with a great deal more caution. Use it sparingly. When choosing a steamer, metal sieve (strainer) or colander for steaming the couscous, check that it fits neatly over the pan in which you intend to cook the vegetables.

1 Heat the oil in a large, non-stick pan. Add the onion and garlic and cook gently for 5 minutes. Add the cumin and paprika and cook for 1 minute, stirring.

2 Add the tomatoes, stock, cinnamon stick, saffron, aubergines, courgettes and carrots, with water to cover. Season with salt. Bring to the boil, then reduce the heat, cover and cook for 20 minutes until the vegetables are just tender.

3 Line a steamer with muslin (cheesecloth). Steam the couscous according to the instructions on the packet. Add the chickpeas and prunes to the vegetables and cook for 5 minutes.

4 Place the couscous on top of the vegetable pan, cover, and cook for 5 minutes until the couscous is hot.

5 Stir the parsley and coriander into the vegetables. Heap the couscous on to a warmed serving plate. Using a slotted spoon, arrange the vegetables over the couscous. Spoon over a little of the remaining liquid and combine.

6 Stir the harissa into the remaining reserved liquid and serve separately.

Energy 396Kcal/1667kJ; Protein 15.1g; Carbohydrate 73.2g, of which sugars 28.3g; Fat 6.6g, of which saturates 0.9g; Cholesterol 0mg; Calcium 138mg; Fibre 12.2g; Sodium 43mg.

PEPPERS FILLED WITH SPICED VEGETABLES ★★

INDIAN SPICES SEASON THE POTATO AND AUBERGINE STUFFING IN THESE COLOURFUL LOW-FAT BAKED PEPPERS. THEY ARE GOOD WITH BROWN RICE AND A LENTIL DHAL. ALTERNATIVELY, SERVE THEM WITH A SALAD, LOW-FAT INDIAN BREADS AND A LIGHT CUCUMBER OR MINT AND YOGURT RAITA.

SERVES SIX

INGREDIENTS

6 large evenly shaped red or yellow (bell) peppers
500g/1¼lb waxy potatoes
1 small onion, chopped
4–5 garlic cloves, chopped
5cm/2in piece of fresh root ginger, chopped
1–2 fresh green chillies, seeded and chopped
105ml/7 tbsp water
45–60ml/3–4 tbsp sunflower oil
1 aubergine (eggplant), diced
10ml/2 tsp cumin seeds
5ml/1 tsp kalonji seeds
2.5ml/½ tsp ground turmeric
5ml/1 tsp ground coriander
5ml/1 tsp ground toasted cumin seeds
a pinch of cayenne pepper
about 30ml/2 tbsp lemon juice
salt and ground black pepper
30ml/2 tbsp chopped fresh coriander (cilantro), to garnish

1 Cut the tops off the red or yellow peppers, then remove and discard the seeds. Cut a thin slice off the base of the peppers, if necessary, to make them stand upright.

COOK'S TIP
The hottest part of a chilli is the white membrane that connects the seeds to the flesh. Removing the seeds and membrane before cooking gives a milder flavour.

2 Bring a large pan of lightly salted water to the boil. Add the peppers and cook for 5–6 minutes. Drain and leave them upside down in a colander.

3 Cook the potatoes in a pan of lightly salted boiling water for 10–12 minutes until just tender. Drain, cool and peel, then cut into 1cm/½in dice.

4 Put the onion, garlic, ginger and green chillies in a blender or food processor with 60ml/4 tbsp of the water and process to a purée.

5 Heat 30ml/2 tbsp of the sunflower oil in a large, deep, non-stick frying pan and cook the diced aubergine until it is evenly browned on all sides, stirring occasionally. Remove the aubergine from the pan and set aside. Add another 15ml/1 tbsp of the sunflower oil to the pan, add the diced potatoes and cook until lightly browned on all sides. Remove the potatoes from the pan and set aside.

6 If necessary, add another 10ml/2 tsp sunflower oil to the pan, then add the cumin and kalonji seeds. Cook briefly until the seeds darken, then add the turmeric, coriander and ground cumin. Cook for 15 seconds. Stir in the onion and garlic purée and cook until the onions begin to brown, scraping the pan with a spatula.

7 Return the potatoes and aubergine to the pan, season with salt, pepper and 1–2 pinches of cayenne. Add the remaining water and 15ml/1 tbsp lemon juice and cook until the liquid evaporates, stirring. Preheat the oven to 190°C/375°F/Gas 5.

8 Fill the peppers with the spiced vegetable mixture and place on a lightly greased baking tray. Lightly brush the peppers with the remaining oil and bake in the oven for 30–35 minutes until they are cooked. Allow to cool slightly, then sprinkle with a little more lemon juice, garnish with coriander and serve.

COOK'S TIP
Kalonji, or nigella as it is also known, is a tiny black seed. It is widely used in Indian cookery, especially sprinkled over breads or in potato dishes. It has a mild, slightly nutty flavour and is best toasted for a few seconds in a dry or lightly oiled frying pan over a medium heat before using in a recipe. This helps to bring out its flavour, as with most spices.

Energy 151Kcal/633kJ; Protein 3.2g; Carbohydrate 21.2g, of which sugars 8.3g; Fat 6.5g, of which saturates 0.9g; Cholesterol 0mg; Calcium 38mg; Fibre 4.1g; Sodium 17mg.

SPICY CHICKPEA AND AUBERGINE STEW ★★

SPICES ARE ESPECIALLY TYPICAL OF DISHES FROM THE NORTH OF GREECE, ALTHOUGH AUBERGINES AND CHICKPEAS ARE ENJOYED ALL OVER THE COUNTRY. THIS IS A HEARTY AND AROMATIC STEW.

SERVES FOUR

INGREDIENTS
3 large aubergines (eggplants), diced
200g/7oz/generous 1 cup dried
   chickpeas, soaked overnight
   in cold water
25ml/5 tsp olive oil
3 garlic cloves, finely chopped
2 large onions, chopped
2.5ml/½ tsp ground cumin
2.5ml/½ tsp ground cinnamon
2.5ml/½ tsp ground coriander
3 x 400g/14oz cans chopped
   tomatoes
salt and ground black pepper
hot cooked rice, to serve
For the garnish
10ml/2 tsp extra virgin olive oil
1 onion, sliced
1 garlic clove, sliced
a few sprigs of fresh coriander
   (cilantro)

1 Place the diced aubergines in a colander and sprinkle them with plenty of salt. Sit the colander in a bowl and leave for at least 30 minutes, to allow the bitter juices to escape. Rinse thoroughly with cold water and pat dry on kitchen paper. Set aside.

2 Drain the chickpeas and put them in a large pan with enough water to cover them. Bring to the boil over a medium heat, then reduce the heat and simmer for 30 minutes, or until tender. Drain them thoroughly. Set aside.

3 Heat the oil in a large, non-stick pan. Add the garlic and onions and cook gently until soft. Add the ground spices and cook for a few seconds, stirring. Add the diced aubergine and stir to coat with the spices and onions. Cook for 5 minutes. Add the tomatoes, chickpeas and seasoning. Cover and simmer for 20 minutes.

4 To make the garnish, heat the olive oil in a non-stick frying pan and, when very hot, add the sliced onion and garlic. Fry until golden and crisp.

5 Serve the thick stew with cooked rice, topped with the crispy fried onion and garlic, and garnished with sprigs of fresh coriander.

Energy 303Kcal/1281kJ; Protein 15.3g; Carbohydrate 45.3g, of which sugars 19.2g; Fat 8.2g, of which saturates 1.2g; Cholesterol 0mg; Calcium 141mg; Fibre 12.8g; Sodium 53mg.

AROMATIC CHICKPEA AND SPINACH CURRY ★★

HIGH IN FIBRE, THIS HEARTY, WARMING LOW-FAT CURRY TASTES GREAT AND BOOSTS VITALITY WITH ESSENTIAL VITAMINS. SERVE IT WITH SPICY MANGO CHUTNEY COMBINED WITH COOLING MINT RAITA.

SERVES FOUR

INGREDIENTS

15ml/1 tbsp sunflower oil
1 large onion, finely chopped
2 garlic cloves, crushed
2.5cm/1in piece of fresh root ginger,
  finely chopped
1 fresh green chilli, seeded and
  finely chopped
30ml/2 tbsp medium curry paste
10ml/2 tsp ground cumin
5ml/1 tsp ground turmeric
225g/8oz can chopped tomatoes
1 green or red (bell) pepper, seeded
  and chopped
300ml/½ pint/1¼ cups
  vegetable stock
15ml/1 tbsp tomato purée (paste)
450g/1lb fresh spinach
425g/15oz can chickpeas, rinsed
  and drained
45ml/3 tbsp chopped fresh
  coriander (cilantro)
5ml/1 tsp garam masala (optional)
salt

1 Heat the oil in a large, heavy, non-stick pan and cook the onion, garlic, ginger and chilli over a gentle heat for about 5 minutes, or until the onion has softened, but not browned. Stir in the curry paste, mix thoroughly and cook for a further minute, then stir in the ground cumin and turmeric. Stir over a low heat for a further minute.

2 Add the tomatoes and pepper and stir to coat with the spice mixture. Pour in the stock, then stir in the tomato purée. Bring to the boil, reduce the heat, cover and simmer for 15 minutes.

3 Remove any coarse stalks from the spinach, then rinse the leaves thoroughly, drain them and tear into large pieces. Add them to the pan, in batches, adding a handful more as each batch cooks down and wilts.

4 Stir in the chickpeas, cover and cook gently for a further 5 minutes. Add the chopped coriander, season to taste with salt and stir well. Spoon into a warmed serving bowl and sprinkle with the garam masala, if using. Serve immediately.

VARIATION
Use 4–6 shallots in place of onion.

Energy 239Kcal/1000kJ; Protein 12.9g; Carbohydrate 32.7g, of which sugars 13.9g; Fat 7.2g, of which saturates 0.9g; Cholesterol 0mg; Calcium 274mg; Fibre 9.5g; Sodium 397mg.

MIXED BEAN AND AUBERGINE TAGINE WITH MINT YOGURT ★★

IN THIS TRADITIONAL-STYLE, HEARTY BUT LOW-FAT MOROCCAN DISH, THE MIXED BEANS AND AUBERGINE PROVIDE BOTH TEXTURE AND FLAVOUR, WHICH ARE ENHANCED BY THE HERBS AND CHILLIES.

SERVES SIX

INGREDIENTS

115g/4oz/generous ½ cup dried red
  kidney beans, soaked overnight in
  cold water and drained
115g/4oz/generous ½ cup dried
  black-eyed beans (peas) or
  cannellini beans, soaked overnight
  in cold water and drained
600ml/1 pint/2½ cups water
2 bay leaves
2 celery sticks, each cut into
  4 batons
45ml/3 tbsp olive oil
1 aubergine (eggplant), about 350g/
  12oz, cut into small chunks
1 onion, thinly sliced
3 garlic cloves, crushed
1–2 fresh red chillies, seeded
  and chopped
30ml/2 tbsp tomato purée (paste)
5ml/1 tsp paprika
2 large tomatoes, roughly chopped
300ml/½ pint/1¼ cups
  vegetable stock
15ml/1 tbsp each chopped fresh mint,
  parsley and coriander (cilantro)
salt and ground black pepper
fresh herb sprigs, to garnish
For the mint yogurt
150ml/¼ pint/⅔ cup low-fat natural
  (plain) yogurt
30ml/2 tbsp chopped fresh mint
2 spring onions (scallions), chopped

COOK'S TIPS
When using dried beans, first rinse them
in a sieve (strainer) under cold running
water to wash off any loose, floury matter
before cooking, as this will minimise the
formation of scum during cooking. Then,
soak the beans in plenty of cold water,
overnight, then drain and use as
required. When you store dried beans in
a jar or container, always make a note
of the 'best-before' date. Older dried
beans will still be quite edible, but
fresh ones will need less cooking time.

1 Place the soaked and drained kidney
beans in a large pan of unsalted boiling
water. Bring back to the boil and boil
rapidly for 10 minutes, then drain.
Place the soaked and drained black-
eyed or cannellini beans in a separate
large pan of unsalted boiling water and
boil rapidly for 10 minutes, then drain.

2 Place the 600ml/1 pint/2½ cups of
water in a large tagine or casserole, and
add the bay leaves, celery and beans.
Cover and place in an unheated oven.
Set the oven temperature to 190°C/
375°F/Gas 5. Cook for 1–1½ hours or
until the beans are tender, then drain.
Discard the bay leaves and celery.

3 Heat 30ml/2 tbsp of the oil in a large,
non-stick frying pan or cast-iron tagine
base. Add the aubergine chunks and
cook for 4–5 minutes, until evenly
browned, stirring. Remove the
aubergines from the pan and set aside.

4 Add the remaining oil to the frying
pan or tagine base, then add the onion
and cook for about 4–5 minutes, until
softened, stirring. Add the garlic and
red chillies and cook for a further
5 minutes until the onion is golden,
stirring frequently.

5 Reset the oven temperature to
160°C/325°F/Gas 3. Add the tomato
purée and paprika to the onion mixture
and cook for 1–2 minutes. Add the
tomatoes, aubergine chunks, beans
and stock, then season to taste with
salt and pepper.

6 Cover the tagine base with the lid or,
if using a frying pan, transfer the
contents to a clay tagine or casserole.
Place in the oven and cook for 1 hour.

7 Meanwhile, mix together the yogurt,
mint and spring onions in a small
serving bowl. Just before serving, add
the chopped mint, parsley and
coriander to the tagine and lightly mix
through the vegetables. Garnish with
fresh herb sprigs and serve with the
mint yogurt.

Energy 210Kcal/885kJ; Protein 12.1g; Carbohydrate 26.8g, of which sugars 8.8g; Fat 6.9g, of which saturates 1.1g; Cholesterol 0mg; Calcium 145mg; Fibre 8.5g; Sodium 55mg.

CREAMY LEMON PUY LENTILS ★★

THE COMBINATION OF LENTILS, SPRING ONIONS, TOMATO, LEMON, PEPPER AND CRÈME FRAÎCHE MAKES FOR A TANGY MEDITERRANEAN DISH. THE LENTILS PROVIDE A SLIGHTLY EARTHY FLAVOUR.

SERVES SIX

INGREDIENTS

250g/9oz/generous 1 cup Puy lentils
1 bay leaf
15ml/1 tbsp olive oil
4 spring onions (scallions), sliced
2 large garlic cloves, chopped
15ml/1 tbsp Dijon mustard
finely grated rind and juice of
   1 large lemon
4 plum tomatoes, seeded and diced
6 eggs
60ml/4 tbsp reduced-fat
   crème fraîche
salt and ground black pepper
30ml/2 tbsp chopped fresh flat leaf
   parsley, to garnish

1 Put the Puy lentils and bay leaf in a large pan, cover with cold water, and slowly bring to the boil. Reduce the heat and simmer, partially covered, for about 25 minutes, or until the lentils are tender. Stir the lentils occasionally and add more water, if necessary. Drain.

2 Heat the oil in a non-stick frying pan and cook the spring onions and garlic for about 1 minute or until softened. Add the Dijon mustard and lemon rind and juice and stir to mix.

COOK'S TIP
Puy lentils are the most superior of all lentils and they originate from Puy in France. They are tiny grey-green lentils, with a distinctive flavour. Unlike some lentils, they keep their shape and colour when cooked.

3 Stir the tomatoes and seasoning into the onion mixture, then cook gently for 1–2 minutes until the tomatoes are heated through, but still retain their shape. Add a little water if the mixture becomes too dry.

4 Meanwhile, poach the eggs in a separate pan of lightly salted barely simmering water for 4 minutes, adding them one at a time.

Energy 244Kcal/1026kJ; Protein 17.3g; Carbohydrate 23.2g, of which sugars 3.1g; Fat 9.9g, of which saturates 3g; Cholesterol 190mg; Calcium 75mg; Fibre 4.5g; Sodium 85mg.

BALTI STIR-FRIED VEGETABLES WITH CASHEWS ★★

THIS VERSATILE STIR-FRY RECIPE WILL ACCOMMODATE MOST COMBINATIONS OF VEGETABLES SO FEEL FREE TO EXPERIMENT. THE CASHEW NUTS ADD A DELICIOUS TEXTURE AND INTEREST.

SERVES FOUR

INGREDIENTS
    2 carrots
    1 red (bell) pepper, seeded
    1 green (bell) pepper, seeded
    2 courgettes (zucchini)
    115g/4oz green beans, halved
    a bunch of spring onions (scallions)
    15ml/1 tbsp extra virgin olive oil
    4–6 curry leaves
    2.5ml/½ tsp cumin seeds
    4 dried red chillies
    10–12 cashew nuts
    5ml/1 tsp salt
    30ml/2 tbsp lemon juice
    fresh mint leaves, to garnish

1 Cut the carrots, peppers and courgettes into matchsticks, halve the beans and chop the spring onions. Set aside.

2 Heat the oil in a non-stick frying pan or wok and stir-fry the curry leaves, cumin seeds and dried chillies for 1 minute.

COOK'S TIP
When making stir-fries, it is a good idea to use a non-stick wok (or frying pan) to minimize the amount of oil needed. However, it cannot be heated to the same high temperature as a conventional wok.

3 Add the prepared vegetables and nuts and toss them over the heat for 3–4 minutes. Add the salt and lemon juice and stir-fry for a further 2 minutes, until the vegetables are tender-crisp.

4 Transfer to a warm dish and serve garnished with mint leaves. Serve with cooked brown or white rice or warm naan bread.

Energy 105Kcal/436kJ; Protein 4.2g; Carbohydrate 11.2g, of which sugars 10.1g; Fat 5.1g, of which saturates 0.9g; Cholesterol 0mg; Calcium 56mg; Fibre 3.9g; Sodium 510mg.

TOFU AND VEGETABLE THAI CURRY ★★

TRADITIONAL THAI INGREDIENTS — COCONUT MILK, CHILLIES, GALANGAL, LEMON GRASS AND KAFFIR LIME LEAVES — GIVE THIS LIGHT CURRY A WONDERFULLY FRAGRANT AROMA AND A LOVELY FLAVOUR.

SERVES FOUR

INGREDIENTS
175g/6oz firm tofu, drained
45ml/3 tbsp dark soy sauce
15ml/1 tbsp sesame oil
5ml/1 tsp chilli sauce
2.5cm/1in piece of fresh root ginger,
　finely grated
225g/8oz cauliflower
225g/8oz broccoli
10ml/2 tsp vegetable oil
1 onion, sliced
400ml/14fl oz/1⅔ cups coconut milk
150ml/¼ pint/⅔ cup water
1 red (bell) pepper, seeded and
　chopped
175g/6oz green beans, halved
115g/4oz/1½ cups fresh shiitake or
　button (white) mushrooms, halved
shredded spring onions (scallions),
　to garnish
boiled Thai fragrant rice or noodles,
　to serve
For the curry paste
2 fresh green chillies, seeded
　and chopped
1 lemon grass stalk, chopped
2.5cm/1in piece of fresh galangal,
　chopped
2 kaffir lime leaves
10ml/2 tsp ground coriander
a few sprigs of fresh coriander
　(cilantro), including the stalks

COOK'S TIP
Thai fragrant rice is also known as jasmine rice. Before cooking, rinse it at least three times in cold water until the water runs clear. Place it in a large pan and add 750ml/1¼ pints/3 cups cold water for every 450g/1lb/generous 2 cups rice. Bring to a vigorous boil over a high heat, then stir and reduce the heat to low. Cover and simmer for 15–20 minutes, until all the water has been absorbed. Remove from the heat and leave to stand, still covered, for 10 minutes. Remove the lid and gently stir the rice with a fork or chopsticks to fluff up the grains before serving.

1　Cut the tofu into 2.5cm/1in cubes and place in an ovenproof dish. Mix together the soy sauce, sesame oil, chilli sauce and fresh ginger and pour over the tofu. Toss gently to coat all the cubes evenly, then leave to marinate in a cool place for at least 4 hours or overnight if possible, turning and basting the tofu occasionally.

2　To make the curry paste, place the chillies, lemon grass, galangal, kaffir lime leaves, ground coriander and fresh coriander in a blender or food processor and process for a few seconds until well blended. Add 45ml/3 tbsp water and process to a thick paste.

3　Preheat the oven to 190°C/375°F/Gas 5. Cut the cauliflower and broccoli into small florets and cut any stalks into thin slices.

4　Heat the vegetable oil in a non-stick frying pan, add the onion and cook gently for about 8 minutes, or until soft and lightly browned. Stir in the prepared curry paste and the coconut milk. Add the water and bring to the boil.

5　Stir in the red pepper, green beans, cauliflower and broccoli. Transfer to a Chinese sand pot or earthenware casserole. Cover and place in the oven.

6　Stir in the tofu and marinade, then place this ovenproof dish in the top of the oven, at the same time as the curry, and cook for 30 minutes, then stir the tofu and marinade into the curry with the mushrooms. Reduce the oven temperature to 180°C/350°F/Gas 4 and cook the curry for a further 15 minutes, or until the vegetables are tender. Garnish with spring onions and serve with boiled Thai fragrant rice or noodles.

VARIATION
Use thinly sliced carrots in place of cauliflower or broccoli florets.

Energy 169Kcal/707kJ; Protein 11g; Carbohydrate 13.7g, of which sugars 12.3g; Fat 8.2g, of which saturates 1.3g; Cholesterol 0mg; Calcium 356mg; Fibre 5.4g; Sodium 932mg.

TOFU AND GREEN BEAN RED CURRY ★

THIS IS ONE OF THOSE VERSATILE RECIPES THAT SHOULD BE IN EVERY COOK'S REPERTOIRE. THIS VERSION USES GREEN BEANS, BUT OTHER TYPES OF VEGETABLE WORK EQUALLY WELL.

SERVES FOUR

INGREDIENTS

- 600ml/1 pint/2½ cups canned coconut milk
- 15ml/1 tbsp Thai red curry paste
- 10ml/2 tsp palm sugar or honey
- 225g/8oz/3¼ cups button (white) mushrooms
- 115g/4oz/scant 1 cup green beans, trimmed
- 175g/6oz firm tofu, rinsed, drained and cut into 2cm/¾in cubes
- 4 kaffir lime leaves, torn
- 2 fresh red chillies, seeded and sliced
- fresh coriander (cilantro) leaves, to garnish

1 Pour about one-third of the coconut milk into a wok or pan. Cook until it starts to separate and an oily sheen appears on the surface.

2 Add the red curry paste and palm sugar or honey to the coconut milk. Mix thoroughly, then add the mushrooms. Stir and cook for 1 minute.

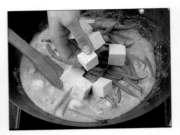

3 Stir in the remaining coconut milk. Bring back to the boil, then add the green beans and tofu cubes. Simmer gently for 4–5 minutes more.

4 Stir in the kaffir lime leaves and sliced red chillies. Spoon the curry into a serving dish, garnish with the coriander leaves and serve immediately.

Energy 89kcal/375kJ; Protein 5.7g; Carbohydrate 11.3g, of which sugars 10.7g; Fat 2.7g, of which saturates 0.6g; Cholesterol 0mg; Calcium 282mg; Fibre 1.2g; Sodium 437mg

CHINESE OMELETTE VEGETABLE PARCELS ★★

STIR-FRIED FRESH VEGETABLES COOKED IN CHINESE SAVOURY BLACK BEAN SAUCE MAKE A REALLY INTERESTING OMELETTE FILLING, FOR AN UNUSUAL MAIN MEAL.

SERVES FOUR

INGREDIENTS
130g/4½oz broccoli, cut into
  small florets
15ml/1 tbsp groundnut (peanut) oil
1cm/½in piece of fresh root ginger,
  finely grated
1 large garlic clove, crushed
2 fresh red chillies, seeded and
  thinly sliced
4 spring onions (scallions),
  sliced diagonally
175g/6oz/3 cups pak choi (bok
  choy), shredded
50g/2oz/2 cups fresh coriander
  (cilantro) leaves, plus extra to
  garnish
115g/4oz/½ cup beansprouts
45ml/3 tbsp black bean sauce
4 eggs
salt and ground black pepper

1 Blanch the broccoli in a pan of salted boiling water for 2 minutes, drain well, then refresh under cold running water. Set aside.

2 Meanwhile, heat 5ml/1 tsp oil in a non-stick frying pan or wok. Add the ginger, garlic and half the chilli and stir-fry for 1 minute. Add the spring onions, broccoli and pak choi and stir-fry for 2 minutes, tossing the vegetables to prevent them sticking.

3 Chop three-quarters of the coriander and add it to the frying pan or wok. Add the beansprouts and stir-fry for 1 minute, then add the black bean sauce and heat through for a further minute. Remove the pan from the heat and keep warm.

4 Beat the eggs lightly and season well with salt and pepper. Heat a little of the remaining groundnut oil in a small, non-stick frying pan and add a quarter of the beaten egg. Swirl the egg until it covers the base of the pan, then sprinkle over a quarter of the reserved coriander leaves. Cook until set, then carefully turn out on to a plate and keep warm in the oven while you make three more omelettes, adding a little more oil when necessary.

5 Spoon the vegetable stir-fry on to the omelettes and roll up. Cut in half crossways and serve garnished with coriander leaves and the remaining sliced chilli.

VARIATIONS
Use cauliflower florets or green beans (cut into 5cm/2in lengths), in place of broccoli. Use sesame oil in place of groundnut (peanut) oil.

COOK'S TIP
Black bean sauce is available in jars or cans from most large supermarkets.

Energy 148Kcal/614kJ; Protein 10.4g; Carbohydrate 6.2g, of which sugars 5.4g; Fat 9.3g, of which saturates 2.2g; Cholesterol 190mg; Calcium 152mg; Fibre 3g; Sodium 323mg.

DESSERTS

Even though you may be watching your calorie and fat intake, this doesn't mean you have to miss out on enticing puddings and desserts. Desserts round off many meals perfectly and the dessert recipes that follow are both delicous and low in fat. Choose from hot delights such as Caribbean Baked Bananas, Filo-topped Apple Pie and Blackberry Charlotte, or select from cool temptations including Mango Sorbet with Mango Sauce, Summer Berry Frozen Yogurt and Autumn Pudding.

MANGO SORBET WITH MANGO SAUCE ★

*THIS INDIAN SPECIALITY MAKES A VERY REFRESHING, LOW-FAT DESSERT. REMOVE FROM THE
FREEZER 10 MINUTES BEFORE SERVING TO ALLOW IT TO SOFTEN AND RELEASE THE FULL FLAVOUR.*

SERVES FOUR

INGREDIENTS
    900g/2lb/5 cups mango pulp
    2.5ml/½ tsp lemon juice
    finely grated rind of 1 orange and
        1 lemon
    4 egg whites
    50g/2oz/¼ cup caster
        (superfine) sugar
    120ml/4fl oz/½ cup low-fat Greek
        (US strained plain) yogurt
    50g/2oz/½ cup icing
        (confectioners') sugar

1 In a large, chilled bowl that can
safely be used in the freezer, mix half
of the mango pulp with the lemon juice
and the grated orange and lemon rinds.

COOK'S TIP
Ripe mangoes should yield when gently
pressed. The colour of a mango is no
guide to ripeness as the skin colour
varies from one variety to another. A
green mango can be as ripe as a bright
red one.

2 Beat the egg whites in a separate
grease-free bowl until soft peaks form,
then fold into the mango mixture,
with the caster sugar. Cover and freeze
for at least 1 hour.

3 Remove the sorbet from the freezer
and beat well. Transfer to an ice-cream
container, and freeze until solid.

4 Lightly whisk the yogurt with the icing
sugar and the remaining mango pulp.
Spoon into a bowl and chill for 24 hours.
Scoop out individual servings of sorbet
and cover each with mango sauce.

Energy 206Kcal/881kJ; Protein 6.1g; Carbohydrate 47.1g, of which sugars 46.4g; Fat 0.8g, of which saturates 0.4g; Cholesterol 0mg; Calcium 92mg; Fibre 5.9g; Sodium 91mg.

LYCHEE AND ELDERFLOWER SORBET ★

THE TASTE OF ELDERFLOWERS IS WELL-KNOWN FOR BRINGING OUT THE FLAVOUR OF GOOSEBERRIES, BUT IT ALSO COMPLEMENTS LYCHEES WONDERFULLY, AS WITH THIS TEMPTING DESSERT.

SERVES FOUR

INGREDIENTS

175g/6oz/generous ¾ cup caster (superfine) sugar
400ml/14fl oz/1⅔ cups water
500g/1¼ lb fresh lychees, peeled and stoned
15ml/1 tbsp undiluted elderflower cordial
dessert biscuits, to serve (optional)

1 Heat the sugar and water in a pan until the sugar has dissolved. Boil for 5 minutes, then add the lychees. Reduce the heat and simmer for 7 minutes. Remove from the heat and allow to cool.

2 Process the lychees and syrup in a blender or food processor to form a purée. Place a sieve (strainer) over a bowl. Pour the purée into it and press through with a wooden spoon.

3 Stir the elderflower cordial into the strained purée, then pour the mixture into a shallow freezerproof container. Freeze for approximately 2 hours, or until ice crystals start to form around the edges.

4 Remove the sorbet from the freezer and process briefly in a blender or food processor to break up the crystals. Repeat this freezing and processing procedure twice more, then freeze until firm.

5 Transfer the sorbet to the fridge for 10 minutes to soften slightly before serving in scoops. Serve with dessert biscuits, if you like.

COOK'S TIP
Ripe lychees have a prickly shell which can be reddish-brown, deep pink or white in colour, depending on the variety. The pearly white aromatic flesh of lychees tastes sweet yet slightly acidic.

COOK'S TIP
Crisp dessert biscuits can be served with the sorbet, but aren't really necessary. If you do serve them, remember that they will increase the fat and calorie contents of the dessert.

Energy 249Kcal/1064kJ; Protein 1.4g; Carbohydrate 64.7g, of which sugars 64.7g; Fat 0.1g, of which saturates 0g; Cholesterol 0mg; Calcium 31mg; Fibre 0.9g; Sodium 4mg.

TROPICAL COCONUT SORBET ★

DELICIOUSLY REFRESHING AND COOLING, THIS LOW-FAT TROPICAL SORBET CAN BE FOUND IN DIFFERENT VERSIONS ALL OVER SOUTH-EAST ASIA.

SERVES SIX

INGREDIENTS

175g/6oz/scant 1 cup caster
(superfine) sugar
120ml/4fl oz/½ cup coconut milk
50g/2oz/⅔ cup grated or desiccated
(dry unsweetened shredded) coconut
a squeeze of fresh lime juice
fresh mint leaves, to decorate

1 Place the sugar in a heavy pan and add 200ml/7fl oz/scant 1 cup water. Bring to the boil, stirring constantly until the sugar has dissolved completely. Reduce the heat and simmer for 5 minutes to make a light syrup.

2 Stir the coconut milk into the syrup, along with most of the coconut and the lime juice. Pour the mixture into a shallow bowl or freezer container and freeze for 1 hour.

3 Take the sorbet out of the freezer and beat it, or process it in a blender or food processor, until smooth and creamy, then return it to the freezer and leave until frozen.

4 Before serving, allow the sorbet to stand at room temperature for 10–15 minutes to soften slightly. Serve in small bowls and decorate with the remaining coconut and the mint leaves.

COOK'S TIP
Desiccated (dry unsweetened shredded) coconut is the shredded white flesh of fresh coconut from which all the moisture has been extracted. It is available either flaked or in fine or medium shredded strands. Desiccated coconut is suitable for both sweet and savoury dishes.

Energy 196Kcal/834kJ; Protein 1.1g; Carbohydrate 40.1g, of which sugars 40.1g; Fat 4.7g, of which saturates 3.9g; Cholesterol 0mg; Calcium 71mg; Fibre 0.9g; Sodium 209mg.

LEMON SORBET ★

EATING THIS SMOOTH, TANGY COMPLETELY FAT-FREE SORBET, PROVIDES A REFRESHING CHANGE OF TASTE TO THE PALATE AFTER A MORE SPICY OR FULL-BODIED MAIN MEAL.

SERVES SIX

INGREDIENTS
  200g/7oz/1 cup caster
    (superfine) sugar
  300ml/½ pint/1¼ cups water
  4 lemons, washed
  1 large (US extra large) egg white
  a little granulated sugar,
    for sprinkling

1 Put the caster sugar and water into a heavy pan and bring slowly to the boil, stirring occasionally until the sugar has just dissolved.

2 Using a swivel vegetable peeler, thinly pare the rind from two of the lemons directly into the pan. Simmer for about 2 minutes without stirring, then remove the pan from the heat. Leave the syrup to cool, then chill.

3 Squeeze the juice from all the lemons and carefully strain it into the syrup, making sure all the pips are removed. Take the lemon rind out of the syrup and set it aside until you make the decoration.

4 If you have an ice cream maker, strain the syrup into the machine tub and churn for 10 minutes until it thickens.

5 Lightly whisk the egg white with a fork and pour it into the machine. Continue to churn for 10–15 minutes, until firm enough to scoop.

6 Working by hand, strain the syrup into a plastic tub or a similar shallow freezerproof container and freeze for 4 hours, until the mixture is mushy.

7 Scoop the mushy mixture into a food processor and process until smooth. Lightly whisk the egg white with a fork until it is just frothy. Spoon the sorbet back into its container and beat in the egg white. Return to the freezer for 1 hour.

8 To make the sugared rind decoration, use the blanched rind from Step 2. Cut it into very thin strips and sprinkle with granulated sugar on a plate. Scoop the sorbet into bowls or glasses and decorate with sugared lemon rind.

VARIATION
Sorbet can be made from any citrus fruit. As a guide, you will need 300ml/½ pint/ 1¼ cups of fresh fruit juice and the pared rind of half the squeezed fruits. For example, use four oranges or two oranges and two lemons, or, to make a grapefruit sorbet, use the rind of one ruby grapefruit and the juice of two.

Energy 135Kcal/574kJ; Protein 0.7g; Carbohydrate 35.1g, of which sugars 35.1g; Fat 0g, of which saturates 0g; Cholesterol 0mg; Calcium 19mg; Fibre 0g; Sodium 12mg.

SUMMER BERRY FROZEN YOGURT ★

ANY COMBINATION OF SUMMER FRUITS WILL WORK WELL FOR THIS EXTREMELY LOW-FAT DESSERT, AS LONG AS THEY ARE FROZEN, BECAUSE THIS HELPS TO CREATE A COOL CHUNKY TEXTURE. WHOLE FRESH FROZEN BERRIES MAKE AN ATTRACTIVE DECORATION AND ARE TASTY IN THEIR OWN RIGHT.

SERVES SIX

INGREDIENTS
  350g/12oz/3 cups frozen mixed
    summer fruits
  200g/7oz/scant 1 cup low-fat Greek
    (US strained plain) yogurt
  25g/1oz/¼ cup icing
    (confectioners') sugar

COOK'S TIP
Packets of frozen mixed summer fruits or summer berries are available in many supermarkets, and are ideal for this recipe.

VARIATION
To make a rich and creamy ice cream, use double (heavy) cream in place of the yogurt. It's a lot less healthy and contains a much higher calorie and fat content, but it's delicious for an occasional treat.

1 Put all the ingredients into a blender or food processor and process until combined but still quite chunky. Spoon the mixture into six 150ml/¼ pint/ ⅔ cup ramekin dishes.

2 Cover each dish with clear film (plastic wrap) and place in the freezer for about 2 hours, or until firm.

3 To turn out the frozen yogurts, dip the dishes briefly in hot water, then invert them on to small serving plates. Tap the base of the dishes and the yogurts should come out. Serve immediately.

Energy 51Kcal/215kJ; Protein 2.2g; Carbohydrate 10.4g, of which sugars 10.4g; Fat 0.4g, of which saturates 0.2g; Cholesterol 0mg; Calcium 75mg; Fibre 0.7g; Sodium 32mg.

JUNGLE FRUITS IN LEMON GRASS SYRUP ★

THIS EXOTIC AND REFRESHING VIRTUALLY FAT-FREE FRUIT SALAD CAN BE MADE WITH ANY COMBINATION OF TROPICAL FRUITS — JUST GO FOR A GOOD BALANCE OF COLOUR, FLAVOUR AND TEXTURE. YOU CAN ALSO FLAVOUR THE SYRUP WITH GINGER RATHER THAN LEMON GRASS, IF YOU LIKE.

SERVES SIX

INGREDIENTS

1 firm papaya
1 small pineapple
2 small star fruit (carambola), sliced
   into stars
400g/14oz can preserved lychees or
   12 fresh lychees, peeled and stoned
2 firm yellow or green bananas,
   peeled and cut diagonally
   into slices

For the syrup
115g/4oz/generous ½ cup caster
   (superfine) sugar
2 lemon grass stalks, bruised

1 To make the syrup, put 225ml/ 7½fl oz/scant 1 cup water into a heavy pan with the sugar and bruised lemon grass stalks. Bring the liquid to the boil, stirring constantly until the sugar has dissolved, then reduce the heat and simmer for 10–15 minutes. Remove the pan from the heat and leave to cool.

2 Prepare the fruit. Peel and halve the papaya, remove the seeds and slice the flesh crossways. Peel the pineapple and slice it into rounds. Remove the core and cut each round in half.

3 Put all the prepared fruit into a bowl. Pour the syrup, including the lemon grass stalks, over the fruit and toss lightly to combine. Cover and chill for at least 6 hours, or overnight, to allow the flavours to mingle. Remove and discard the lemon grass stalks before serving.

Energy 199Kcal/849kJ; Protein 1.6g; Carbohydrate 50.3g, of which sugars 49.7g; Fat 0.4g, of which saturates 0g; Cholesterol 0mg; Calcium 49mg; Fibre 3.5g; Sodium 8mg.

PISTACHIO AND ROSE WATER ORANGES ★

THIS LIGHT AND CITRUSY DESSERT COMBINES, ALONG WITH PISTACHIO NUTS, TWO FAVOURITE MIDDLE EASTERN INGREDIENTS. IT IS DELIGHTFULLY FRAGRANT AND REFRESHING.

SERVES FOUR

INGREDIENTS
4 large oranges
30ml/2 tbsp rose water
30ml/2 tbsp shelled pistachio nuts, roughly chopped

VARIATION
Use hazelnuts if you don't have pistachio nuts.

COOK'S TIP
Rose-scented sugar is delicious sprinkled over fresh fruit salads. Wash and thoroughly dry a handful of rose petals and place in a sealed container filled with caster (superfine) sugar for 2–3 days. Remove and discard the petals before using the sugar.

1 Slice the top and bottom off one of the oranges to expose the flesh. Using a small serrated knife, slice down between the pith and the flesh, working round the orange, to remove all the peel and pith. Slice the orange into six rounds, reserving any juice. Repeat with the remaining oranges.

2 Arrange the orange rounds on a serving dish. Mix the reserved juice with the rose water and drizzle over the oranges. Cover the dish with clear film (plastic wrap) and chill for about 30 minutes. Sprinkle the chopped pistachio nuts over the oranges to serve.

Energy 123Kcal/518kJ; Protein 3.7g; Carbohydrate 18.5g, of which sugars 18.3g; Fat 4.4g, of which saturates 0.6g; Cholesterol 0mg; Calcium 107mg; Fibre 4g; Sodium 50mg.

BLUSHING PEARS ★

PEARS POACHED IN ROSÉ WINE AND SWEET SPICES ABSORB ALL THE SUBTLE FLAVOURS AND TURN A SOFT PINK COLOUR, TO CREATE THIS ALLURING VIRTUALLY FAT-FREE DESSERT.

SERVES SIX

INGREDIENTS

6 firm eating pears
300ml/½ pint/1¼ cups rosé wine
150ml/¼ pint/⅔ cup cranberry or
    clear apple juice
a strip of thinly pared orange rind
1 cinnamon stick
4 whole cloves
1 bay leaf
75ml/5 tbsp caster (superfine) sugar
extra small bay leaves, to decorate

1 Thinly peel the pears with a sharp knife or vegetable peeler, leaving the stalks attached.

2 Pour the wine and cranberry or apple juice into a large, heavy pan. Add the orange rind, cinnamon stick, cloves, bay leaf and sugar.

COOK'S TIP
Check the pears by piercing with a skewer or sharp knife towards the end of the poaching time, because some may cook more quickly than others.

3 Heat gently until the sugar has dissolved, stirring constantly. Add the pears and stand them upright in the pan. Pour in enough cold water to barely cover them. Cover and cook gently for 20–30 minutes, or until just tender, turning and basting occasionally.

4 Using a slotted spoon, gently lift the pears out of the syrup and transfer them to a serving dish.

5 Bring the syrup to the boil, then boil it rapidly for 10–15 minutes, or until it has reduced by half.

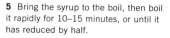

6 Strain the syrup, then pour it over the pears. Serve hot or well-chilled, decorated with small bay leaves.

VARIATION
Use 6 firm, fresh peaches or nectarines in place of pears.

Energy 154Kcal/652kJ; Protein 0.6g; Carbohydrate 31.8g, of which sugars 31.8g; Fat 0.2g, of which saturates 0g; Cholesterol 0mg; Calcium 31mg; Fibre 3.3g; Sodium 8mg.

FRESH FRUIT SALAD ★

ORANGES ARE AN ESSENTIAL INGREDIENT FOR A DELICIOUS AND REFRESHING LIGHT FRUIT SALAD, WHICH CAN INCLUDE ANY FRUIT IN SEASON. STRAWBERRIES, PEACHES AND APPLES ENTICE THE TASTE BUDS.

SERVES SIX

INGREDIENTS
2 eating apples
2 oranges
2 peaches
16–20 strawberries
30ml/2 tbsp lemon juice
15–30ml/1–2 tbsp orange
   flower water
icing (confectioners') sugar,
   to taste (optional)
a few sprigs of fresh mint,
   to decorate

COOK'S TIP
There are no rules with this fruit salad, and you could use almost any fruit that you like. Oranges, however, should form the base and apples give a delightful contrast in texture.

1 Peel and core the apples and cut into thin slices. Cut a thin slice of peel and pith from both ends of the oranges, then cut off the remaining peel and pith. Cut out each segment leaving the membrane behind. Squeeze the juice from the membrane and retain.

2 Blanch the peaches in a pan of boiling water for 1 minute. Peel off the skin and cut the flesh into thick slices.

3 Hull the strawberries, if you like, and halve or quarter them if large. Place all the prepared fruit in a large serving bowl.

4 Mix together the lemon juice, orange flower water and any orange juice. Taste and add a little icing sugar to sweeten, if you like. Pour the fruit juice mixture over the salad and serve decorated with mint leaves.

Energy 47Kcal/202kJ; Protein 1.2g; Carbohydrate 11g, of which sugars 11g; Fat 0.1g, of which saturates 0g; Cholesterol 0mg; Calcium 32mg; Fibre 2.1g; Sodium 5mg.

DRIED FRUIT SALAD ★

A WONDERFUL COMBINATION OF FRESH AND DRIED FRUIT FLAVOURED WITH HONEY AND LEMON, THIS MAKES AN EXCELLENT LOW-FAT DESSERT. YOU CAN SUBSTITUTE FROZEN RASPBERRIES OR BLACKBERRIES.

SERVES FOUR

INGREDIENTS
115g/4oz/½ cup dried apricots
115g/4oz/½ cup dried peaches
1 eating pear
1 eating apple
1 orange
115g/4oz/⅔ cup mixed raspberries
   and blackberries
1 cinnamon stick
50g/2oz/¼ cup caster
   (superfine) sugar
15ml/1 tbsp clear honey
30ml/2 tbsp lemon juice

1 Place the apricots and peaches in a bowl and add water to cover. Set aside to soak for 1–2 hours until plump, then drain well and halve or quarter the fruit.

2 Peel and core the pear and apple, then dice the flesh. Cut a thin slice of peel and pith from each end of the orange, then cut off the remaining peel and pith. Cut the orange into wedges. Place all the prepared fruit in a large pan with the raspberries and blackberries.

3 Add 600ml/1 pint/2½ cups water, the cinnamon stick, sugar and honey, and bring to the boil. Cover and simmer gently for about 10 minutes, then remove the pan from the heat. Stir in the lemon juice. Leave to cool completely, then transfer the fruit and syrup to a bowl and chill for 1–2 hours before serving.

Energy 185Kcal/790kJ; Protein 2.9g; Carbohydrate 45.3g, of which sugars 45.3g; Fat 0.5g, of which saturates 0g; Cholesterol 0mg; Calcium 64mg; Fibre 5.8g; Sodium 12mg.

CARIBBEAN BAKED BANANAS ★

TENDER BAKED BANANAS IN A RICH AND SPICY SAUCE OF GROUND ALLSPICE AND GINGER CREATES THIS DELICIOUS LOW-FAT DESSERT, IDEAL FOR THOSE WITH A SWEET TOOTH.

SERVES FOUR

INGREDIENTS

30ml/2 tbsp reduced-fat spread
8 firm ripe bananas
juice of 1 lime
75g/3oz/scant ½ cup soft dark
  brown sugar
5ml/1 tsp ground allspice
2.5ml/½ tsp ground ginger
seeds from 6 cardamom pods crushed
30ml/2 tbsp rum
pared lime rind, to decorate
half-fat crème fraîche, to serve
  (optional)

COOK'S TIPS
Choose firm, ripe bananas for this dessert, but avoid very ripe bananas with brown speckled skins as these may be slightly too ripe and soft for this recipe. Use a stainless steel knife to cut the bananas, to help prevent them browning or discolouring, before you add the spicy topping.

1 Preheat the oven to 200°C/400°F/ Gas 6. Use a little of the reduced-fat spread to grease a shallow baking dish large enough to hold the bananas snugly in a single layer.

2 Peel the bananas and cut them in half lengthways. Arrange the bananas in the dish and pour over the lime juice.

3 Mix the sugar, allspice, ginger and crushed cardamom seeds in a bowl. Scatter the mixture over the bananas. Dot with the remaining reduced-fat spread. Bake in the oven for 15 minutes, or until the bananas are soft, basting once.

4 Remove the dish from the oven. Warm the rum in a small pan or metal soup ladle, pour it over the bananas and set it alight.

5 As soon as the flames die down, decorate the dessert with the pared lime rind. Serve while still hot and add a small dollop of reduced-fat crème fraîche to each portion, if you like.

VARIATION
For a version that will appeal more to children, use orange juice instead of lime and leave out the rum.

Energy 253Kcal/1069kJ; Protein 2.2g; Carbohydrate 52.1g, of which sugars 48.9g; Fat 3.5g, of which saturates 1g; Cholesterol 0mg; Calcium 21mg; Fibre 1.6g; Sodium 51mg.

FILO-TOPPED APPLE PIE ★

WITH ITS SCRUNCHY FILO TOPPING AND ONLY A SMALL AMOUNT OF REDUCED-FAT SPREAD, THIS RECIPE CREATES A REALLY LIGHT AND HEALTHY DESSERT.

SERVES SIX

INGREDIENTS

900g/2lb Bramley or other cooking apples
75g/3oz/6 tbsp caster (superfine) sugar
finely grated rind of 1 lemon
15ml/1 tbsp lemon juice
75g/3oz/generous ½ cup sultanas (golden raisins)
2.5ml/½ tsp ground cinnamon
4 large sheets filo pastry, thawed if frozen
30ml/2 tbsp reduced-fat spread, melted
icing (confectioners') sugar, for dusting

1 Peel, core and dice the apples. Place them in a pan with the caster sugar and lemon rind. Drizzle the lemon juice over. Bring to the boil, stir well, then cook for 5 minutes or until the apples soften.

2 Stir in the sultanas and cinnamon. Spoon the mixture into a 1.2 litre/2 pint/5 cup pie dish and level the top. Leave to cool.

COOK'S TIP

Filo pastry is available frozen or as chilled fresh pastry in sheets of varying sizes. Thaw frozen filo thoroughly (according to the instructions on the packet) and let both defrosted and chilled fresh filo pastry come to room temperature in its box before you use it.

3 Preheat the oven to 180°C/350°F/Gas 4. Place a pie funnel in the centre of the fruit. Brush each sheet of filo pastry with melted reduced-fat spread. Scrunch up the pastry loosely and place on the fruit to cover it completely.

4 Bake in the oven for 20–30 minutes or until the filo is golden. Dust the pie with sifted icing sugar before serving.

VARIATIONS

• To make filo crackers, cut the greased filo into 20cm/8in wide strips. Spoon a little of the filling along one end of each strip, leaving the sides clear. Roll up and twist the ends to make a cracker. Brush with a little more melted reduced-fat spread, and bake in the oven for 20 minutes.

• Use raisins or chopped ready-to-eat dried apricots in place of sultanas (golden raisins). Use ground mixed spice or ginger in place of ground cinnamon.

Energy 198Kcal/843kJ; Protein 2.2g; Carbohydrate 44.8g, of which sugars 35.3g; Fat 2.4g, of which saturates 0.6g; Cholesterol 0mg; Calcium 38mg; Fibre 3g; Sodium 44mg.

APPLE AND BLACKCURRANT PANCAKES ★

THESE TASTY, LIGHT PANCAKES ARE MADE WITH A WHOLEWHEAT BATTER AND ARE FILLED WITH A FRESH ZESTY BERRY FRUIT MIXTURE. HALF-FAT CRÈME FRAÎCHE TOPS OFF THIS TEMPTING DESSERT.

MAKES TEN PANCAKES

INGREDIENTS
  115g/4oz/1 cup plain wholemeal
    (whole-wheat) flour
  300ml/½ pint/1¼ cups
    skimmed milk
  1 egg, beaten
  30ml/2 tbsp sunflower oil
  half-fat crème fraîche, to serve
    (optional)
  toasted nuts or sesame seeds, for
    sprinkling (optional)
For the filling
  450g/1lb cooking apples
  225g/8oz blackcurrants
  30–45ml/2–3 tbsp water
  30ml/2 tbsp demerara (raw) sugar

COOK'S TIP
If you wish, substitute other combinations of fruit such as pears and blueberries for apples and blackcurrants.

1 To make the pancake batter, put the flour in a mixing bowl and make a well in the centre.

2 Add a little of the milk with the egg and 15ml/1 tbsp of the oil. Beat the flour into the liquid, then gradually beat in the remaining milk, keeping the batter smooth and free from lumps. Cover the batter and chill it while you prepare the filling.

3 Quarter, peel and core the apples. Slice them into a pan, then add the blackcurrants and water. Cook over a gentle heat for 10–15 minutes until the fruit is soft. Stir in enough demerara sugar to sweeten.

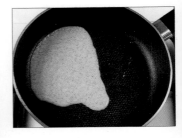

4 Meanwhile, lightly grease a non-stick frying pan with just a smear of the remaining oil. Heat the pan, whisk the batter, then pour about 30ml/2 tbsp of the batter into the pan, swirl it around to cover the base of the pan evenly and cook for about 1 minute until golden underneath. Flip the pancake over with a palette knife or metal spatula and cook the other side until golden. Put a sheet of baking parchment on a plate and keep hot while cooking the remaining pancakes.

5 Fill the pancakes with the apple and blackcurrant mixture and roll them up. Serve with a small dollop of crème fraîche, if using, and sprinkle with nuts or sesame seeds, if you like.

Energy 96Kcal/409kJ; Protein 3.5g; Carbohydrate 17.3g, of which sugars 10.2g; Fat 2g, of which saturates 0.4g; Cholesterol 20mg; Calcium 61mg; Fibre 2.6g; Sodium 22mg.

CASSAVA SWEET ★

SWEET AND STICKY, THIS LOW-FAT SNACK IS MORE LIKE AN INDIAN HELVA THAN A DESSERT. THIS RECIPE CAN ALSO BE MADE USING SWEET POTATOES OR YAMS IN PLACE OF THE CASSAVA.

SERVES SIX TO EIGHT

INGREDIENTS
15g/½oz/1 tbsp butter, for greasing
350ml/12fl oz/1½ cups coconut milk
115g/4oz/generous ½ cup palm sugar
2.5ml/½ tsp ground aniseed
a pinch of salt
675g/1½lb cassava root, peeled
   and grated

1 Preheat the oven to 190°C/375°F/ Gas 5. Grease an ovenproof baking dish with the butter. In a bowl, whisk the coconut milk with the sugar, aniseed and salt, until the sugar has dissolved.

2 Beat the grated cassava root into the coconut mixture, then pour it into the baking dish. Bake in the oven for about 1 hour, or until nicely golden on top. Leave the dessert to cool in the dish before serving.

COOK'S TIPS
• Cassava is a tropical plant (originally from Brazil where it is called manioc), cultivated for its starchy roots. It looks somewhat similar to the yam, with a tough brown, often waxy skin, and creamy white or yellow hard flesh. In North American it is made into tapioca. The root's flavour spoils in a day or so, even if kept unskinned and under refrigeration. The skinned root must be kept under water until it is ready to be cooked.
• To prepare the cassava for grating, use a sharp knife to slit the whole length of the root and then carefully peel off the skin. Simply grate the peeled root using a coarse grater.

Energy 176Kcal/752kJ; Protein 1.5g; Carbohydrate 41g, of which sugars 17.8g; Fat 1.9g, of which saturates 1.2g; Cholesterol 4mg; Calcium 33mg; Fibre 1.1g; Sodium 62mg.

SUMMER BERRY CRÊPES ★

LIGHT AND DELICIOUS CRÊPES MAKE A PERFECT FLUFFY 'ENVELOPE' FOR THIS MIXTURE OF TANGY BERRY FRUITS. ADDING AND FLAMBÉING A LIQUEUR TAKES IT INTO ANOTHER DESSERT DIMENSION.

SERVES FOUR

INGREDIENTS
115g/4oz/1 cup self-raising
  (self-rising) flour
1 large (US extra large) egg
300ml/½ pint/1¼ cups
  skimmed milk
a few drops of pure vanilla extract
spray oil, for greasing
icing (confectioners') sugar,
  for dusting
For the fruit
15ml/1 tbsp reduced-fat spread
50g/2oz/¼ cup caster
  (superfine) sugar
juice of 2 oranges
thinly pared rind of ½ orange
350g/12oz/3 cups mixed summer
  berries, such as sliced strawberries,
  yellow or red raspberries,
  blueberries and redcurrants
45ml/3 tbsp Grand Marnier or other
  orange-flavoured liqueur

1 Preheat the oven to 150°C/300°F/
Gas 2. To make the crêpes, sift the flour
into a large bowl and make a well in the
centre. Break in the egg, then gradually
whisk in the milk to make a smooth,
creamy batter. Stir in the vanilla extract.
Set the batter aside in a cool place for
up to 30 minutes.

VARIATIONS
• Use self-raising (self-rising) wholemeal
(whole-wheat) flour in place of white flour.
• Use soft light brown sugar in place of
caster (superfine) sugar.

2 Apply a light, even coat of spray oil
to an 18cm/7in non-stick frying pan.
Whisk the batter, then pour a little of
it into the hot pan, swirling to cover the
base of the pan evenly. Cook until the
mixture comes away from the sides and
the crêpe is golden underneath.

3 Flip the crêpe over with a large
palette knife or metal spatula and cook
the other side briefly until it appears
golden. Slide the crêpe on to a
heatproof plate.

4 Make seven or so more crêpes in the
same way layering the crêpes one on
top of the other, with sheets of baking
parchment in between each one. Cover
the crêpes with foil or another ovenproof plate and keep them hot in a
warm oven.

5 To prepare the fruit, melt the
reduced-fat spread in a heavy non-stick
frying pan over a gentle heat, then stir
in the caster sugar and cook gently. Add
the orange juice and pared rind and
cook until syrupy. Add the fruits and
warm through (reserving some for
decoration), then add the liqueur and
set it alight. Shake the pan until the
flames die down.

6 Fold the pancakes into quarters and
arrange two on each serving plate. Spoon
over the fruit mixture and dust with
sifted icing sugar. Serve the remaining
fruit separately in a serving bowl.

COOK'S TIPS
• Choose firm, ripe, plump summer berries
that are uniform in colour and showing no
signs of mould or rot. Choose berries such
as strawberries with hulls or stalks intact
(then remove them before use).
• For safety, when igniting a mixture for
flambéing, use a long taper or long
wooden match. Stand back as you set
the mixture alight.

Energy 260Kcal/1099kJ; Protein 8g; Carbohydrate 45.9g, of which sugars 24.6g; Fat 3.5g, of which saturates 0.9g; Cholesterol 51mg; Calcium 235mg; Fibre 2.4g; Sodium 184mg.

AUTUMN PUDDING ★

SUMMER PUDDING IS FAR TOO GOOD TO BE RESERVED FOR THE SOFT FRUIT SEASON. HERE IS A DELICIOUS LOW-FAT AUTUMN VERSION, COMBINING APPLES, PLUMS AND BLACKBERRIES.

SERVES SIX

INGREDIENTS

450g/1lb eating apples
450g/1lb plums, halved and stoned
225g/8oz/2 cups blackberries
60ml/4 tbsp apple juice
a little granulated sugar or honey,
to sweeten (optional)
8 slices wholemeal (whole-wheat)
bread, crusts removed
a fresh mint sprig and a blackberry,
to decorate
half-fat crème fraîche, to serve
(optional)

VARIATIONS
Use white bread in place of wholemeal (whole-wheat) bread. Use autumn raspberries in place of blackberries.

1 Quarter the apples, peel and core them, then slice the apples into a pan. Add the plums, blackberries and apple juice. Cover and cook gently for 10–15 minutes until tender. Sweeten, if necessary, with a little sugar or honey, although the fruit should be sweet enough.

2 Line the bottom and sides of a 1.2 litre/2 pint/5 cup heatproof bowl with slices of bread, cut to fit. Press together tightly.

3 Spoon the fruit mixture into the bowl. Pour in just enough juice to moisten. Reserve any remaining juice.

4 Cover the fruit completely with the remaining bread. Fit a plate on top, so that it rests on the bread just below the rim. Stand the basin in a larger bowl to catch any juice. Place a weight on the plate and chill overnight.

5 Turn the pudding out on to a serving plate and pour the reserved juice over any areas that have not absorbed the juice. Decorate with the mint sprig and blackberry. Serve with a little crème fraîche, if you like.

Energy 153Kcal/654kJ; Protein 4.8g; Carbohydrate 33g, of which sugars 17.3g; Fat 1.4g, of which saturates 0.2g; Cholesterol 0mg; Calcium 71mg; Fibre 5.6g; Sodium 199mg.

BLACKBERRY CHARLOTTE ★

A CLASSIC LOW-FAT HOT, MOULDED FRUIT PUDDING, THE PERFECT REWARD FOR AN AFTERNOON'S
BLACKBERRY PICKING. USE WHITE BREAD AND A LOW-FAT SPREAD INSTEAD OF BUTTER.

SERVES FOUR

INGREDIENTS

30ml/2 tbsp reduced-fat spread
175g/6oz/3 cups fresh white
  breadcrumbs
50g/2oz/¼ cup soft light brown sugar
60ml/4 tbsp golden (light corn) syrup
finely grated rind and juice of
  2 lemons
450g/1lb cooking apples
450g/1lb/4 cups blackberries

1 Preheat the oven to 180°C/350°F/
Gas 4. Melt the reduced-fat spread in a
non-stick pan with the breadcrumbs.
Cook gently for 5–7 minutes, until the
crumbs are golden and fairly crisp,
stirring frequently. Remove the pan from
the heat and leave to cool slightly.

2 Gently heat the sugar, syrup and
lemon rind and juice in a separate small
pan. Add the crumbs and mix well.

3 Cut the apples into quarters, then
peel them and remove the cores. Slice
the wedges thinly.

4 Arrange a thin layer of blackberries
in an ovenproof baking dish. Top with a
thin layer of crumbs, then a thin layer of
apples, topping the fruit with another
thin layer of crumbs. Repeat the
process with another layer of
blackberries, followed by a layer of
crumbs, then apples.

5 Continue until you have used up all
the ingredients, finishing with a layer
of crumbs.

6 Bake in the oven for 30 minutes, or
until the crumbs are golden and the
fruit is soft. Serve immediately.

VARIATION
Use blueberries or raspberries in place
of blackberries.

COOK'S TIP
When layering the fruit and crumbs, the
mixture should be piled well above the
top edge of the dish, because it shrinks
during cooking.

Energy 346Kcal/1468kJ; Protein 7g; Carbohydrate 74.6g, of which sugars 41.8g; Fat 4.2g, of which saturates 0.9g; Cholesterol 0mg; Calcium 120mg; Fibre 6.3g; Sodium 427mg.

MANGO AND AMARETTI STRUDEL ★

FRESH MANGO AND CRUSHED AMARETTI WRAPPED IN WAFER-THIN FILO PASTRY MAKE A SPECIAL LOW-FAT TREAT THAT IS EQUALLY DELICIOUS MADE WITH FRESH APRICOTS OR PLUMS.

SERVES 4

INGREDIENTS
1 large mango
finely grated rind of 1 lemon
2 amaretti
25g/1oz/2 tbsp demerara (raw) sugar
60ml/4 tbsp fresh wholemeal
 (whole-wheat) breadcrumbs
2 sheets filo pastry, each 48 x 28cm/
 19 x 11in, thawed if frozen
20g/¾oz/4 tsp non-hydrogenated soft
 margarine, melted
15ml/1 tbsp chopped almonds
icing (confectioners') sugar,
 for dusting

2 Crush the amaretti and mix them with the demerara sugar and breadcrumbs in a separate bowl.

4 Sprinkle the filo rectangle with the amaretti mixture, leaving a 5cm/2in border on each long side. Arrange the mango cubes over the top.

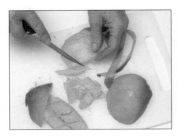

1 Preheat the oven to 190°C/375°F/ Gas 5. Lightly grease a large baking sheet and set aside. Halve, stone and peel the mango (see Cook's Tip). Cut the flesh into cubes, then place them in a bowl, and sprinkle with grated lemon rind. Set aside.

3 Lay one sheet of filo pastry on a flat surface and brush with a quarter of the melted margarine. Top with the second sheet of filo, brush with one-third of the remaining margarine, then fold both sheets over, if necessary, to make a rectangle measuring about 28 x 23cm/ 11 x 9in. Brush with half the remaining margarine.

COOK'S TIP
The easiest way to prepare a mango is to cut horizontally through the fruit, keeping the knife blade close to the stone. Repeat on the other side of the stone and peel off the skin. Remove the remaining skin and flesh from around the stone.

VARIATIONS
Use the finely grated rind of 1 lime or 1 small orange in place of lemon rind. Use chopped (shelled) pistachio nuts or hazelnuts in place of almonds.

5 Roll up the filo from one of the long sides like a Swiss roll (jelly roll). Lift the strudel on to the baking sheet making sure that the seam is underneath. Brush with the remaining melted margarine and sprinkle evenly with the chopped almonds

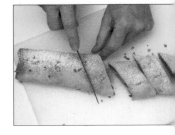

6 Bake in the oven for 20–25 minutes or until golden brown, then transfer to a chopping board. Dust with sifted icing sugar, slice diagonally and serve warm.

Energy 190Kcal/803kJ; Protein 3.4g; Carbohydrate 35.2g, of which sugars 13.2g; Fat 4.9g, of which saturates 0.2g; Cholesterol 0mg; Calcium 48mg; Fibre 1.7g; Sodium 164mg.

CAKES, BAKES, AND BREADS

It's hard to resist the delicious aroma of freshly baked bread, cakes and bakes wafting through your kitchen, and you can enjoy many of these home-baked delights as part of a healthy low-fat vegetarian eating plan. Included here is a selection of satisfying breads from all over the world, including Soda Bread, Pitta Bread and Focaccia, as well as tasty treats in the shape of low-fat cakes and bakes such as Cinnamon Apple Gateau, Carrot and Courgette Cake, Fresh Raspberry Muffins and Oaty Crisps.

PITTA BREAD ★

LOW IN FAT, PITTA BREAD IS FUN TO MAKE, AND LOOKS ALL THE BETTER FOR A LITTLE WOBBLINESS AROUND THE EDGES. IT ADDS SO MUCH BODY WHEN YOU EAT WITH LOW-FAT SOUPS AND STEWS.

MAKES TWELVE PITTA BREAD

INGREDIENTS
25g/1oz fresh yeast
500g/1¼lb/5 cups unbleached strong
   white bread flour, or half strong
   white and half strong wholemeal
   (whole-wheat) bread flour
15ml/1 tbsp sea salt
15ml/1 tbsp olive oil
250ml/8fl oz/1 cup water

1 Dissolve the yeast in 120ml/4fl oz/
½ cup warm water. Allow to stand for
10 minutes. Put the flour(s) and salt in
a large mixing bowl and stir in the yeast
mixture. Mix together the oil and water,
and stir enough of this liquid into the
flour mixture to make a stiff dough.

2 Place the dough in a lightly oiled
bowl, cover with a clean dish towel and
leave in a warm place for at least 30
minutes and up to 2 hours.

3 Knead the dough on a lightly floured
surface for 10 minutes, or until smooth.
Lightly oil the bowl again, place the
dough in it, cover once more and leave
to rise in a warm place for about 1 hour,
or until doubled in size.

4 Divide the dough into 12 equal
pieces. With lightly floured hands,
flatten each piece, then roll out into a
round measuring about 20cm/8in in
diameter and about 5mm–1cm/¼–½in
thick. Keep the rolled breads covered
with a clean dish towel.

5 Heat a large, heavy frying pan over a
medium-hot heat. When smoking hot,
gently lay one piece of flattened dough
in the pan and cook for 15–20 seconds.
Carefully turn it over and cook the
second side for about 1 minute.

6 When large bubbles start to form on
the bread, turn it over again. It should
puff up. Using a folded clean dish
towel, gently press on the bread where
the bubbles have formed. Cook for a
total of 3 minutes, then remove the
pitta from the pan. Repeat with the
remaining flattened dough pieces until
all the pittas have been cooked.

7 Wrap the pitta breads in a clean dish
towel, stacking them as each one is
cooked. Serve the pittas hot while they
are soft and moist.

VARIATION
To cook the breads in the oven, preheat
the oven to 220°C/425°F/Gas 7. Fill an
unglazed or partially glazed ovenproof
dish with hot water and place in the
bottom of the oven. Alternatively, soak
a handful of unglazed tiles in hot water
and arrange them in the bottom of the
oven. Use either a non-stick baking sheet
or a lightly oiled ordinary baking sheet
and heat in the oven for a few minutes.
Place two or three pieces of flattened
dough on to the hot baking sheet and
place in the hottest part of the oven.
Bake for 2–3 minutes. They should puff
up. Repeat with the remaining dough
until all the pittas have been cooked.

Energy 150Kcal/638kJ; Protein 3.9g; Carbohydrate 32.4g, of which sugars 0.6g; Fat 1.5g, of which saturates 0.2g; Cholesterol 0mg; Calcium 58mg; Fibre 1.3g; Sodium 165mg.

SODA BREAD ★

THIS DELICIOUS SODA BREAD RECIPE TAKES ONLY A FEW MINUTES TO MAKE AND NEEDS NO RISING OR PROVING. IF POSSIBLE, EAT SODA BREAD WHILE STILL WARM FROM THE OVEN AS IT DOES NOT KEEP WELL.

SERVES EIGHT

INGREDIENTS
    450g/1lb/4 cups plain (all-purpose)
      flour, plus extra for sprinkling
    5ml/1 tsp salt
    5ml/1 tsp bicarbonate of soda
      (baking soda)
    5ml/1 tsp cream of tartar
    350ml/12fl oz/1½ cups buttermilk

1 Preheat the oven to 220°C/425°F/ Gas 7. Flour a baking sheet and set aside. Sift all the dry ingredients into a mixing bowl and make a small well in the centre.

2 Add the buttermilk and mix quickly to form a soft dough. Turn on to a floured surface and knead lightly. Shape into a round about 18cm/7in in diameter and place on the baking sheet.

VARIATION
Use plain (all-purpose) wholemeal (whole-wheat) flour in place of some or all of the white flour.

3 Cut a deep cross in the top of the loaf and sprinkle with a little flour. Bake in the oven for about 25 to 30 minutes, then transfer the soda bread to a wire rack to cool down. Best served still warm in slices or wedges.

COOK'S TIP
Soda bread needs a light hand. The ingredients should be bound together quickly in the bowl and kneaded very briefly. The aim is to get rid of the largest cracks, as the dough will become tough if it is handled for too long.

COOK'S TIP
Buttermilk is high in lactic acid, and when, in recipes such as this one, it is mixed with an alkali such as bicarbonate of soda (baking soda), the chemical reaction that results produces a gas called carbonic acid. This has the effect of aerating the dough and making it much lighter. Sour cream can be used in place of buttermilk, as it is also acidic.

Energy 206Kcal/875kJ; Protein 6.8g; Carbohydrate 45.6g, of which sugars 2.8g; Fat 0.9g, of which saturates 0.2g; Cholesterol 2mg; Calcium 132mg; Fibre 1.7g; Sodium 267mg.

ROSEMARY AND SEA SALT FOCACCIA ★

FOCACCIA IS A DELICIOUS ITALIAN FLAT BREAD MADE WITH A LITTLE OLIVE OIL. HERE IT IS GIVEN ADDED FLAVOUR WITH ROSEMARY AND COARSE SEA SALT.

SERVES EIGHT

INGREDIENTS
   350g/12oz/3 cups plain
     (all-purpose) flour
   2.5ml/½ tsp salt
   10ml/2 tsp easy-blend (rapid-rise)
     dried yeast
   about 250ml/8fl oz/1 cup
     lukewarm water
   45ml/3 tbsp olive oil
   1 small red onion
   leaves from 1 large fresh
     rosemary sprig
   5ml/1 tsp coarse sea salt

1 Sift the flour and salt into a large mixing bowl. Stir in the yeast, then make a well in the centre of the dry ingredients. Pour in the water and 30ml/2 tbsp of the oil. Mix well, adding a little more water if the mixture seems too dry.

2 Turn the dough on to a lightly floured surface and knead for about 10 minutes or until smooth and elastic.

3 Place the dough in a lightly oiled bowl, cover and leave to rise in a warm place for about 1 hour or until doubled in size. Knock back (punch down), then knead the dough for 2–3 minutes.

4 Meanwhile, preheat the oven to 220°C/425°F/Gas 7. Grease a baking sheet and set aside. Roll out the dough to form a large round or oval about 1cm/½in thick, then transfer it to the baking sheet. Brush with the remaining oil.

COOK'S TIP
Use flavoured olive oil, such as chilli or herb oil, for extra flavour. Wholemeal (whole-wheat) flour or a mixture of wholemeal and white flour works well with this recipe.

VARIATIONS
• Use 2–3 shallots or 1 small standard onion in place of red onion.
• Use fresh thyme in place of rosemary.
• Use salt flakes in place of coarse sea salt granules.

5 Halve the onion and slice it into thin wedges. Sprinkle the onion over the dough, with the rosemary and sea salt, pressing them lightly into the dough.

6 Using a finger, make deep indentations all over the surface of the dough. Cover with greased clear film (plastic wrap), then leave to rise in a warm place for 30 minutes. Remove the clear film and bake in the oven for 25–30 minutes or until golden. Serve warm in slices or chunks.

Energy 189Kcal/798kJ; Protein 4.2g; Carbohydrate 34.6g, of which sugars 1.1g; Fat 4.7g, of which saturates 0.7g; Cholesterol 0mg; Calcium 63mg; Fibre 1.5g; Sodium 2mg.

CHAPATIS ★

THESE CHEWY, UNLEAVENED BREADS ARE EATEN THROUGHOUT NORTHERN INDIA. THEY ARE IDEAL SERVED AS AN ACCOMPANIMENT TO LOW-FAT SPICY VEGETARIAN DISHES. CHAPATIS ARE BEST WHEN MADE AT HOME BY HAND RATHER THAN SHOP-BOUGHT.

MAKES SIX CHAPATIS

INGREDIENTS
175g/6oz/1½ cups Atta or plain
   (all-purpose) wholemeal
   (whole-wheat) flour
2.5ml/½ tsp sea salt
about 120ml/4fl oz/½ cup water
5ml/1 tsp sunflower oil
a little melted ghee, butter or
   non-hydrogenated margarine, for
   brushing (optional)

1 Sift the flour and salt into a large mixing bowl. Add the water and mix to a soft dough using your hand or a round-bladed knife. Knead in the oil, then turn the dough out on to a lightly floured surface.

2 Knead for 5–6 minutes until smooth. Place the dough in a lightly oiled bowl, cover with a damp dish towel and leave to rest for 30 minutes. Turn out on to a floured surface. Divide the dough into six equal pieces. Shape each piece into a ball.

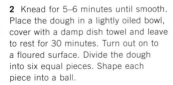

3 Press each ball of dough into a larger round with the palm of your hand, then roll into a 13cm/5in round. Stack, layered between clear film (plastic wrap), to keep moist.

4 Heat a griddle or heavy frying pan over a medium heat for a few minutes until hot. Take one chapati, brush off any excess flour, and place on the griddle. Cook for 30–60 seconds, or until the top begins to bubble and white specks appear on the underside.

5 Turn the chapati over using a metal spatula and cook for a further 30 seconds. Remove from the pan and keep warm, layered between a folded dish towel, while cooking the remaining chapatis. If you like, the chapatis can be brushed lightly with melted ghee or butter immediately after cooking. Serve warm.

COOK'S TIP
• *Atta* or *ata* is a very fine wholemeal (whole-wheat) flour, which is only found in Indian stores and supermarkets. It is sometimes simply labelled chapati flour.
• Atta can also be used for making rotis and other Indian flat breads.

Energy 99Kcal/422kJ; Protein 3.7g; Carbohydrate 20g, of which sugars 0.5g; Fat 1.1g, of which saturates 0.2g; Cholesterol 0mg; Calcium 38mg; Fibre 1.9g; Sodium 165mg.

SPRING ONION FLATBREADS ★

OVEN-BAKED FLATBREAD IS A STAPLE FOOD FROM INDIA TO NORTH AFRICA AND THE CAUCASUS. USE THESE DELICOUSLY SPICY FLATBREADS AS SOON AS THEY'RE COOKED TO WRAP AROUND CHARGRILLED VEGETABLES AND CHUNKY VEGETABLE SALADS, OR SERVE WITH TASTY VEGETARIAN DIPS SUCH AS HUMMUS.

MAKES SIXTEEN FLATBREADS

INGREDIENTS

450g/1lb/4 cups strong white bread
  flour, plus extra for dusting
5ml/1 tsp salt
7g/¼oz packet easy-blend (rapid-rise)
  dried yeast
4 spring onions (scallions),
  finely chopped

1 Place the flour in a large mixing bowl and stir in the salt, yeast and spring onions. Make a well in the centre and pour in about 300ml/½ pint/1¼ cups lukewarm water. Mix to form a soft, but not sticky, dough.

2 Turn out the dough on to a floured work surface and knead for about 5 minutes, until smooth.

3 Put the dough back in the bowl, cover with a damp dish towel and leave to rise in a warm place until doubled in size.

4 Knock back (punch down) the dough to get rid of any excess air, then turn it out on to a floured work surface or board. Divide the dough into 16 equal pieces and roll each piece into a smooth ball. Roll out each ball to flatten it to a 13cm/5in round.

5 Heat a large, heavy frying pan until hot. Dust off any excess flour from one dough round and cook for 1 minute, until slightly browned in parts, then flip over and cook for a further 30 seconds. Repeat with the remaining dough rounds.

VARIATION

To make garlic flatbreads, use 2 finely chopped garlic cloves in place of the spring onions (scallions).

Energy 97Kcal/410kJ; Protein 2.7g; Carbohydrate 21.9g, of which sugars 0.5g; Fat 0.4g, of which saturates 0.1g; Cholesterol 0mg; Calcium 40mg; Fibre 0.9g; Sodium 124mg.

LEMON CHIFFON CAKE ★

LEMON MOUSSE PROVIDES A TANGY FILLING FOR THIS DELICIOUS LIGHT LEMON SPONGE, IDEAL SERVED AS A TASTY LOW-FAT DESSERT OR SPECIAL TREAT.

SERVES EIGHT

INGREDIENTS
  2 eggs
  75g/3oz/6 tbsp caster
    (superfine) sugar
  finely grated rind of 1 lemon
  50g/2oz/½ cup sifted plain
    (all-purpose) flour
  lemon shreds, to decorate
For the filling
  2 eggs, separated
  75g/3oz/6 tbsp caster
    (superfine) sugar
  grated rind and juice of 1 lemon
  30ml/2 tbsp water
  15ml/1 tbsp vegetarian gelatine
    equivalent (see Cook's Tip)
  120ml/4fl oz/½ cup low-fat plain
    fromage frais or low-fat soft cheese
For the icing
  15ml/1 tbsp lemon juice
  115g/4oz/1 cup icing (confectioners')
    sugar, sifted

1 Preheat the oven to 180°C/350°F/ Gas 4. Grease and line a 20cm/8in loose-bottomed cake tin (pan). Whisk the eggs, sugar and lemon rind together in a mixing bowl with a hand-held electric whisk, until the mixture is thick and mousse-like. Gently fold in the flour, then turn the mixture into the prepared tin, levelling the surface.

COOK'S TIP
The mousse should be just setting when the egg whites are added. Speed up this process by placing the bowl of mousse in iced water.

2 Bake in the oven for 20–25 minutes until the cake springs back when lightly pressed in the centre. Turn on to a wire rack to cool. Once cold, split the cake in half horizontally and return the lower half to the clean cake tin.

3 Make the filling. Put the egg yolks, sugar and lemon rind and juice in a clean bowl. Beat with a hand-held electric whisk until thick, pale and creamy.

4 Pour the water into a heatproof bowl and sprinkle the gelatine equivalent on top, then stir over simmering water until dissolved or follow the packet instructions. Cool, then whisk into the egg yolk mixture. Fold in the fromage frais or soft cheese, mixing well.

5 When the mixture begins to set, whisk the egg whites to soft peaks in a separate grease-free bowl. Fold the whisked egg whites into the lemon mousse mixture.

6 Pour the lemon mousse over the sponge in the cake tin, spreading it to the edges. Set the second layer of sponge on top and chill until set.

7 Slide a palette knife or metal spatula dipped in hot water between the tin and the cake to loosen it, then carefully transfer the cake to a serving plate.

8 Make the icing by adding enough lemon juice to the icing sugar in a bowl to make a mixture thick enough to coat the back of a wooden spoon. Pour the icing over the cake and spread evenly to the edges. Decorate with the lemon shreds. Serve in slices.

COOK'S TIP
Vegetarian equivalents to gelatine include agar-agar (based on seaweed) or products such as Gelozone which is made from locust bean, guargum and carrageen, or Irish moss. Follow the instructions on the packet which will tell you how much to use and how to prepare it before adding it to the recipe.

Energy 208Kcal/883kJ; Protein 6.1g; Carbohydrate 40g, of which sugars 35.2g; Fat 4.1g, of which saturates 1.6g; Cholesterol 99mg; Calcium 58mg; Fibre 0.2g; Sodium 103mg.

ANGEL CAKE ★

A DELICIOUS LIGHT CAKE TO SERVE AS A LOW-FAT DESSERT FOR A SPECIAL OCCASION.

SERVES TEN

INGREDIENTS

40g/1½oz/⅓ cup cornflour
    (cornstarch)
40g/1½oz/⅓ cup plain
    (all-purpose) flour
8 egg whites
225g/8oz/generous 1 cup caster
    (superfine) sugar, plus extra
    for sprinkling
5ml/1 tsp vanilla extract
90ml/6 tbsp orange-flavoured glacé
    icing, 4–6 physalis and a little icing
    (confectioners') sugar, to decorate

VARIATION
Use lemon-flavoured glacé icing,
if you prefer.

1 Preheat the oven to 180°C/350°F/
Gas 4. Sift both flours on to a sheet of
baking parchment. Set aside.

2 Whisk the egg whites in a clean, dry
large bowl until very stiff, then gradually
add the caster sugar and vanilla extract,
whisking until the mixture is thick
and glossy.

3 Gently fold in the flour mixture with a
large metal spoon. Spoon into an
ungreased 25cm/10in angel cake tin
and smooth the surface. Bake in the
oven for about 45–50 minutes, until the
cake springs back when lightly pressed
in the centre.

4 Sprinkle a piece of baking parchment
with caster sugar and set an egg cup in
the centre. Invert the cake tin over the
paper, balancing it carefully on the egg
cup. When cold, the cake will drop out
of the tin.

5 Transfer the cake to a serving
plate, spoon over the glacé icing,
spreading it evenly, arrange the physalis
on top and then dust with sifted icing
sugar. Serve in slices.

COOK'S TIP
If you prefer, omit the glacé icing and
physalis and simply dust the cake with a
little sifted icing (confectioners') sugar – it
is delicious to serve as a coffee-time treat,
and also makes the perfect accompaniment
to vanilla yogurt ice for a dessert.

Energy 126Kcal/536kJ; Protein 2.8g; Carbohydrate 30.3g, of which sugars 23.6g; Fat 0.1g, of which saturates 0g; Cholesterol 0mg; Calcium 19mg; Fibre 0.1g; Sodium 52mg.

CINNAMON APPLE GATEAU ★

APPLE AND CINNAMON ARE A TRIED AND TESTED COMBINATION TO GIVE YOU A MOREISH CAKE.

SERVES TWELVE

INGREDIENTS
  3 eggs
  115g/4oz/generous ½ cup caster
    (superfine) sugar
  75g/3oz/⅔ cup plain (all-purpose) flour
  5ml/1 tsp ground cinnamon
For the filling and topping
  4 large eating apples
  60ml/4 tbsp clear honey
  15ml/1 tbsp water
  75g/3oz/generous ½ cup sultanas
    (golden raisins)
  2.5ml/½ tsp ground cinnamon
  350g/12oz/1½ cups low-fat
    soft cheese
  60ml/4 tbsp low-fat plain fromage
    frais or low-fat soft cheese
  10ml/2 tsp lemon juice
  45ml/3 tbsp apricot glaze or apricot
    jam, heated until melted
  fresh mint sprigs, to decorate

1 Preheat the oven to 190°C/375°F/ Gas 5. Grease and line a 23cm/9in shallow round cake tin (pan). Place the eggs and caster sugar in a bowl and beat with a hand-held electric whisk until thick and mousse-like. (When the whisk is lifted, a trail should remain on the surface of the mixture for at least 15 seconds.)

2 Sift the flour and cinnamon over the egg mixture and fold in with a large metal spoon. Pour the mixture evenly into the prepared tin and bake in the oven for 25–30 minutes, or until the cake springs back when lightly pressed. Turn the cake on to a wire rack to cool.

3 To make the filling, peel, core and slice 3 of the apples and put them in a pan. Add 30ml/2 tbsp of the honey and the water. Cover and cook over a gentle heat for about 10 minutes. Remove the pan from the heat, add the sultanas and cinnamon, stir well, replace the lid and leave to cool.

4 Put the soft cheese in a bowl with the remaining honey, the fromage frais – or soft cheese if you prefer – and half the lemon juice. Beat until the mixture is smooth.

5 Halve the cake horizontally, place the bottom half on a chopping board and drizzle over any liquid from the apples. Spread with two-thirds of the cheese mixture, then top with the apple filling. Fit the top of the cake in place.

6 Swirl the remaining cheese mixture over the top of the sponge. Core and slice the remaining apple, sprinkle with the remaining lemon juice and use to decorate the edge of the cake. Brush the apple slices with the apricot glaze and decorate with mint sprigs.

Energy 166Kcal/704kJ; Protein 6.8g; Carbohydrate 29g, of which sugars 24.2g; Fat 3.9g, of which saturates 1.9g; Cholesterol 55mg; Calcium 60mg; Fibre 0.9g; Sodium 153mg.

CARROT AND COURGETTE CAKE ★

IF YOU CAN'T RESIST A SLICE OF ICED CAKE, YOU'LL LOVE THIS MOIST, SPICED SPONGE WITH ITS DELICIOUS CREAMY TOPPING, WHICH IS FULL OF FLAVOUR, BUT LOW IN FAT TOO!

SERVES TEN

INGREDIENTS

1 medium carrot
1 medium courgette (zucchini)
3 eggs, separated
115g/4oz/½ cup soft light brown sugar
30ml/2 tbsp ground almonds
finely grated rind of 1 orange
150g/5oz/1¼ cups self-raising (self-rising) wholemeal (whole-wheat) flour
5ml/1 tsp ground cinnamon
5ml/1 tsp icing (confectioners') sugar, to dust
fondant carrots and courgettes (zucchini), to decorate
For the topping
175g/6oz/¾ cup low-fat soft cheese
5ml/1 tsp clear honey

1 Preheat the oven to 180°C/350°F/ Gas 4. Line an 18cm/7in square cake tin (pan) with baking parchment. Coarsely grate the carrot and courgette. Set aside.

2 Put the egg yolks, sugar, ground almonds and orange rind into a bowl and whisk until very thick and light.

3 Sift together the flour and cinnamon and fold into the mixture together with the grated vegetables. Add any bran left over from the flour in the sieve (strainer).

4 In a separate bowl, whisk the egg whites until stiff, then carefully fold them into the flour mixture, half at a time. Spoon evenly into the prepared tin. Bake in the oven for 1 hour, covering the top with foil after 40 minutes.

5 Leave to cool in the tin for 5 minutes, then turn out onto a wire rack and carefully remove the lining paper.

6 For the topping, beat together the cheese and honey in a bowl, then spread evenly over the cake. Decorate with fondant carrots and courgettes. Serve in slices or cut into squares.

Energy 148Kcal/625kJ; Protein 6.9g; Carbohydrate 24.4g, of which sugars 15.1g; Fat 3.5g, of which saturates 1.5g; Cholesterol 61mg; Calcium 48mg; Fibre 1.8g; Sodium 102mg.

FRUITED MALT LOAF ★

*THIS IS A RICH AND STICKY MALT LOAF THAT IS LOW IN FAT AND IDEAL FOR VEGETARIANS.
IF IT LASTS LONG ENOUGH TO GO STALE, TRY TOASTING IT FOR A DELICIOUS TEATIME TREAT.*

SERVES EIGHT

INGREDIENTS
150ml/¼ pint/⅔ cup lukewarm
  skimmed milk
5ml/1 tsp active dried yeast
a pinch of caster (superfine) sugar
350g/12oz/3 cups plain
  (all-purpose) flour
1.5ml/¼ tsp salt
30ml/2 tbsp light muscovado
  (brown) sugar
175g/6oz/generous 1 cup sultanas
  (golden raisins)
15ml/1 tbsp sunflower oil
45ml/3 tbsp malt extract
For the glaze
30ml/2 tbsp caster (superfine) sugar
30ml/2 tbsp water

1 Place the milk in a bowl. Sprinkle the yeast on top and add the sugar. Leave for 30 minutes until frothy. Sift the flour and salt into a mixing bowl, stir in the muscovado sugar and sultanas, and make a well in the centre.

2 Add the yeast mixture with the oil and malt extract. Gradually incorporate the flour and mix to a soft dough, adding a little extra milk, if necessary.

3 Turn on to a floured surface and knead for about 5 minutes until smooth and elastic. Grease a 450g/1lb loaf tin (pan).

4 Shape the dough and place it in the prepared tin. Cover with a damp dish towel and leave to rise in a warm place for 1–2 hours or until well risen. Preheat the oven to 190°C/375°F/Gas 5.

5 Bake the loaf in the oven for 30–35 minutes, or until it sounds hollow when it is tapped underneath.

6 Meanwhile, prepare the glaze by dissolving the sugar in the water in a small pan. Bring to the boil, stirring, then reduce the heat and simmer for 1 minute. Place the loaf on a wire rack and brush with the glaze while still hot. Leave the loaf to cool before serving.

COOK'S TIP
Sultanas are basically dried grapes and are packed with nutrients including iron.

Energy 260Kcal/1103kJ; Protein 5.3g; Carbohydrate 58.6g, of which sugars 25.3g; Fat 2.1g, of which saturates 0.3g; Cholesterol 1mg; Calcium 97mg; Fibre 1.8g; Sodium 38mg.

CHOCOLATE AND BANANA BROWNIES ★

NUTS TRADITIONALLY GIVE BROWNIES THEIR CHEWY TEXTURE. HERE OAT BRAN IS USED INSTEAD, CREATING A MOIST, MOREISH, YET HEALTHY ALTERNATIVE.

MAKES NINE BROWNIES

INGREDIENTS

75ml/5 tbsp reduced-fat
  cocoa powder
15ml/1 tbsp caster (superfine) sugar
75ml/5 tbsp skimmed milk
3 large bananas, peeled and mashed
215g/7½oz/scant 1 cup soft light
  brown sugar
5ml/1 tsp vanilla extract
5 egg whites
75g/3oz/⅔ cup self-raising
  (self-rising) flour
75g/3oz/¾ cup oat bran
15ml/1 tbsp icing (confectioners')
  sugar, for dusting

1 Preheat the oven to 180°C/350°F/ Gas 4. Line a 20cm/8in square cake tin (pan) with baking parchment. Set aside.

2 Blend the cocoa powder and caster sugar with the skimmed milk in a mixing bowl. Add the mashed bananas, soft light brown sugar and vanilla extract and mix well.

3 In a separate bowl, lightly beat the egg whites with a fork. Add the chocolate mixture and continue to beat well. Sift the flour over the mixture and fold in with the oat bran until well mixed. Pour evenly into the prepared tin.

4 Bake in the oven for 40 minutes or until firm. Cool in the tin for 10 minutes, then turn out on to a wire rack. Cut into squares and lightly dust with sifted icing sugar before serving.

COOK'S TIPS
• Store these brownies in an airtight container for a day before eating – they improve with keeping.
• You'll find reduced-fat cocoa powder in health food shops. If you can't find it, ordinary cocoa powder will work just as well, but, of course, the fat content will be higher!

Energy 200Kcal/846kJ; Protein 7g; Carbohydrate 37.2g, of which sugars 29.2g; Fat 3.6g, of which saturates 1.3g; Cholesterol 64mg; Calcium 61mg; Fibre 3.9g; Sodium 118mg.

BANANA AND GINGERBREAD SLICES ★

THESE LOW-FAT SLICES ARE VERY QUICK TO MAKE AND ARE DELICIOUSLY MOIST BECAUSE OF THE ADDITION OF MASHED BANANAS TO COMPLEMENT THE GINGER.

MAKES TWENTY SLICES

INGREDIENTS
 275g/10oz/scant 2½ cups plain
  (all-purpose) flour
 20ml/4 tsp ground ginger
 10ml/2 tsp mixed spice
 5ml/1 tsp bicarbonate of soda
  (baking soda)
 115g/4oz/½ cup soft light
  brown sugar
 60ml/4 tbsp sunflower oil
 30ml/2 tbsp molasses or black treacle
 30ml/2 tbsp malt extract
 2 eggs, beaten
 60ml/4 tbsp orange juice
 3 bananas
 115g/4oz/scant 1 cup raisins

1 Preheat the oven to 180°C/350°F/
Gas 4. Lightly grease and line an 18 x
28cm/7 x 11in baking tin (pan). Set aside.

2 Sift the flour into a bowl with the
ground spices and bicarbonate of soda.
Stir in the sugar, mixing well.

VARIATION
To make Spiced Honey and Banana Slices:
omit the ground ginger and add another
5ml/1 tsp mixed spice; omit the malt
extract and the molasses or black treacle
and add 60ml/4 tbsp strong-flavoured
clear honey instead; and replace the
raisins with either sultanas (golden raisins),
or coarsely chopped ready-to-eat dried
apricots, or semi-dried pineapple.
If you choose to use the pineapple, then
you could also replace the orange juice
with pineapple juice.

3 Make a well in the centre, add the
oil, molasses or black treacle, malt
extract, eggs and orange juice and mix
together thoroughly.

4 Peel and mash the bananas, add
them to the bowl with the raisins and
mix together well.

5 Pour the mixture evenly into the
prepared tin and bake in the oven for
about 35–40 minutes, or until the
centre of the cake springs back when
lightly pressed.

6 Leave the cake to cool in the tin for
5 minutes, then turn out on to a wire
rack and leave to cool completely. Cut
into 20 slices to serve.

Energy 133Kcal/563kJ; Protein 2.3g; Carbohydrate 25.9g, of which sugars 15.2g; Fat 3g, of which saturates 0.5g; Cholesterol 19mg; Calcium 37mg; Fibre 0.7g; Sodium 18mg.

APRICOT SPONGE BARS ★

THESE LOW-FAT SPONGE FINGERS ARE DELICIOUS AT TEATIME — THE APRICOTS WILL KEEP THE BARS MOIST FOR SEVERAL DAYS AT LEAST AND THEY ARE BEST KEPT IN A COOL DRY, PLACE.

MAKES EIGHTEEN

INGREDIENTS
    225g/8oz/2 cups self-raising
      (self-rising) flour
    115g/4oz/½ cup soft light
      brown sugar
    50g/2oz/⅓ cup semolina
    175g/6oz/¾ cup ready-to-eat dried
      apricots, chopped
    30ml/2 tbsp clear honey
    30ml/2 tbsp malt extract
    2 eggs, beaten
    60ml/4 tbsp skimmed milk
    60ml/4 tbsp sunflower oil
    a few drops of almond extract
    30ml/2 tbsp flaked (sliced) almonds

1 Preheat the oven to 160°C/325°F/
Gas 3. Lightly grease and then line an
18 x 28cm/7 x 11in baking tin (pan).
Set aside.

2 Sift the flour into a mixing bowl, then
stir in the sugar, semolina and apricots.
Make a well in the centre and add the
honey, malt extract, eggs, milk, oil and
almond extract. Mix the ingredients
together until smooth and well mixed.

3 Spoon the mixture into the prepared
tin, spreading it evenly to the edges,
then sprinkle the flaked almonds
over the top.

COOK'S TIPS
Use a sharp knife to cut the cooled cake
into even bars or slices. Use a pair of
kitchen scissors to snip the apricots into
small pieces.

4 Bake in the oven for 30–35 minutes,
or until the centre springs back when
lightly pressed. Remove from the tin
and turn on to a wire rack to cool. Cut
into 18 slices to serve.

COOK'S TIP
If you don't have pre-soaked (ready-to-
eat) dried apricots, just chop ordinary
dried apricots, soak them in boiling water
for 1 hour, then drain well and add to
the mixture.

VARIATIONS
Use self-raising (self-rising) wholemeal
(whole-wheat) flour in place of white
flour. Use ready-to-eat dried pears or
peaches, or raisins or sultanas (golden
raisins) in place of apricots.

Energy 134Kcal/566kJ; Protein 2.7g; Carbohydrate 24.8g, of which sugars 13.2g; Fat 3.3g, of which saturates 0.5g; Cholesterol 21mg; Calcium 36mg; Fibre 1.1g; Sodium 16mg.

SPICED PEAR AND SULTANA TEABREAD ★

THIS IS AN IDEAL TEABREAD TO MAKE WHEN PEARS ARE PLENTIFUL — AN EXCELLENT USE FOR
WINDFALLS AND IT CREATES A TASTY, LOW-FAT SNACK OR SWEET TREAT.

SERVES EIGHT

INGREDIENTS
  25g/1oz/¼ cup rolled oats
  50g/2oz/¼ cup light muscovado
    (brown) sugar
  30ml/2 tbsp pear or apple juice
  30ml/2 tbsp sunflower oil
  1 large or 2 small eating pears
  115g/4oz/1 cup self-raising
    (self-rising) flour
  115g/4oz/scant 1cup sultanas
    (golden raisins)
  2.5ml/½ tsp baking powder
  10ml/2 tsp mixed spice
  1 egg, beaten

VARIATION
Use eating apple(s) in place of pear(s).

1 Preheat the oven to 180°C/350°F/
Gas 4. Grease and line a 450g/1lb loaf
tin (pan) with baking parchment. Put
the oats in a bowl with the sugar, then
pour over the pear or apple juice and
oil, mix well and leave to stand for
15 minutes.

2 Quarter, core and coarsely grate the
pear(s). Add to the oat mixture with the
flour, sultanas, baking powder, mixed spice
and egg, then mix together thoroughly.

3 Spoon the mixture into the prepared
loaf tin and level the surface. Bake in
the oven for 50–60 minutes, or until a
skewer inserted into the centre comes
out clean.

4 Turn out the teabread on to a wire
rack and peel off the lining paper. Leave
to cool completely. Serve in slices.

Energy 176Kcal/743kJ; Protein 3g; Carbohydrate 34.1g, of which sugars 20.8g; Fat 4g, of which saturates 0.6g; Cholesterol 24mg; Calcium 40mg; Fibre 1.8g; Sodium 20mg.

FRESH RASPBERRY MUFFINS ★

THESE AMERICAN-STYLE MUFFINS ARE MADE USING BAKING POWDER AND LOW-FAT BUTTERMILK,
GIVING THEM A LIGHT AND SPONGY TEXTURE.

MAKES TEN TO TWELVE

INGREDIENTS
275g/10oz/scant 2½ cups plain
  (all-purpose) flour
15ml/1 tbsp baking powder
115g/4oz/generous ½ cup caster
  (superfine) sugar
1 egg, beaten
250ml/8fl oz/1 cup buttermilk
60ml/4 tbsp sunflower oil
150g/5oz/scant 1 cup fresh raspberries

1 Preheat the oven to 200°C/400°F/
Gas 6. Arrange 12 paper muffin cases
in a deep muffin tin (pan). Sift the flour
and baking powder into a mixing bowl,
stir in the sugar, then make a well in
the centre.

2 Mix the egg, buttermilk and oil together
in a separate bowl, then pour it into the
flour mixture and mix gently but quickly.

VARIATION
If fresh raspberries are not available,
use frozen small raspberries (not
defrosted) instead.

3 Add the raspberries and lightly fold
in with a metal spoon. Spoon the
mixture into the paper cases, dividing it
evenly between each one.

4 Bake the muffins in the oven for
20–25 minutes until golden brown and
firm in the middle. Transfer to a wire
rack and serve warm or cold.

Energy 165Kcal/696kJ; Protein 3.6g; Carbohydrate 29.3g, of which sugars 11.9g; Fat 4.5g, of which saturates 0.6g; Cholesterol 17mg; Calcium 68mg; Fibre 1g; Sodium 17mg.

DROP SCONES ★

ALSO KNOWN AS PIKELETS, THESE POPULAR LITTLE LOW-FAT DROP SCONES ARE DELICIOUS SERVED WARM, SPREAD WITH A LITTLE JAM, FRUIT PURÉE OR HONEY.

MAKES EIGHTEEN DROP SCONES

INGREDIENTS

225g/8oz/2 cups self-raising
    (self-rising) flour
2.5ml/½ tsp salt
15ml/1 tbsp caster (superfine) sugar
1 egg, beaten
300ml/½ pint/1¼ cups skimmed milk
15–30ml/1–2 tbsp sunflower oil

COOK'S TIP

For savoury drop scones, add 2 chopped spring onions (scallions) and 15ml/1 tbsp of grated fresh Parmesan cheese to the batter. Serve with cottage cheese.

3 Lightly oil the griddle or pan. Drop tablespoons of batter on to the surface, leaving them until they bubble on the surface and the bubbles begin to burst.

4 Turn the drop scones over with a palette knife or metal spatula and cook until the underside is golden brown. Keep the cooked drop scones warm and moist by wrapping them in a clean cotton napkin while cooking others.

1 Preheat a griddle or heavy frying pan until hot. Sift the flour and salt into a mixing bowl. Stir in the sugar, then make a well in the centre.

2 Add the egg and half the milk, then gradually incorporate the surrounding flour to make a smooth batter. Beat in the remaining milk.

Energy 59Kcal/252kJ; Protein 2g; Carbohydrate 11.1g, of which sugars 1.8g; Fat 1.1g, of which saturates 0.2g; Cholesterol 11mg; Calcium 66mg; Fibre 0.4g; Sodium 56mg.

OATY CRISPS ★

THESE LIGHT OAT BISCUITS ARE VERY CRISP, CRUNCHY AND EXTREMELY MOREISH — IDEAL TO SERVE WITH MORNING OR AFTERNOON TEA OR COFFEE.

MAKES EIGHTEEN OATY CRISPS

INGREDIENTS

175g/6oz/1¾ cups rolled oats
75g/3oz/½ cup light muscovado
(brown) sugar
1 egg, beaten
60ml/4 tbsp sunflower oil
30ml/2 tbsp malt extract

COOK'S TIP

To give these biscuits (cookies) a coarser texture, substitute jumbo oats for some or all of the rolled oats. Once cool, store the biscuits in an airtight container to keep them as crisp and fresh as possible.

VARIATIONS

Add 5–7.5ml/1–1½ tsp ground cinnamon or mixed spice with the oats, if you like. Add the finely grated rind of 1 lemon or 1 small orange with the oil, if you like.

1 Preheat the oven to 190°C/375°F/Gas 5. Lightly grease two baking sheets and set aside. Mix the rolled oats and sugar in a bowl, breaking up any lumps in the sugar. Add the egg, sunflower oil and malt extract, mix well, then leave to stand for 15 minutes.

2 Using a teaspoon, place small heaps of the mixture well apart on the prepared baking sheets. Press the heaps into 7.5cm/3in rounds with the back of a dampened fork.

3 Bake the biscuits in the oven for 10–15 minutes, or until golden brown. Leave them to cool for 1 minute, then remove with a palette knife or metal spatula and cool on a wire rack.

Energy 86Kcal/364kJ; Protein 1.6g; Carbohydrate 12.8g, of which sugars 5.7g; Fat 3.6g, of which saturates 0.4g; Cholesterol 11mg; Calcium 9mg; Fibre 0.7g; Sodium 12mg.

OATCAKES ★

TRY SERVING THESE OATCAKES WITH REDUCED-FAT HARD CHEESES FOR A TASTY LOW-FAT SNACK.
THEY ARE ALSO DELICIOUS TOPPED WITH THICK-SET HONEY FOR BREAKFAST.

MAKES EIGHT OATCAKES

INGREDIENTS
  175g/6oz/1½ cups medium oatmeal,
    plus extra for sprinkling
  2.5ml/½ tsp salt
  a pinch of bicarbonate of soda
    (baking soda)
  15g/½oz/1 tbsp butter
  75ml/5 tbsp water

1 Preheat the oven to 150°C/300°F/
Gas 2. Mix the oatmeal with the salt and
bicarbonate of soda in a mixing bowl.
Set aside.

2 Melt the butter with the water in a
small pan. Bring to the boil, then
remove the pan from the heat, add the
butter mixture to the oatmeal mixture
and stir together to form a moist dough.

COOK'S TIP
To achieve a neat round, place a 25cm/
10in cake board or plate on top of the
oatcake. Cut away any excess dough with
a blunt (round-bladed) knife.

3 Turn the dough on to a surface
sprinkled with oatmeal and knead to a
smooth ball. Turn a large baking sheet
upside down, lightly grease it, sprinkle it
lightly with oatmeal and place the ball
of dough on top. Sprinkle the dough
with oatmeal, then roll out to form a
25cm/10in round.

4 Cut the round into eight equal
sections, ease them apart slightly,
then bake in the oven for about
50–60 minutes, or until crisp. Leave to
cool on the baking sheet, then remove
the oatcakes with a palette knife or
metal spatula. Once cool, store in an
airtight container.

Energy 102Kcal/429kJ; Protein 2.7g; Carbohydrate 15.9g, of which sugars 0g; Fat 3.5g, of which saturates 1g; Cholesterol 4mg; Calcium 12mg; Fibre 1.5g; Sodium 141mg.

INDEX

ACKNOWLEDGEMENTS

Recipes: Pepita Aris, Catherine Atkinson, Mary Banks, Alex Barker, Ghillie Basan, Judy Bastyra, Angela Boggiano, Jacqueline Clark, Maxine Clark, Trish Davies, Roz Denny, Joanna Farrow, Jennie Fleetwood, Brian Glover, Nicola Graimes, Carole Handslip, Christine Ingram, Becky Johnson, Lucy Knox, Sally Mansfield, Christine McFadden, Jane Milton, Sallie Morris, Rena Salaman, Jenni Shapter, Marlena Spieler, Liz Trigg, Jenny White, Kate Whiteman, Lucy Whiteman, Jeni Wright.

Home economists: Eliza Baird, Alex Barker, Caroline Barty, Joanna Farrow, Annabel Ford, Christine France, Carole Handslip, Kate Jay, Becky Johnson, Jill Jones, Bridget Sargeson, Jennie Shapter, Carol Tennant, Sunil Vijayakar, Jenny White.

Photographers: Frank Adam, Tim Auty, Martin Brigdale, Louisa Dare, Nicki Dowey, Gus Filgate, Ian Garlick, Michelle Garrett, John Heseltine, Amanda Heywood, Janine Hosegood, Dave Jordan, Dave King, William Lingwood, Thomas Odulate, Craig Roberson, Simon Smith, Sam Stowell.